Evaluating Sure Start
Interprofessionalism and parental involvement in local programmes

Evaluating Sure Start

Interprofessionalism and parental involvement in local programmes

Nigel Malin and Gillian Morrow

w&b

MMXII

Published by Whiting & Birch Ltd,
Forest Hill, London SE23 3HZ

This edition © Nigel Malin and Gillian Morrow 2012
ISBN 9781861770292 (paperback)

Firs Edition © Nigel Malin and Gillian Morrow 2008
ISBN 9781861770547 (hardback)

Printed in England and the United States by Lightning Source

Contents

Foreword

AS A CHILDREN'S SERVICES researcher in the field of early intervention and family support, I am delighted to have the opportunity to contribute a foreword to this really important book. Its subject matter provides a case study of the inter-relationship between two high profile issues in recent social policy . Firstly, and most obviously, the book explores the extent to which government's efforts to enhance community level services for children and families have-or have not , so far , been successful. Secondly, it makes a valuable contribution to the knowledge base which needs to underpin the development and maintenance of high quality services for children and their families. The researchers resist any counter-productive pressures to identify services and approaches which might constitute a *silver bullet* which will remove for ever, the risk of disappointing child and family level outcomes. However their conclusions about a range of crucial issues such as partnership working ; inter-professional working ; the pre-requisites of accessible services; and the facilitation of parental involvement in service use and design, provide a set of invaluable insights for practitioners and managers. At the same time they reinforce the value of collecting data from local, as well as from national evaluations, by making a range of pertinent links between their own work and current international and national literature.

Between 2000 and 2007 I was privileged to have been a team member of the National Evaluation of Sure Start, which was commissioned by the then Department for Education and Skills to study the implementation and impact of the first Rounds 1-4 Sure Start Local Programmes. Our national evaluation brief included the provision of research support for the sort of local evaluations described here. These were seen by government as playing a crucial role in building up an accessible knowledge base for practitioners as well as policy makers. The richness of the data presented in this volume reinforces the importance of studying area –based initiatives such as Sure Start Local Programmes at both local and national level. This book brings alive the experiences of children, parents and workforce members in a particular northern authority. The researchers and all the respondents who contributed to this multi-faceted evaluation are to be congratulated for helping ensure that in Sunderland, the word *evaluation* is seen as a tool for progress in service delivery and the search for a better deal for children and their parents. Their work provides a very positive example of how researchers themselves can make a contribution to this task, in both the local and national context, and at the level of both practice and theory. The example they set clearly has relevance well beyond Sure Start itself, and will hopefully inspire similar agency/academic research partnerships beyond the borders of Sunderland.

Jane Tunstill,
Emeritus Professor of Social Work,
Royal Holloway, London University.
Director, Implementation Module,
National Evaluation of Sure Start, 2000-2007.

Acknowledgements

WE WOULD LIKE to acknowledge the contribution of all the parents, carers, volunteers, staff and other professionals involved in the work of Sure Start and Sure Start Plus to the evaluations. We acknowledge also the funding provided by Sunderland Social Services Department and the Tyne & Wear Sure Start Plus Partnership and Health Action Zone that made this work possible.

Dedication

In loving memory of Anthony Sedgeley Malin.

To Sarah and Sean Morrow and in loving memory of John.

SETTING
THE SCENE

1
Introduction

What is Sure Start?

ANNOUNCED BY THE UK Labour Government in 1998 as a major cross-departmental initiative aiming to close the gap in outcomes between children living in poverty and the wider child population, Sure Start was described as representing a large scale, area-based effort to enhance the health and development of children under 4 years and their families who live in socially-deprived communities in England; however the national programme now covers all children up to the age of 16. Sure Start Local Programmes (SSLPs) were set up to improve services and create new ones in small areas with average populations of just under 13,000 people, including about 800 children aged 0-4. The Government furthermore announced a significant level of funding to support the programme – many hundreds of millions of pounds- at a time when the new Labour Government was committed elsewhere to no increase in public expenditure. The first 60 'trailblazer' SSLPs hence began in 1999 with an original investment of £4.52 million to set up 250 SSLPs across England and the Year 2000 Spending Review provided the resources to double the number of SSLPs to 500 by 2004 – by mid-2004 there were 524; claiming to reach over 400,000 children estimated at about a third of all children aged under 4 living in poverty. In this initial announcement Sure Start was further described as a key part of New Labour's strategy to end child poverty by 2020 and tackle social exclusion.

Sure Start is claimed to be founded on evidence that early comprehensive and sustained support for children can help them succeed at school, help reduce crime, unemployment and teenage pregnancy and enhance life prospects of disadvantaged children, in that all children but particularly aged 0-4 years and their families living in a prescribed area are 'targets' of intervention, hence intended features of Sure Start are that it is universal within catchment areas and non-stigmatising. A central focus of Sure Start is upon parenting and supporting parents aiming to transform the life chances of young children through better access to family support, health services and early education. Because of their local autonomy, SSLPs do not have a 'protocol' to promote adherence to a prescribed model, for example, a fixed set of interventions, as do other early interventions that are known to be effective (Belsky et al, 2006). All SSLPs are expected however to provide core services of outreach or home visiting; family support; support for good quality play, learning, and childcare experiences; primary and community health care; advice about child and family health and development; and support for people with special needs. Community participation is central to the mission of SSLPs through local partnerships that bring together people concerned with children in the local community, for example, health, social, education services; the private sector; the voluntary sector; and parents.

What are the aims of Sure Start?

The aims of Sure Start can be identified broadly and specifically. The broad aims were translated by central government into SSLP objectives and targets, the attainment of which have become the responsibility of local Sure Start partnerships. Objectives were:

1. improving social and emotional development;
2. improving health;
3. improving children's ability to learn; and
4. strengthening families and communities.

Each objective had a number of affiliated targets, for example, making parenting support and information available for all parents of young children; reducing the number of children aged 0-3 admitted to hospital as an emergency; increasing children's speech, language, communication and literacy skills; and building the community's capacity to create pathways out of poverty through evidence of parents acknowledging improved family support, through increases in child care provision, and through bringing more parents into training, FE and helping them find jobs. In 2005 an additional objective of increasing child care provision was issued by the national Sure Start Unit.

Since the publication of the Green Paper Every Child Matters (w, 2003) introducing local children's centres the national policy focus has shifted towards identifying outcomes. The Government argued that Sure Start has provided a foundation for planning future children's centres based on five outcomes: being healthy, staying safe, enjoying and achieving, making a positive contribution, and achieving economic well-being. However from the outset SSLPs were expected to identify their own specific complementary targets relating to the identified needs of young children and their families in their local area. As main SSLP objectives / targets have been established centrally, likewise there is a central monitoring process gathering data on overall progress. Yet SSLPs have been able to exercise discretion over priority they give to individual targets, what methods of working they choose and the type / number of staff to employ. SSLPs are run by Partnerships (LPBs) which include representatives from voluntary, community organisations, practitioners from health, social services, education, other relevant local government departments and local parents and were intended to work closely with other similar local initiatives not through providing a specific service rather by changing existing services by reshaping and by increasing coordination.

The original aim and Public Service Agreement (PSA) / Service Delivery Agreement (SDA) targets were published in 1998 following the Government's Spending Review and were intended to be achieved by 2002. The 2000 Spending Review looked at how the economic and policy context had changed since the 1998 Review. It noted that the UK had the highest percentage of children living in poverty in Europe, and that there was a clear correlation between workless households and child poverty, and that this should be a key issue for Sure Start. The 2000 Spending Review considered that Sure Start was a vital part of the New Labour Government's anti-poverty strategy and commitment to breaking the cycle of deprivation, but also concluded that some changes in programme design were needed. In particular, these concerned a sharper focus on poverty supporting the Government's commitment to eradicate child poverty within 20 years; more work with parents in the prebirth period, and focusing on the importance of quality childcare and the problem of unmet demand for childcare. The Review also concluded that the core services and key principles should remain unchanged, the focus should remain on very young children but with more work on the transition into school; and Sure Start should remain universal within catchment areas and non-stigmatising. Thus the original aim for Sure Start (1999-2002 PSA):

> To work with parents and children to promote the physical, intellectual and social development of preschool children, particularly those who are disadvantaged, to ensure that they are ready to thrive when they get to school,

was amplified as follows (2001 – 2004 PSA):

> To work with parents-to-be, parents and all children to promote the physical, intellectual and social development of babies and young children, particularly those who are disadvantaged, so that they can flourish at home and when they get to school, and thereby break the cycle of disadvantage for the current generation of young children.

The key modifications to Sure Start's overall aim thus concerned working with parents to be as well as parents and children; working with parents of school-age children and aiming to break the cycle of disadvantage, so the link between Sure Start and eradicating child poverty is thus made explicit. The sharper focus on eradicating poverty and concern with the impact of unemployment and low income on child poverty were reflected in the change to Objective Four: Strengthening families and communities. The emphasis changed from involving parents in the community and improving the sensitivity of services to local needs to one of requiring programmes to involve families in building the community's capacity to sustain the programme into the future and thereby create pathways out of poverty. Thus there is an emphasis on people as workers as well as parents. This relates both to paid work and the provision of childcare and to the work of participation in the design and running of the programme.

Hence the official aim has been to combine two different approaches to tackling poverty and social exclusion. The national Sure Start Unit has set out aims, objectives and targets for SSLPs to follow, indicated core services to be included and set out key principles to be adhered to. In this respect it is very much a Government-directed Programme. At the same time there is a commitment to involving parents and other members of the community as key participants in the running and reshaping of services. In this respect Sure Start is thus also very much a community-focused Programme with a community capacity building approach. This combination of approaches has represented a significant challenge for SSLPs. The interdepartmental Sure Start Unit was officially launched in December 2002. It covers children from minus nine months through to age fourteen, including those with special educational needs and for those with disabilities up to age sixteen. The emphasis has been on bringing together early education, childcare and health and family support.

The theoretical framework of Sure Start

Sure Start builds on strategies developed in earlier area-based initiatives, in focusing on concentrations of disadvantage and the co-ordination of service provision for families with pre-school children. Previous research has revealed three broad sets of variables operating as protective factors that may impede or halt the impact of adverse experiences and enable individuals to fully develop their resources. These factors include: attributes of the children themselves; characteristics of their families; and aspects of the wider social context (Masten et al, 1990; Garmezy, 1985; Rutter, 1987; Werner and Smith, 1982).

Children from disadvantaged areas have, on average, poorer health and educational achievement and an increased likelihood of social exclusion later. This may involve unemployment, teenage pregnancy and crime. Interventions aimed at parents, particularly mothers and their children, were a key focus of the recommendations of the Independent Inquiry, chaired by Donald Acheson, into Inequalities in Health (Report, 1998), thereby aiming to influence those environmental factors that have the greatest potential in affecting critical periods of early childhood development. The aim of Sure Start has been to improve the health and wellbeing of families and children *before and after birth,* so children are thriving and fully prepared when they begin school. The Government Green Paper *Supporting Families* (1998) emphasizes the *centrality of family policy* to the New Labour project and the need for wide-ranging policies, linking family support, health visiting, employment policy, education and crime prevention. The Sure Start Evaluation Development Project Report (1999:10) identifies in addition to social exclusion two other major strands that can be seen in the development of the organisation, strategies and practices promoted through Sure Start i.e. British EPAs/CDPs, US 'Head Start'; Early Years Intervention Studies. Each of these strands entails a combination of family intervention approaches, social/educational experiment and an objective to compensate for disadvantage within a designated geographical community:

British Educational Priority Areas (EPAs) / Community Development Programmes (CDPs), US 'Head Start'

The first strand comes from earlier British experience gained through such interventions as the four-year Educational Priority Areas Programme (EPA), which ran from 1968-72. One of the major innovations arising from the 1967 Plowden Report 'Children and their Primary Schools', the EPA programme took place in four designated areas: highly disadvantaged parts of Birmingham, Liverpool, London and South Yorkshire. Similarly from 1969 three local authorities (Coventry, Liverpool, Southwark) agreed to take part in the Community Development Project (CDP) described in the UK Parliamentary announcement as:

> a neighbourhood-based experiment aimed at finding new ways of meeting the needs of people living in areas of high social deprivation: by bringing together the work of all the social services under the leadership of a special project team and also by tapping resources of self-help and mutual help which may exist among the people of the neighbourhood. (quoting from Halsey, 1978:152)

Further quoting from Halsey (1978:153):

> A basic assumption of the EPA programmes is that the most advantageous point at which to break into the vicious poverty circle is in early childhood, in the primary school or in the pre-school period,

and this approach tends to lead to considerable emphasis on work with families, thus raising fundamentally the question of limits to the right of the State, through its agencies to intervene in the relation between parents and children.

Local EPA projects set up a range of different local programmes designed to raise educational standards, increase teachers' morale and involve young families and their children more fully in education. Halsey (1978:154) names 'inadequate social parenthood' and 'the other socialising institution – the school' as the two prominent factors in causing poverty and cultural deprivation which, he argued, needed to be addressed in the EPA projects. In relation to inadequate social parenthood, Halsey claims:

> '(that) the cure consists of improved socialisation with the implication that the main thrust must be towards family casework. In the EPA context this means that the sub-working-class family is held to be the major villain of the piece, failing to provide the early training in literacy, numeracy, and acceptance of work and achievement habits which constitute the normal upbringing of the middle-class child and which prepare the child to take advantage of the opportunities provided in school' (Halsey, 1978:154)

Halsey's second interpretation focused upon the school:

> 'It is the theory that the cause of poverty is educational deprivation. The blame is transferred here to the school teacher who fails to provide adequate educational stimulus to the sub-working-class child' (op.cit)

These two interpretations – parenting and school – were linked in the EPA projects, which emphasized both pre-schooling and the development of the so-called community school. The strong element devoted to pre-school programmes was influenced by US experience with 'compensatory education' and the national 'Head Start' programme that had just preceded the EPA programme. The latter took a similar experimental approach to that used in Headstart where evaluation was a central element involving the allocation of an early language programme to existing pre-school groups in a number of communities. Children's progress over the year was assessed on formal measures so that children in groups using the language kit could be compared with children in groups without this addition. In addition there was national monitoring of educational conditions, and parental and teachers' attitudes to education and pupil performance in each area (Sure Start Evaluation Development Project, Report to Sure Start Unit, November 1999: 1.6).

Early years intervention studies, for example home support to mothers:

The general consensus of research into the effects of pre-school programmes is that, if they are of high quality and have appropriate educational components, they lead to positive outcomes for children in the short and long-term. These positive outcomes cover a wide range of variables, including educational attainment, pro-social behavior and employment prospects (Sylva and Wiltshire, 1993). Pugh (1996:23) writing about the concept of quality in early years intervention identifies three key issues: the provision of an appropriate curriculum, well-trained staff and good relationships between staff and parents. Sparkes and Glennerster (2001:200) state:

> 'The evidence we have reviewed confirms that intervention in a child's early years is among the most effective means of improving educational performance later and the likelihood of escaping social exclusion. The Government's Sure Start programme was heavily influenced by the American evidence of the kind Waldfogel (1998) reviewed'.

This strand covering early years intervention research draws more directly on recent US and UK experience, and particularly on evidence of the long-term returns to the tax and benefits system of investment in pre-school intervention (Sure Start Evaluation Development Project, Report Sure Start Unit, op. cit 2:4). One of the few longitudinal studies to have measured the impact of pre-school programmes upon the life trajectories of children is the Perry Preschool (High/Scope) Project (Schweinhart, Barnes and Weikart, 1997) carried out in Ypsilanti, Michigan. This involved a randomised trial in which families were allocated at random either to an intensive pre-school programme or to a control group with no additional pre-school support. Following up the two groups over twenty years demonstrated strong and lasting effects for the intervention group. They were more likely to have completed high school, to be in employment, and to avoid teenage pregnancy or a police record. Demonstrable economic benefits accompanied these positive outcomes calculated in terms of reduced cost to the taxpayer in the areas of welfare and the criminal justice system. Although the numbers of children in the intervention group were less than 100, the results supported much other US research pointing to the long-term value of interventions directed at disadvantaged families with pre-school children (Lazar and Darlington, 1982; Sylva, 1994; Waldfogel, 1999).

The Perry Pre-School Project is important also because it was shown to be especially effective in improving the life prospects of poor black children and therefore illustrates the value of pre-school experiences as providing 'add protection' against social disadvantage and discrimination. The scheme was also shown to protect against the risk of delinquency and the need for special education (Shepherd and Farrington, 1995). The educative role of play during the early years is widely acknowledged (David, 1996). Studies of pre-school programmes in the UK focusing upon play demonstrate better outcomes for children in contrast with curriculum-based schemes, which showed more behaviour problems and lack of commitment to school during primary years (e.g. Schweinhart, Weikart and Larner, 1986).

The US orientation towards enhancing child development through work with mothers contrasts with the UK community-led approach. However in both countries home visiting has played an important part - in the UK it may be a natural extension of health visiting, or can be done by parents from the community or by other staff. Drysdale and Purcell (1999) evaluated a community parent's programme in four areas within the UK (East Anglia, Dublin, North Tyneside and Tilbury), which demonstrated positive outcomes for mother's wellbeing, general health and diet. An evaluation of a similar scheme in Ireland (Johnson, Howell and Molloy, 1993) found that where first time mothers received support from experienced community mothers monthly for a year children were more likely to have received all their primary immunisations and to be read to daily, to play more cognitive games and be exposed to more nursery rhymes. Mothers and children were more likely to have a better diet, and mothers were less likely to feel tired or depressed, and had more positive feelings.

The value of home visiting or early intervention schemes of various kinds in guiding parents on the best methods of promoting their child's development was recognised for infants with learning disabilities in the 1970s/early 1980s – the best known of these schemes is Portage (Cameron and While, 1982; Ward 1982). Pugh (1981) described the basic principles of Portage and its operation in Wessex and South Glamorgan as a home visiting scheme in which parents were trained by a home teacher how to teach their children specific skills/tasks. The home teacher would initially assess the child and, on the basis of this assessment, the mother and teacher would select and put into practice tasks for the former to teach the child during the forthcoming week, the results recorded on an activity chart. Jones (1995:153) states that Portage was still used by a number of LEAs in the UK and 'involved a team of teachers working with pre-school children and their families before the child is placed in school'. Burke and Cigno's study (1996:66) of support to 67 families of disabled children stated that 'almost all parents who used nursery school Portage and respite care found them helpful'. Portage, in particular, was described as both effective with regard to improving the child's development and skills and supportive to the family (ibid: 130).

How is Sure Start being evaluated?

A defining feature of Sure Start is its identity as an example of policy-making based on evidence. Norman Glass, the Treasury civil servant associated with its beginnings, described Sure Start as a prime example of:

> 'joined-up government and evidence-based policy-making, with its origins grounded in a thorough analysis of the research literature of 'what works' (as) there was an accumulation of evidence that successful intervention in the earliest years offered the greatest potential for making a difference' (Glass, 1999:260).

In addition to this underpinning and pre-existing empirical evidence, Glass also describes how a commitment was made to commission a National Evaluation as 'the programme offers a unique opportunity to contribute to the knowledge base of the impact of early intervention on children and families in areas of multiple disadvantage' (op-cit: 262). Subsequently, following a competitive commissioning process, the National Evaluation of Sure Start (NESS) was initiated and began work in 2000. It has 4 modules: Impact; Implementation;

Cost Effectiveness and Local Context Analysis, whose aggregate brief (NESS Research Team, 2004) was to address three key questions:

- Do existing services change? (how, and if so, for which populations and under what conditions?)
- Are delivered services improved? (how, and if so, for which populations and under what conditions?)
- Do children, families & communities benefit? (how, and if so, for which populations and under what conditions?)

Toward the end of 2005 the NESS team claims that it is still exploring the nature of the relationship between different sets of programme characteristics and outcomes for individual children (Tunstill et al, 2005). This has been undertaken through a Programme Variability Study which considers links between aspects of SSLP implementation and the level of effectiveness on child and parenting outcomes for the 150 SSLPs included in the Impact Study. The study developed ratings of 18 dimensions of implementation. These 18 dimensions related to what was implemented (service quantity, service delivery, identification of users, reach strategies, service innovation and service flexibility), the processes underpinning proficient implementation of services (partnership composition, partnership functioning, leadership, multi-agency working, access to services, evaluation use and staff turnover) and holistic aspects of implementation (vision, communications, empowerment and ethos).

The focus of this book is upon findings from local evaluations of Sure Start conducted in the North-East of England; however, the objective is to try and blend findings from the 'local' with the emerging 'national' findings. The intended nature/scope for local evaluations was specified in: *Information on Evaluation* (National Sure Start Unit, August 2001) the principal focus being upon monitoring and feedback for the local Sure Start Partnership to whom a local evaluation study is accountable. Requirements on local evaluation since July 2003 however have been more prescriptive:

'As a condition of funding there is a requirement to evaluate three main issues: *Progress towards Sure Start PSA and SDA targets and objectives* (addressing the issue of the short-term impact of the programme and services on children, families & communities); *Cross-cutting issues*, for example partnership and interagency working, programme management, parental involvement (addressing how the programme is working in practice); and *Cost-effectiveness.*' (National Sure Start Unit, 2003)

The methodology is evidence-based comprising indepth interviews, case studies, (non) participant observation, focus groups and ethnography; and broadly attempts to address questions from participants' perspectives. Evidence is gathered from two main groups: professionals and parents. The term evidence-based practice is an amalgam of the terminology of science and professional practice: 'evidence-based' implies the concepts of scientific rationality, and 'practice' is about individual practitioner behaviour (Lockett, 1997). It is about finding, appraising and applying scientific evidence to understanding social problems.

The Sure Start local evaluations which follow have been undertaken collaboratively i.e. between researchers and the programmes themselves. The intended benefit of local evaluation to programme managers is to provide information enabling a more strategic focus; to professionals to help them evaluate their practice and support decision-making; and to parents to provide a forum for their views, and increase their knowledge and awareness about Sure Start.

2
Policy background and concepts

The Third Way

Sure Start was designed against a background of New Labour 'Third Way' politics- opportunity, responsibility, community being the central rhetorical trinity. White (2004) portrays the 'Third Way' as having four welfare policy themes each of which is applicable to ideology behind the Sure Start project.

1. Asset-based egalitarianism

State welfare provision should seek not merely to alleviate disadvantage but to build assets so that people are more able to avoid disadvantage. This enables us to expand opportunity, and so increase fairness, and efficiency (see Commission on Social Justice 1994; Brown 1999; Giddens 1998). Linked to this is the idea of the 'social investment state' (Lister, 2004) which for a number of 'Third Way' thinkers and politicians, figures as a normative ideal in which children and the community stand as emblems of a future prosperous, cohesive and inclusive society. The values of responsibility, inclusion and opportunity (RIO), as articulated by New Labour in particular, are its watchwords (Lister, 2000; 2002). Important to the development of the 'social investment state' is a series of service-based initiatives e.g. Sure Start. The argument goes that one major focus of concern must be human capability i.e. a better educated workforce is essential to improving the perceived trade-off between employment and earnings equality in post-industrial economies. *This brings educational policy to centre stage and underscores the importance of early-years intervention to foster child development in pre-school years.*

2. Welfare contractualism

'Opportunity must be combined with "responsibility"; thus benefits for the out-of-work should be made conditional on active job search and retraining' (Giddens, 1998:65, 116-17). In post-industrial labour markets, it is essential to redistribute to boost the incomes of the low-paid since low pay for some is the price of high employment. But the form of redistribution should be seen to reward work rather than laziness, pointing towards programmes such as the Earned Income Tax Credit (Clinton) and Working Families Tax Credit (New Labour). The core policy ideas of New Labour's 'Third Way' according to Le Grand (1998) are CORA- community, opportunity, responsibility, accountability. Contractualism, in a context of supportive, asset-building policies blends views from both the Left i.e. explaining social problems such as poverty, unemployment and crime in terms of structural barriers and from the Right i.e. in terms of individual agency. *This conception of social problems and of how to tackle them is reflected in Sure Start philosophy by focusing upon families who choose to become engaged with the programme in return for expected benefits, for example help with parenting, educational and work opportunities, and child care.*

3. Re-engineering public services

This identifies the state as guarantor, not necessarily provider, hence to meet the objective of 'opportunity,' the state endeavours to secure the provision of certain basic services to all such as health care and education. This does not imply that the state should always be the provider as in some cases it may be appropriate for the state to finance the service while contracting out immediate provision to private, for-profit companies or to the voluntary sector. Where the state retains a provider role, it may be appropriate to reorganize the system of service delivery, employing devices such as quasi-markets and making greater use of performance indicators backed up by inspection regimes. No specific approach is to be singled-out; the key is open-minded experimentation with a view to finding what works. *This is applicable to Sure Start as central and local government set objectives/targets for SSLPs to achieve leaving the methods to be chosen by individual programmes themselves.*

4. Mutualism and the re-engagement of civil society

The theme of re-engineering public services is linked to a 4th policy theme which is 'mutualism' and the effort to build and engage associations within civil society to help address social problems and deliver public services. Credit Unions have a vital role in combating financial exclusion (Brown, Conaty and Mayo, 2003). 'Public interest companies' with mandates to involve the communities they serve in managing service provision may have a role in running hospitals or schools (Lea and Mayo, 2003). Time banks can be used to help encourage volunteering (New Economics Foundation, 2001). More generally, policy objectives will not be met if the government simply does things to or for individuals. The government needs intermediaries close to the ground and to work with, and so must design policy interventions and services in ways that build and engage communities of relevant stakeholders with whom it can work in partnership. A theme for New Labour activists has been *how* to involve the public as co-producers of change requiring new forms of participation. With partnership as the defining feature of the mixed economy of welfare, New Labour's mission has been to invigorate rather than to attack the public services. *For Sure Start the emphasis has been upon the importance of a shared public service ethos between providers from different sectors.*

Social Exclusion

Sure Start as a contributor to the 'progressive' New Labour project has been positioned as playing an important role in its approach to social exclusion, disadvantaged neighbourhoods, low income families and childcare such as measures to integrate functionality of social care and education professionals.

Beyond getting people off welfare and into work and achieving some measure of income redistribution in favour of poorer families with children, New Labour (SEU, 2001:5) identified a range of interconnected social problems that they wished to address because of: 'the huge human costs to individuals and society, and the impact on the public finances and the competitiveness of the economy. The human costs were faced by individuals who experience social exclusion through underachievement in education and the labour market, low income, poor access to services, stress, ill-health and the impact on children and by wider society through reduced social cohesion, higher crime and fear of crime, and higher levels of stress and reduced mobility.' The centrality of work, education and training to New Labour's policies to tackle social exclusion in general, and particularly amongst young people, has been described extensively (Mooney, 2004; Fergusson, 2004).

The term social exclusion entered British policy debate in the early 1990s; and includes poverty and low income but is broader and addresses wider causes and consequences of poverty. Anderson and Sim (2000:11) claim that the term is *comprehensive* because, unlike the term 'poverty' it covers different dimensions of integration-civic, social, economic and interpersonal and *dynamic* in that it directs attention to processes rather than outcomes. The concept can be traced to Weber, who identified exclusion as one form of social closure (Parkin 1979). He saw exclusionary closure as the attempt of one group to secure for itself a privileged position at expense of some other group through a process of subordination.

According to Lund (2002:192) the meaning is opaque yet supporters of its use claim it poses the right questions, a view seemingly endorsed by New Labour's SEU (2001:1.2): '(it is) a shorthand term for what can happen when people or areas suffer from a combination of linked problems such as unemployment, poor skills, low incomes, poor housing, high crime, bad health and health breakdown'. The term social exclusion probably originated in France where it was used to refer primarily to those who slipped through the social insurance system; the socially excluded were those who were administratively excluded by the state (Lenoir 1974; Duffy 1997). *Les exclus* (the excluded) were those who fell through the net of social protection: in the 1970s, disabled people, lone parents, and the uninsured unemployed, especially young adults (Evans 1998). The increasing intensity of social problems on peripheral estates in large cities led to a broadening of the definition to include disaffected youth and isolated individuals. Later French thinking has emphasized the importance of unemployment (Paugam 1993).

In emphasizing *unemployment* this usage of the term overlaps with American views, although the Americans use terms such as ghettoization, marginalization and the underclass rather than social exclusion (Wilson 1996). The socially excluded become a matter for government as they constitute a threat to social solidarity. The concern with unemployment, especially long-term unemployment, was picked up by other continental European countries and together with an increasing recognition of the impact of globalization on national and regional economic structure, this led to the establishment of the European Observatory on social exclusion, and to the adoption of various 'social inclusion' resolutions at EU levels (Burchardt, Le Grand, Piachaud 2002:2). In Britain New Labour's concern has been focused on workless households (DSS 1998). The idea that social exclusion is 'a necessary and inherent characteristic of unequal post-industrial capitalism founded around a flexible labour market' (Byrne, 2002:45) does not distinguish a permanent underclass, but rather a reserve army of labour, continually changing places with those in low-status employment and serving to keep the power of the working-class in check.

Levitas suggests that the term *social exclusion* is simply a currently fashionable way of talking about poverty. She describes three narratives of government: the redistributionist discourse (RED) i.e. *the poor* have no money involving redistributional policies where the focus is on how to address financial inequalities; the social integrationist discourse (SID) i.e. *the poor* have no work where the focus is on policy responses to improve work/educational opportunities; and the moral underclass discourse (MUD) i.e. *the poor* have no morals where the focus is on policy responses to change individual/group behaviour. Stemming from the last of these her principal concern is with single mothers assessing consequences for New Labour's conception, not focusing primarily on low income but including polarization, differentiation and inequality i.e. the need to understand the processes by which individuals and their communities become polarized, socially differentiated and unequal. Washington and Paylor (1998:332) contend that central to most definitions is the notion of *separateness* from the life experiences common to the majority within society:

> 'Social exclusion is multidimensional disadvantage which dislocates people from the major social and economic opportunities in society: from citizenship, housing, adequate living standards or employment. The processes which locate people in these positions may well be different and their exact position on the margins may be varied but the characteristic definition of the terrain is that it is occupied by people who are apart from the mainstream of social living.'

Burchardt, Le Grand and Piachaud (1999) take up the issue of *voluntary/involuntary* social exclusion:

> 'An individual is socially excluded if (a) he or she is geographically resident in a society but (b) for reasons beyond his or her control he or she cannot participate in the normal activities of citizens in that society and (c) he or she would like to so participate. Condition (a) is necessary so as not to describe as socially excluded those who happen to live within the geographical confines of another society, but who nonetheless meet conditions (b) and (c).'

Conditions (b) and (c) address voluntary/involuntary social exclusion and the right of individuals to self-exclude:

> 'Condition (b) implies that an individual who voluntarily withdraws him or herself from society – a hermit, a recluse, a Scrooge- is not socially excluded. There are a number of reasons why we might be unhappy with this condition. First there might be a question in specific cases as to whether an apparently voluntary act of self exclusion is really voluntary' (op.cit 1999)

If a group faced with continuous hostility from a wider society withdraws into itself developing its own independent or counter-culture, then the context still makes it a case of social exclusion where people are being made to do things against their will. Even if a particular case of *self exclusion* is genuinely voluntary it may still be classified as social exclusion. If social exclusion is preferred by the individuals themselves it is not good for the wider society to have people resident in that society but not part of it. New Labour's view is that they need to be converted towards inclusion. Condition (c) assumes that individuals have a desire to participate whereas circumstances appear not to allow this. What then if a resident is excluded from a society's normal activities by factors beyond his or her control but does not care? Burchardt et al describe this as *problematic* i.e. whom to count in research on the subject. Fergusson (2004:291) has emphasized the centrality of participation i.e. social exclusion as being denied a range of forms of social participation that make people integrated, interdependent, networked-in 'stakeholders' and members of society.

In establishing the Social Exclusion Unit (SEU) the then Prime Minister Tony Blair (1998:2) described social exclusion 'as broadly covering those people who do not have the means, material or otherwise, to participate in social, economic, political and cultural life'. This Unit set up in the Cabinet Office in Britain after the 1997 General Election avoided becoming enmeshed in definitional issues as New Labour's approach to reducing social exclusion was based upon a broad policy of *work for those who can* and *security for those who cannot work*. Robinson and Oppenheim (1998) propose four lead indicators of the level of social exclusion in Britain: the proportion of the population falling below 50% of average household income; the International Labour Office (ILO) unemployment rate; the proportion of 16 year olds failing to get at least 20 GCSE points; and the Standard Mortality Ratio in Social Class IV/V in relation to other social classes. This approach correlates with one prescribing *normal activities* such as that of Burchardt, Le Grand & Piachaud (1999) who suggest the following five dimensions: *consumption activity* - being able to consume at least up to some minimum level the goods and services considered normal for the society and as a dimension is closest to traditional measures of poverty or deprivation (Townsend 1979; Mack and Lansley 1985); *savings activity* - accumulating savings, pension entitlements or owning property; *production activity* - engaging in an economically or socially valued activity such as paid work, education or training, retirement if over state pension age, or looking after a family; *political activity* - engaging in some collective effort to improve or protect the immediate or wider social or physical environment and includes voting; and *social activity* - engaging in significant social interaction with family or friends, and identifying with a cultural group or community. Measures of social exclusion attempt to identify not only those who lack resources but also those whose non-participation arises in different ways through discrimination, chronic ill-health, geographical location or cultural identification, however lack of material resources remains a central and important cause of non-participation.

Lupton and Power (2002: 118-140) have examined how poverty and social exclusion in Britain are spatially concentrated demonstrating that poverty has become more concentrated in certain neighbourhoods stating that the nature of neighbourhoods actually contributes to the social exclusion of their residents in three ways:

'Firstly, neighbourhoods have intrinsic characteristics well-established and difficult to change. These include their location, transport infrastructure, housing and economic base. Such characteristics are not wholly determined at neighbourhood level; for example, an over-supply of housing might be the result of national trends or local depopulation; weak labour market prospects might reflect wider regional trends. Secondly, residential sorting takes place concentrating the most disadvantaged people in the least advantaged neighbourhoods. Part of the sorting process is driven by market responses to intrinsic neighbourhood characteristics, such as the quality of the housing or the type of work available which affect the desirability of neighbourhoods. Thirdly, once this concentration of disadvantage is established, neighbourhoods can acquire even more damaging characteristics. Acquired characteristics include the area's reputation, its environment, services and facilities, levels of crime and disorder, and aspects of social life such as extent of social interaction and residents' levels of confidence in the neighbourhood. When these characteristics are negative they limit opportunities for residents and reduce the quality of life, and they can contribute to a sense of powerlessness and alienation that is in itself excluding.'

There is a case for targeting measures on poorest neighbourhoods involving other sorts of special initiatives, e.g. programmes to improve skills, qualifications of the unemployed, helping them to find/keep jobs; increased benefit levels, schemes to supply free childcare, family support services which should not only apply to individuals in poor areas, but those who are at risk of social exclusion anywhere (Smith 1999). New Labour's SEU (2001: 42) reported that: 'In many cases the structure of Government has meant that the joined-up problems of social exclusion did not receive a joined-up response hence the demand for agency partnership'. New Labour launched a series of initiatives targeted on selected local areas aimed mainly at *people change* which was a reversal of ideas and policies associated with previous Labour governments where measures were aimed more at structural changes and socio-economic development more broadly.

The notion arose that high unemployment was associated with areas having populations with relatively poor skills, educational attainment and a wide range of health-related problems. Programmes directed to deprived areas included Education Action Zones, Employment Zones, the Crime Reduction Programme, Health Action Zones, the New Deal for communities, the Neighbourhood Renewal Fund, Sure Start, Healthy Living Centres and the Social Regeneration Budget which was revamped to concentrate on sixty-five most deprived local authorities. A SEU report (1998:3) concluded that the impact of earlier initiatives to combat neighbourhood deprivation had been limited because: 'there had been too many different schemes each parachuted from outside that had lacked coordination and had concentrated too much on physical renewal and not enough on people.' Inclusive mainstream became a policy effort to focus attention of education and health care services set for special initiatives aimed at reducing health and social inequalities in the UK involving specially-funded projects becoming partners with mainstream services to create additionality and sustainability.

Partnership

Sure Start is claimed to be based upon partnership-working and is planned at local level via Partnership Boards (LPBs). What is meant by the term 'partnership'? It has been presented as a critique of market-led and state-led forms of governance, whereas in policy discourse, according to Mcdonald (2005), it offers the potential for a more resource-efficient, outcome-effective and inclusive-progressive form of policy delivery. Variously identified as interagency, interprofessional, collaborative or joined-up working, joined-up thinking or a whole systems or holistic approach, that which we have chosen to call 'partnership-working' exists along a broad continuum of theory and practice (Balloch and Taylor, 6:2002). Partnership became the mantra of the 1997 Labour Government in its efforts to reform public services to break down 'old-fashioned demarcations between staff and barriers between services' (DoH, 1998). Two particular White Papers, namely 'Modernizing Social Services' and ' The New NHS: Modern, Dependable', set out approaches to facilitate closer working between local agencies e.g. 'Health Improvement Programmes and Health Action Zones provide the means for health and local authorities to work together with other independent bodies, as well as local communities and individuals to pursue joint objectives to improve health and reduce inequalities'. (NSC 1999/152: LAC (99) 26, para 10). New Labour's emphasis on finding 'joined-up' solutions to social problems triggered enormous rhetoric on partnership choosing terms such as interagency working, joined-up government and seamless services to characterize their 'collaborative discourse' (Clarence and Painter, 1998).

One definition (Lowndes & Skelcher, 1998:314) is that partnership is analytically distinct from a network as a mode of governance and means by which social coordination is achieved and does not imply that relations between actors are conducted on the basis of mutual benefit, trust and reciprocity but that each actor has a vested interest in belonging to it eg by representing a particular voice. Partnerships are associated with a variety of forms of social coordination including networks, hierarchies and markets (Powell and Exworthy, 2002:16). According to Huxham (2000:339) many words are used to describe governance structures that involve cross-organisational working such as partnership, alliance, collaboration, coordination, cooperation, network, joint working and multi-party working. Practitioners claim different meanings for these labels, typically arguing that a particular situation is a 'collaboration' but *not* a 'partnership' or vice-versa as there appears to be no consistency in usage of such terms. Mitchell and Shortell (2000: 242) equate the term 'partnership' with coalitions, alliances, consortia and related forms of inter-organisational relations. McDonald (2005) argues that research into partnerships remains 'theoretically undeveloped' and does not address deeper contradictions relating to the structuring relations of power which underpin conceptions of partnership. However it is important to recall why partnerships were originally so positively evaluated as they were seen to represent one mechanism for bringing government departments and local authorities, professional groups both within and between agencies, those who deliver services and those who receive them to work together towards a common goal (Audit Commission,

2000). Partnership is claimed as a mode of 'disciplined pluralism' linked to 'progressive governance' defining the management of New Labour public sector agencies (Kettle, 2003).

A different version of partnership lays emphasis on mutual benefit, trust and reciprocity as highly relevant, thereby potentially acting wherein the whole becomes greater than the sum of the parts (Gambetta, 1998). In this case each partner in sharing their ideas, knowledge and resources stands to gain from the additional ideas, knowledge and resources that other members of the partnership bring to it by offering partners opportunity to influence each other to behave differently and in ways in which actions can become more aligned allowing partners to achieve their goals more economically and effectively. Considering trust as an endemic attribute, partnership is viewed as an organizational arrangement with normative rules, determining what behaviour is permissible and what constitutes a violation of trust. The rules are designed to facilitate exchange in a situation otherwise open to exploitation. Whenever agents need or choose to cooperate with each other the presence or absence of trust is overwhelmingly important (Lorenz, 1998:206).

Williams (1988) considers the idea of a 'motivation to cooperate' and the relation of that idea to the concept of trust. His assumption is: 'Two agents cooperate when they engage in a joint venture for the outcome of which the actions of each are necessary, and where a necessary action by at least one of them is not under the immediate control of the other' (op.cit:7). Under this definition, a situation in which two agents cooperate necessarily involves at least one of them depending on the other, or being, a dependent party. The notion of 'cooperation' does not fall under this definition, because everyone involved is under the immediate control of everyone: if a party does not do his bit, this can be immediately detected. In the instance where one party depends on another, the notion of trust comes in. Williams (op.cit:7) makes the following distinction: 'Cooperation is a symmetrical relation: if x cooperates with y, y cooperates with x (if that seems unnatural, read 'cooperates' as 'engages in a cooperative venture with'). Depends on, however, is a non-symmetrical relation: if x depends on y-in the sense that his getting what he wants of the venture depends on y doing his part-it may or may not be the case that y depends on x.' The question posed by this author is: what motivations do there need to be for there to be cooperation? One possible answer to the question is that the only way to produce practices of cooperation is by confining them to persons whose disposition and character are individually known to one another (they rely on what might be called 'thick trust'). People will not do this unless they have some assurance that the other, non-dependent, party will not defect. Cooperation requires trust in the sense that dependent parties need some degree of assurance that non-dependent parties will not defect. Cooperation is conditional on the belief that the other party is disposed to grant trust blindly, but also on the belief that he will be well disposed towards us if we make the right move. Thus tit for tat can be equilibrium only if both players believe the other will abide by it, otherwise other equilibria are just as possible and self-confirming. 'We can trust and distrust distrust, and we learn that it can be rewarding to behave as if we trusted even in unpromising situations' (Gambetta: 228).

Partnership as a mode of governance became applied to the development of children's provision with New Labour publishing its Green Paper 'Meeting the childcare challenge' in May 1998 requiring local authorities to convene partnerships based on the then recently established Early Years and Development Child Care Partnerships (EYDCPs). These had been set up to regulate the distribution of nursery education places including assembling information on childcare demand and supply in their area and producing local plans covering also expansion of the childcare workforce. EYDCPs provided a forum in which different local agencies met, expressed their own concerns and achieved better understanding of those of others. Partnerships offer in theory provision responsive to idiosyncrasies of local demand together with a sense of local community 'ownership' of child care policy.

Family support

Sure Start is based upon a model of *family support*—an original SDA target was that 75% of families should report personal evidence of an improvement in the quality of services providing family support. What is meant by the term 'family support'?

The term became associated with the 1989 Children Act which empowered local authorities to provide support for families with children 'in need'. The Guidance and Regulations to the Act states that:

'They (local authorities) are required to make provision for advice, guidance, counselling assistance and home help services. They are empowered to provide social, cultural or leisure activities or assistance with holidays. Local authorities are required in addition to provide such family centres as they consider appropriate in their area.' 3.1

Smith (1999) arguing in support of family centres states that: 'locating the debate about 'prevention' (of harm) within the 1989 Children Act, and its association with individual rather than structural definitions and explanations of disadvantage and risk, is unhelpful and that there is need to 'refocus' on mainstream *family support services* rather than specialist child protection.'

Since the 1989 Act was passed there has been a plethora of reports teasing out the implications of *family support,* and its connection with other social policy measures. These include family support as an aspect of community care and empowerment (Stevenson & Parsloe, 1993); as a contribution to better parenting (Pugh et al, 1994; Utting, 1995; Lloyd, 1999); as a way of preventing child abuse (Gough, 1993; National Commission of Inquiry into the Prevention of Child Abuse, 1996); as a service response to cases of child abuse (Thoburn et al, 2000); as a service to children in need (Tunstill, 1995; Tunstill & Aldgate, 2000); and as part of a debate about the value of home-based versus centre-based family support (Buchanan & Hudson, 1998; Duggan et al, 1999). Penn & Gough (2002) assert that social work and health services tend to operate within a model of family support narrowly focused on emotional support and behavioural change, rather than a preferred needs-based model which considers income maintenance, childcare, leisure and education. Family support for parents of children with learning disabilities tends to emphasise respite care, day care / education, and income maintenance (Burke & Cigno, 2002).

One of the key more recent debates in UK child welfare has been about the relationship between family support and child protection (Department of Health, 1995; Association of Directors of Social services, 1996; Parton, 1997). This debate has followed the emergence of an authoritarian style developing in child protection during the 1980s —largely as a result of political and media concern about child deaths and the subsequent inquiry findings. This led to the emergence of a child protection discourse which placed an emphasis on firm and clear action to protect children seen to be abused or at risk of abuse

(Frost, Johnson, Stein & Wallis 2000). The terms of this debate began to be shifted by the events in Cleveland (HMSO, 1988; Campbell, 1988) where it had been perceived that child protection practice was in danger of acting against the best interest of both parents and children by taking children away from their homes without substantive evidence of harm. This shift was confirmed by the Children Act 1989 which provided the platform for the Department of Health to attempt to shift the terms of the place of child protection within family support work (Frost et al, op. cit). They published a summary of many research studies which argued that:

> 'An approach based on the process of Section 47 enquiries (which includes a duty to investigate children at risk of significant harm) and the provision of Section 17 services, might well shift the emphasis in child protection work more towards family support.' (Department of Health, 1995:55)

Smith (1999) observes that this emphasis on family support was confirmed in the Department of Health's guidelines which increased responsibilities of local authorities stating that the definition of 'need' in the Act was:

> 'deliberately wide to reinforce the emphasis on preventive services and support to families and that services should not be confined to children at risk of significant harm which attracts the duty to investigate under section 47'. (Department of Health, 1991: 2.4)

However surveys in the early 1990s of local authorities' interpretation of Section 17 of the Children Act (Aldgate & Tunstill, 1996; Tunstill, 1997) have shown that they have tended to give priority to children for whom social services departments already have responsibility. In other words the surveys showed that children 'at risk of significant harm' or 'neglect', and those already in care or accommodated or on remand, were given priority by seven in ten local authorities, children with disabilities by half, and children or young people involved in crime by one third (Smith, op. cit). Findings showed that children growing up in families with lone parents already facing pressures of low income, unemployment, or poor housing or homelessness figured lower in the priority lists i.e. the emphasis given to preventative family support services was relatively low. More recent studies did not detect any significant change in local authorities' priorities to reflect the

Department of Health's 'refocusing' initiative, or wider definition of eligibility (Social Services Inspectorate, 2002).

The publication of *Child Protection: Messages from Research* (Department of Health, 1995) and of the 'Supporting Families' Green Paper (Home Office, 1998) have both highlighted the importance of developing family support services, in keeping with the word and the spirit of the Children Act 1989. Frost, Johnson, Stein & Wallis (2000) consider Home Start which offers support to mothers with children under 5 through voluntary home visiting, as a measure of family support to deal with child protection. The authors state that 'this wider perspective on family support has been mandated by the Blair government in their support to Home Start, the development of the Sure-Start project and the other programmes outlined in 'Supporting Families' (Home Office, 1998).' They conclude:

> 'Our research illustrates that it is possible to deliver a valued form of *family support* through voluntary organisations such as Home Start, the advantages of which are:
> - they can mobilize local commitment both in recruiting voluntary visitors and management committees;
> - they can contribute to the continuum of local family support services;
> - they can offer a flexible, non-stigmatizing service;
> - they can work in partnership with local professionals.'

The line between family support and child protection is complex, or to put it another way, between 'need' and 'risk'. The over-riding concerns of the Children Act 1989 and Children Act 2004 are the definition and execution of the two tasks of *promoting* and *safeguarding* their welfare. While the detail of policy may change in respect both of measuring the relevant outcomes; and establishing the appropriate balance to be struck between the two tasks, the central duties are perennial and cross-cultural (Tunstill, 2006).

Interprofessionalism

Part of the Sure Start vision is that 'Providers of services and support will work together in new ways that cut across old professional and agency boundaries and focus more successfully on family and community needs' (DFEE, 1999:6) and thereby achieve Government targets/objectives more adroitly. Each SSLP is founded upon a concept of interprofessionalism i.e. ideas of professional collaboration, integration and a need for greater understanding of each other's roles or multi-agency working, although often professionals have simply been exhorted to initiate multi-agency working with little training or guidance (Anning & Edwards, 1999). This is not without challenges, as in multi-agency teamwork professional knowledge boundaries can become blurred and professional identity can be challenged as roles and responsibilities change but there are actual/potential conflicts for professionals working in multi-agency teams about models of understanding, about roles, identities, status and power, about information-sharing, and around links with other agencies (Robinson & Cottrell, 2005). The literature on interprofessional collaboration regarding health, education and social care shows that it is not readily achieved in practice owing to dilemmas associated with reconciling different professional beliefs and practices (Easen et al, 2000; Freeman, Miller & Ross, 2002) and further research is needed regarding outcomes and costs (Nicholas et al, 2003; Barr & Ross, 2006). Difficulties of joint working focus on differences in occupational culture, including professional identity, status and accountability (Johnson et al, 2003); the complexity of managing workers on different conditions of service and pay scales (Atkinson, Wilkin, Scott & Kinder, 2001); problems associated with combining funding streams from distinct service budgets (Roaf, 2002); difficulties in developing a common language for use in multi-agency meetings (Salmon & Rapport, 2005) and the need to invest in joint training and to generate continuing interprofessional learning opportunities that build on the basics (Barr & Ross, 2006). Differences and similarities in professional values for instance in relation to nursing and social work should perhaps be accepted as unavoidable and even desirable, and there may be good arguments for concentrating on optimizing the quality of interprofessional dialogue around values, rather than for seeking to remove those differences (Wilmot, 1995).

The emphasis from Government on partnership within social care and health care agencies has tended to be on strategic inter-agency working rather than interprofessional relationships (Hudson, 1999); and that with the proposal to establish a data-base for each child following the Children Act 2004 the 'top down' implementation model takes for granted professional compliance and trust among professionals (Hudson, 2005). Indicators for positive interprofessional team-working appear to be the personal qualities and commitment of staff, communication within the team and the opportunity to develop creative working methods within the team (Molyneux, 2001); also a culture of commitment at strategic and operational levels to overcome professionally differentiated attitudes (Harker et al, 2004). Issues of 'personhood' cannot be ignored, as professional and disciplinary differences are manifested in terms of who professional persons consider themselves to be in relation to what is expected of them (Dombeck, 1997). When boundaries of distinct groups appear to come under threat from integration of various professional groups, there may be a sense of loss of professional identity, there may be tribalism or feeling of ambivalence, conflict and grief, and the need to maintain the self-confidence of different professional groups is very real (Atkins, 1998). The problem with trying to create professional partnership, according to Sennett (1999: 84) is that it is based upon a 'domain of demeaning superficiality which besets the workplace. Groups, teams tend to hold together through keeping to the surface of things - shared superficiality keeps people together by avoiding difficult, divisive, personal questions'. Hunter (2000:43) asserts that it is the absence of authority or rather the 'leader' figure which mars successful interprofessionalism and that this is prerequisite to delivering agreed objectives; also that : 'deep, lasting partnerships can only be established where there are stable long-term relationships and real trust can emerge ... all the pressures associated with short-term deadlines, and the demand for instant results, militate against such partnerships being given a fair wind'.

Interprofessionalism itself has potentially confusing related concepts since writers differentiate between multi-, inter- and transdisciplinary, with regard to emphasis on sharing and collaboration, seeing only the final term as referring to true collaboration (Orelove and Sobsey, 1991; Rainforth et al, 1992; Leathard, 1994; Lacey and Thomas, 1993; Lacey, 2001). For example, Orelove and Sobsey (op.cit) offer definitions for each of these demonstrating qualitative differences between them. They suggest that the term 'multi-disciplinary' refers to professionals from more than one discipline, working alongside but separately from each other; not referring to working together but to co-existence and suggest that those who work in a multi-disciplinary manner make no attempt to allocate resources to prevent overlap, but work independently of each other, concentrating on the disability or educational need for which they are responsible. The same authors suggest that 'inter-disciplinary' work refers to the way in which professionals share information and decide an education and care programmes together. These programmes are however implemented separately by members of the individual disciplines. Finally, they go on to describe the term 'trans-disciplinary' which involves sharing or transferring information and skills across traditional disciplinary boundaries to enable one or two team members to be the primary workers supported by others working as consultants.

Parent Participation

A key objective of SSLPs is to achieve meaningful parental involvement. What is meant by 'effective participation'? The notion of 'authentic' participation of parents through exercise of contextual power has been examined by Halvorsen (2003). More recent studies e.g. Boehm and Staples (2004) make use of empowerment theory. Tunstill et al (2005:164) conclude from NESS case study data that the only way to make inroads on any or all of the myriad disincentives to service use is to think in terms of an on-going engagement process or 'continuum'. The importance to child development of learning in the home and of parental involvement lies in pre-school education. Recent studies eg Melhuish et al (2001), Sammons et al (2002) demonstrate that learning-at-home with parents combined with high quality pre-school education make a positive difference to children's social and intellectual development. Another study found that: 'the most effective settings shared child-related information between parents and staff and parents were often involved in decision-making about their child's learning programme. There were more intellectual gains for children in centres that encouraged high levels of parental involvement' (Sylva et al, 2003). The principle of partnership between parents and professionals indicates a move away from a *'deficit model'* (Ball, 1994) regarding this relationship which implies compensating for perceived deficiencies.

This notion of partnership goes alongside an emphasis on user involvement and user participation in health and social care policies. The Department of Health (2001:33) states that patients and the public will play a greater role in shaping NHS services than ever before following policy initiatives determining the involvement of service users in service planning, delivery and monitoring at every level. Stacey (1991) notes that partnership implies equality and a division of power that draw parents into decision-making and policy issues going beyond helping and information-sharing. The Start-Right report on early learning (Ball, 1994) noted that the issue of partnership still tended to be seen in terms of 'parental involvement' which is depicted as a hierarchy of levels from non-participation to partnership and control. Ball proposes a 'triangle of care' formed by parents, professionals and the community with parents at the apex, the key issue being the quality of the relationship between parents and professionals. Inherent in such debate is the broader notion of empowerment. Foot et al (2002) suggest that whilst the child's best interests have always been paramount in the notion of partnership between parents and professionals, views over the nature of that partnership have changed with more emphasis on the parents themselves as beneficiaries of parental involvement and hence on empowerment (for example Ball, 1994) and self-efficacy (Bandura, 1997). Empowerment itself tends to be an ill-defined concept. Indeed, its definitions are 'many and varied' (Malin et al, 2002:61). Traditionally, 'to empower' has meant 'to invest legally or formally with power or authority; to authorize, license' (OUP, 1969) and 'to impart or bestow power to an end or for a purpose; to enable, permit' (ibid.). Empowerment has been defined as 'the giving to individuals of power to take decisions in matters relating to themselves, especially [in an organisation] in relation to self-development' (Chambers-Harrap, 1993). Barrow and Milburn (1990:113) suggest that in contemporary usage the word 'empower' is used without reference to what a person is empowered to do making its meaning nebulous. Deutsch (1973:4) identifies that: 'power is a relational concept; it does not reside in the individual but rather in the relationship of the person to his environment'.

Professionals may see empowerment 'as a matter of giving, the granting of something which is in their gift to bestow or withhold' (Farrell and Gilbert, 1996:3) whilst users 'generally feel that it is more to do with playing an active part in their own care or community' (ibid.) Generally the term is used to mean that service users have more control or power to take decisions, take actions, make choices, or work with others which they were previously unable to do which helps to get over problems about whether people can be given or granted power by professionals (Barnes and Bowl, 2001). Pease (2002:135) argues that the modernist concept upon which empowerment rests can have unintended disempowering effects: 'by conceptualizing power as a commodity identities are forced into a powerful-powerless dualism which does not always do justice to diverse experiences, thus we can sometimes contribute to dominance in spite of our liberatory intentions'. Ball (1994:46) proposes that the midwife is an exemplar of a professional who 'empowers he mother to bear and tend the child; that professionals need to do more than pay lip-service to the idea that their relationship with parents is a partnership of equals and that giving the idea reality will involve seeking to enable and empower parents and children to become more confident and self-reliant'. Studies of 'effective participation' of parents show a complex gradual process that operates at different levels (Arnstein, 1969; Shemmings and Shemmings, 1995); not all parents wishing to be included in a way that involves *moving up a hierarchy* (Farrell and Gilbert, 1996). A general conclusion is that whereas tokenism may be easily achieved authentic participation may not; and for professionals the challenge is about how to support parents in different types of working relationships.

FINDINGS FROM LOCAL SURE START EVALUATIONS

3
Accessibility of services

THIS CHAPTER EXPLORES issues relating to the accessibility and acceptability of services, based on a survey of parents and carers carried out in two phases in a trailblazer SSLP. The chapter then discusses the findings of a study regarding targeted work on involving fathers in one Round Five Sure Start Local Programme. Fathers are traditionally regarded as a 'hard-to-reach' group.

ISSUES RELATING TO SERVICE USE

As noted by Garbers et al (2006),

'The facilitation of access to services represents a universal challenge for all those policy-makers and practitioners responsible for designing and delivering services for children and their families in the community' (Garbers et al, 2006: 287).

This section discusses issues such as attitudes towards the use of new services, the acceptability of services and their relationship to the importance of social networks and community links. It is based on selected findings from a study involving two surveys of parents/carers in a Sure Start trailblazer programme. One of the findings was that new initiatives can be viewed with suspicion by the target population, but that attitudes can change over time and are influenced by the overall philosophy and approach of the programme and its workers, and by community networks. These findings may have implications for the development of other services for children and families, such as Sure Start Children's Centres.

The study consisted of two phases, one year apart. The purpose of the first phase was to ascertain current knowledge and understanding of Sure Start, what services were being accessed, what benefits they were perceived to be bringing so far, and in what other ways Sure Start could work with families and the local community. Two members of the research team undertook the initial planning of an interview schedule following discussions with key Sure Start staff. The first draft was discussed by one researcher and three members of the Sure Start team to clarify the appropriateness of the content and the wording of the questions in order to omit areas of jargon and ambiguity and prevent misinterpretation. This was particularly important as three researchers would be carrying out the interviews and it was vital that they did not interpret the questions differently. The comments of these team members were incorporated into a second draft. The interview was then piloted with two parents and some suggestions were incorporated into a third draft of the interview schedule. This was then discussed further with two more members of the team and clarification regarding specific areas of work was sought from three other members. Again, the purpose was to confirm appropriate content, ensure clarity, omit jargon and ambiguity and prevent misinterpretation. Further amendments were made and a final, fourth version of the interview schedule was produced.

The survey was carried out using a stratified sample of families within the Sure Start area. The number of families to include from each of the five geographical areas out of a targeted total of 100 was calculated on a proportionate basis, and a systematic sample was then selected for interview. The population of families with children under four years of age in the Sure Start area ($n=735$) had already been stratified according to postcode within each geographical area. From the proposed total of 100, the number of families to interview within each area was calculated on a proportionate basis in order to reflect the relative numbers of families with children under four years of age in each area (Robson, 1993). The next stage in the selection consisted of forming a stratified systematic sample. This involved choosing a starting point in the sampling frame at random and choosing every seventh family from the population of each area to reach the required total. The survey was conducted face-to-face and the final number of surveys completed was sixty-seven.

The phase two survey was carried out one year later. The purpose was to explore the perspectives of parents and carers on the effectiveness and impact of Sure Start over a period of time. A total of 47 surveys was completed, again conducted face-to-face.

Analysis was undertaken by two researchers through developing coding frames identified from themes emerging from the data.

Attitudes to new initiatives

The National Evaluation of Sure Start (Report 01, June 2002) identified that

'Negotiating a pathway between strategies that tailor services to the needs of specific groups, and those that are seen by potential recipients to target provision in a potentially stigmatising way' (DfES, 2002: 111)

was one of the specific challenges that had faced Sure Start in the implementation stage.

The findings of the initial survey had suggested that Sure Start might be perceived as being for particular groups of people, such as 'underprivileged', 'poor' or 'needy' families or lone parents. For example,

'The impression I got at the beginning was that it was for underprivileged, or people with difficulties, or lone parents. That might put a lot of people off... A lot of people might say they wouldn't use it because they perceive it as being for the underprivileged – that's how it's portrayed in the press, that's the way it comes across'. [generally, nationally rather than locally]

'I think it's seen as more for poor or needy families. I didn't go looking for them, they were referred to me, but they have been very helpful'.

The findings of the second survey confirmed that this had indeed been a common expectation. However, their experience was, for example,

'different to what I thought. It's better because it helps everybody, not just people on benefits and it's for anybody who wants to use it. I realised when I came down and got to know more about it that I could join in with more things'.

It was interesting to note that several respondents had expected Sure Start to have a rather authoritarian role and that they would be told what to do, and they made it clear that this would not have been welcomed. For example,

'I thought it would be like a lot of health visitors and other official people telling you what to do. I thought, 'Nobody's telling me how to bring my child up'. I thought that was what it would be like, but they're not like that'.

In fact, the nature of the client/professional relationship was one of the most significant ways in which experience had differed to and exceeded expectation. Apart from in one case where a young mother felt that *'sometimes it feels like people are watching you'*, Sure Start was not seen as an intrusive service, but as one that provided opportunities for support, was non-judgemental and was available when needed, and where, in normal circumstances, decision-making and choice rested with the family. For example,

'That's one thing about Sure Start – they don't pry. They don't, like, come pushing all the time – they help you when you need them and help the best they can. I like that approach. If you talk to them you get support and they don't criticise'.

'You go at first and you expect them to say do this, do that and get on that, but you're not told what to do, they encourage you to participate in what's going on ... I was expecting it to be like going back to school and being told what to do'.

The efforts made by a toddler group leader to introduce Sure Start and Sure Start staff into her local area in order to provide extra activities, bring greater health awareness to the group, and *'make Sure Start more accessible to people'* so that *'they would realise it wasn't an authority kind of thing and it was more relaxed and people could access services without feeling they would be judged'* give an indication of the importance of Sure Start developing networks in the community in order to develop understanding.

One mother commented that she had been *'dubious'* about Sure Start at first, thinking *'They don't know me – what do they know about me and my family?'* but her experience had surpassed her expectations in terms of the way professionals worked together, for example sharing information and working *'like a community'*.

> *'There doesn't appear to be different departments – like that's the Nursery and that's the health visitor – they all seem quite happy to work with you together, not 'That's my case and this is the little bit in my case I want you to work with'. It's like a little community within Sure Start, rather than different departments. It seems like a community that's happy to intermingle. Everybody is happy to share the information they've got to try and find solutions'.*

This feeling of staff working together, liaising and communicating with each other, together with confidence in their confidentiality, was a common finding amongst those who had had a significant amount of contact with Sure Start professionals.

Furthermore, the evaluation highlighted the importance of recognising that parents are not a homogeneous group. Rather, they are a diverse group who will have diverse needs, aspirations and experiences. It is clear that Sure Start as a project will mean different things to different people, and will be more important for some than others. Some parents will 'pick and choose' aspects that are most relevant to them and/or their children, or that meet particular needs at particular times. For example, parents said, *'I wanted somewhere to go with the bairn, so I go to the [Drop-in]*, or *'my child loves books, so I've just joined the Early Years Library'*. Others said that they had had a lot of support at a particular time of need (e.g. bereavement, family illness, depression), but, as one commented, *'by the time I had my son I was back on track'*. Other parents will choose to 'embrace' the project as a whole. The evidence shows that the approach of this programme had supported parents in making informed choices and had the flexibility and capacity to respond to need as and when appropriate.

The growing perception that being involved Sure Start did not define one as 'needy' or unable to cope, that there is no stigma in being attached to Sure Start, is important in terms of the Sure Start principle that programmes must 'avoid stigma by ensuring that all local families are able to use Sure Start services'. It is also important for the future development of services and possible perceptions of some of those who may be considered 'hard to reach'. In situations where families may still be hesitant about using services, the way Sure Start presents itself is of crucial importance.

Families' perceptions of services

Autonomy vs. Dependency

The attitudes and culture of organisations are important for clients' perceptions of services. Beresford, writing in the context of the Laming Report on the Victoria Climbié Inquiry, suggests that 'Real reform comes from addressing organisational attitudes, cultures and understandings first, and structures second' (Guardian Society, 5.2.03).

As stated above, an analysis of families' initial expectations suggested that some parents thought that they were going to be told what to do and how to bring their children up, which they emphasised would not have been acceptable. As one parent stated, *'I don't want anybody trampling down my views'* and another, *'Nobody's going to tell me how to bring my child up'*. This seems to suggest some initial cynicism about the nature and approach of Sure Start, and a suspicion that their expertise and experience and their own knowledge of their children would be ignored or invisible. It also confirms research that suggests that parents want to be treated with respect and their parenting to be valued. For example, surveys with regard to social work have highlighted that what service users most want from social workers are positive human qualities of openness and honesty, warmth and empathy and the capacity to treat people with respect and equality (Beresford, Guardian Society, 5.2.03). Bad feelings about a service have been found to relate to people feeling that they have not been listened to or have been made to feel like bad parents (Quinton, 2004).

These families' subsequent experience of Sure Start showed a different approach to that expected, with a strong element of choice, and Sure Start was *'not forced down your throat'*. Families were clearly making personal choices and decisions about accessing those services that were seen to meet their own or their children's needs. There was a strong sense of it being down to the individual and that *'it's there for you to use as much or as little as you like'*. Parents felt that *'You're not seen as the problem, but as part of the solution'*, *'They don't make you feel stupid'* and *'you feel on the same level'*. Respondents stressed strongly that they felt that the staff were treating them as equals, and there was a sense of mutuality and a changing symmetry of power relationships. The issue of power relationships is further explored in the second section of this chapter.

Furthermore, there was evidence of consultation, choice and personal decision-making over proposed programmes or interventions, such that parents felt in control. This suggests that the Sure Start local programme was promoting autonomy rather than dependency amongst parents. They appeared to be facilitating and encouraging the development of the confidence, knowledge, skills and self-esteem that enable one to make autonomous decisions as a parent rather than depending on others. In addition, they appeared to be working to the Sure Start principle of 'involving parents, grandparents and carers in ways that build on their existing strengths'. This seemed to be a particular strength of this local programme in its trailblazer period, and a useful message may be that the organisation should continue to remind itself of this guiding principle and that the induction of any new staff should make explicit the values and principles underlying Sure Start.

Accessibility and availability

Parents do not like services that are badly organised, inconvenient and expensive to use and, most important, do not pay attention to their needs as they see them (Quinton, 2004). There was a strong sense of Sure Start being readily accessible by telephone or through personal visit. Sure Start was valued as a community-based service with *'on the doorstep support'* all *'under one roof'*, and with staff who were friendly, approachable, *'ready to listen'* and *'easy to talk to'*. The service was regarded as flexible, with staff working round clients wherever possible with regard to appointment times. Direct access to the building was less easy for some than others, but initiatives whereby Sure Start staff went out into the community, e.g. to local toddler groups, to deliver services and offer support, advice or information on an informal basis were clearly valued. This approach suggests that this SSLP puts clients at the centre of its operations and has developed ways that make the expertise they have to offer not just physically but also 'mentally' accessible.

Professionals working together

Not only were help and advice felt to be easily accessible and readily available from Sure Start, but there was also a sense of staff working together. This related both to:

Sure Start as a 'seamless' service

Penn and Gough (2002) question whether existing family support services, however well co-ordinated, can be anything other than marginally effective 'unless they address the range of resources families need to live a decent life' (Penn and Gough, 2002: 30). They note an emphasis amongst family support services on emotional support and the quality of the interaction between mother and child but suggest that from a family perspective, all families need a range of resources, highlighting income maintenance, healthcare, childcare, education and leisure. They argue that, 'from this family based perspective, the relationship of the mother or carer with a child is only one of a multiplicity of concerns with which she must deal; and arguably, the relationship is shaped by and reflects the many other problems with which she must cope' (ibid: 23).

Parents in this study felt able to phone anybody at Sure Start, often a contact with whom they had built up a relationship through their involvement with one aspect of the service, e.g. a nursery nurse delivering a sleep programme, and knew that *'if they can't help they'll always find someone who can'*. This suggests a notion of Sure Start as a seamless support service in the community which enables parents to access appropriate professional expertise at the point of need. It also highlights the importance of staff knowledge of, and links with, services that address a range of family needs.

At the same time, there may be, as acknowledged by staff and some parents, families who are less receptive to the aims, ideas and services of Sure Start, and the ability of the programme to respond to a range of concerns, any of which may predominate in the lives and minds of families at a particular time, and to build on existing strengths, interests and resources is crucial.

Working in partnership

Parents reported a feeling that staff were communicating with each other and working together with and for families. Some families were involved with a number of different professionals from Sure Start, e.g. a dietician, family worker and family therapist, and reported favourably on the high level of communication between these professionals and the trust they felt in them, for example with regard to confidentiality. Furthermore, there was a clear sense of 'working together' in terms of professionals working with clients to consider what the issues are and what might be done about them, again suggesting mutuality in the relationship rather than asymmetrical power, whilst acknowledging that *'I feel they would step in if they felt something was really wrong'*.

Improvements in Services

This section gives an indication of how parents/carers felt services for families with children under four years of age had improved, either since Sure Start began or over the previous year, thus also providing an indication of what matters to them. What was particularly notable was a perception of a changing nature of support and an emphasis on the community aspect of the service, which were felt to constitute an improvement in the following ways:

- The availability of a wider range of professional support that is more easily accessible, on the doorstep and under one roof

- Advice and support being available in a community setting on an informal basis, e.g. *'If you need to speak about diets you can just talk to the dietician – it doesn't seem as formal here – going to a hospital dietician seems more formal – it makes you feel more relaxed and calm'.*
- The flexible nature of this community based provision, providing *'more opportunities to follow things up ... and they fit round you, they try and work round you and fit appointments in round your family'.*
- A change in the nature of client/professional relationships, including *'the way they think of you'.* Whilst keen to stress that they had previously had a satisfactory relationship with health visitors, for example, parents noted that their relationship with professionals now felt more *'equal'.* There was also a comment that *'It feels like they've got more of an interest in your family because they come out to toddlers, and they're not just coming to do a check'.*
- Greater opportunities for peer support. For example, a mother with children over and under four stated, *'When I was a new parent I didn't have a clue and I had to get on with it, but it's different with* [child]. *There's somewhere to come when you're home alone, somewhere to come to, drop-in sessions, and talking to other parents sometimes makes you feel a lot better'.*
- *'Just the fact that you know there's something there if you need it',* in terms of both advice and company: *'if there's nothing for the kids to do and you're bored in the house you can walk up and know there'd be something there to do and faces there you'd know'.*

The themes of informality, flexibility, accessibility, availability of a wider range of professional support, peer support and back-up were mentioned frequently in perceived improvements to services.

The place of services within the community: Social networks and community links

There was evidence that involvement in Sure Start had led to the development of friendships and social networks and support from other parents, both whilst based at Sure Start (e.g. *'We support each other as parents as well – we meet up and say I'm having trouble with his teething and people say, 'Well, I've tried this and this and this, and it's all in a relaxed, informal atmosphere')* and extending into the wider community. For example, *'You meet people on courses and then we arrange to meet at each other's houses for coffee'.*

There was a reported reduction in isolation and a development of social networks, e.g. *'people talking to each other more'.* It *'stops loneliness and gets people together'* and there are more opportunities to *'get you out of the house and doing things'.* Respondents also commented on an increased range of facilities and learning opportunities and the increased availability of childcare within the local community. There was a comment that Sure Start had *'brought the community more together. Some people from different areas come into the area. I've made friends from different areas that I wouldn't have met'.* Some findings related to instances of where parents themselves felt they were having an influence on Sure Start and on activities within the community. For example, one parent took her children swimming, was known to be involved in Sure Start, and was asked whether she thought they would be interested in aqua natal classes. This suggestion was relayed to Sure Start and was taken up. Another parent had been asked to give feedback on a breastfeeding video and this led to her promoting it in the community. Staff going out into the community more, e.g. to toddler groups, was enabling the formation of relationships and allowing opportunities for parents to make suggestions, e.g. for courses. Some parents were passing on skills gained through courses and interventions, e.g. regarding baby massage and speech and language. There were also instances where a respondent's involvement in Sure Start has led to development in other areas for members of their family, e.g. a gardening project or learning about Job Linkage.

The evidence of developing social networks in the community is significant in four main respects:

Ongoing and future knowledge and use of Sure Start

This study suggests that, even with the provision of relevant information, people will not fully know what to expect from Sure Start, or fully understand it, until they have gained some experience of it themselves.

The survey showed that 'word of mouth' is a highly significant source of information for families. Research has shown that for many parents the preferred source of information is informal: a family member, friend or other parent (NFPI, 1999). Further, information sources themselves find that parents use them because they have heard about the service from another parent (Moorman and Ball, 2001).

A positive personal experience for those in contact with Sure Start seems to be the best guarantee for building knowledge within the community about Sure Start and its potential contribution. The implication for staff is to be reminded of the importance of the particular and the detail, because every interaction is not just with one service user, but also possibly with all their networks in the community.

The finding also suggests an important role for volunteers and for 'community parents' in developing understanding and encouraging use of Sure Start services.

Client/professional relationships

There was evidence that working in different venues in the community and running a variety of activities (e.g. clinics, courses) was providing not only more points of access but also facilitating the development of informal trusting relationships in which parents feel comfortable about raising issues to do with parenting and other aspects of their lives. Sure Start were taking services to the client rather than expecting clients to operate on their terms and on their territory, indicating that it was a genuinely client-responsive service.

This is also important in the light of research by Miller (2002) that found that voicing difficulties around early experiences of mothering, to professionals and others, was difficult for women, who were concerned that admitting to difficulties would signal that they were not coping or were failing as new mothers. At Sure Start, one mother commented, *'It feels different, you're allowed to have a bad day'.*

Friendship and peer support

Mothers clearly valued talking to other women and sharing ideas and experiences. Sure Start is providing opportunities for this, for example through their approach to delivering courses and through services such as the drop-in room. Sometimes friendships were built up in this way and there was evidence that peer support was continuing outside of Sure Start. These findings are also important in the light of a research overview conducted by Moorman and Ball in which a key theme was that parents felt isolated, the main reasons given being newness to their area, going out to work, transport difficulties and lack of confidence, especially where crime rates are high and there are no cheap, accessible meeting places. Lone parents had particular difficulty in making contact. A key antidote to this isolation was contact with other parents (Moorman and Ball, 2001). Research studies have also highlighted that large numbers of parents feel under stress and that there is some evidence that parental stress is relieved by human contact, with other parents and with empathetic practitioners (ibid.). Ghate and Hazel (2002) suggest that enhancing semi-formal services such as mother and toddler groups could also help enhance informal support networks, because of the predominantly 'social' reasons that parents gave for accessing semi-formal services.

Personal and community benefits

Sure Start could be seen to be playing an important role in building new community networks that may continue to develop in the longer term. Gilchrist (2003) suggests that 'insufficient attention is paid to the importance of community participation in its own right, rather than as a vehicle for delivering government objectives' (Gilchrist, 2003: 20). She emphasises the importance of community networking and notes that there is plenty of evidence that 'robust and diverse social networks are of value in themselves, accelerating people's recovery from disease and trauma, reducing levels of anti-social behaviour and fear of crime, enhancing health and happiness generally, and creating a stronger sense of personal identity' (ibid.). At the same time, 'The collective benefits are to be found in increased levels of social trust, an improved capacity to organize, greater tolerance of difference and more coherent impact on decision-making' (ibid.) and 'Anything which creates opportunities and occasions for positive and inclusive networking is useful in developing 'community'' (ibid.). This can be seen as linking to the overall Sure Start objective of 'strengthening families and communities'.

The nature of Sure Start itself brings particular challenges, with a focus both on meeting the needs of individual families and on broader capacity building. Parents are seen as participants in the design and working of the programme as well as service users. At the same time, the programme was operating within a mainstreaming agenda and the development of citywide initiatives. Furthermore, a new interdepartmental Sure Start Unit was officially launched in December 2002, covering children from minus nine months through to age fourteen, with ongoing Sure Start programmes to continue. Taylor (2003) reported that the director of the Sure Start Unit, Naomi Eisenstadt, had expressed concern over the effects of increasing control from central government and fears that the ethos of local participation and ownership that have been developed since Sure Start began could be ruined by involvement from the centre. 'The magic of Sure Start is local community participation and the problem with central government is that they think local means local government. It doesn't – it means [at] street [level]' (Eisenstadt, in Taylor, 2003: 14).

Representation in the formal structures of a programme, whilst clearly important and potentially influential, does not guarantee widespread community ownership of the programme. As Sure Start was becoming more widely known in the community, participation in the design and running of the programme was happening in informal ways through links being established with new and existing services as well as through membership of groups and committees. A strength of Sure Start has been the working of informal networks involving all sorts of people. The informal community networking of clients themselves, as well as more formal participation, is important although less easily measured. Issues of parental participation are further explored in the next chapter.

Encouraging access to services for children and families

It was a fundamental requirement for all SSLPs to reach all families and children living in the areas of high deprivation in which they were set up. A key Sure Start principle has been that 'every family should get access to a range of services that will deliver better outcomes for both children and parents, meeting their needs and stretching their aspirations'. There was a particular emphasis on reaching those families who were most in need and/or 'hard to reach'.

The Sure Start Children's Practice Guidance acknowledges that there are barriers to service use, and that families most vulnerable to poor outcomes, and other families, may not want to use the services that are on offer for a variety of reasons. They 'may not see themselves as needing services or not know there are services that could help them' (Sure Start 2005: 29). They 'may find the attitudes of the professional staff in the services off-putting or not feel that the services are relevant to their needs' (ibid.). They 'may be fearful of using services in case they are judged as not being able to cope' (ibid.). They 'may be worried about possible interference in their lives, about their control being undermined, about being patronised, or that their privacy will be invaded' (ibid.).

The guidance on participation in multi-agency working also points out that families' needs will vary between families and over time, which will mean offering a variety of ways for parents and carers to be involved in the service and influence what is on offer. Further, 'Outreach, home visiting and drop-ins can provide a non-threatening gateway to other more specialist services'. The Sure Start Children's Centre Practice Guidance (2005) has recommended that there should be 'a greater emphasis on outreach and home visiting as a basis for enabling greater access to services for families who are unlikely to visit a centre' (Sure Start, 2005:3). It notes the need for children's centres 'to work effectively with other services, particularly health services, to obtain information and to support vulnerable families. Supporting parents is a key part of the day-to-day business of midwives and health visitors. Offering practical advice early can reduce the need for more extensive interventions' (ibid: 30). Outreach means 'taking services nearer to people's homes: delivering them in small venues that people already know and find welcoming has a good record for increasing the use of services ... Home visiting is an extension of outreach – taking services into people's homes' (ibid.).

This first section of this chapter has highlighted some key factors with regard to the acceptability and accessibility of services for children and families. It has described the initial suspicion in the minds of some, the concern over stigma, and parents' feelings regarding control over their decisions and their relationships with professionals. These are all issues that could face policy-makers and practitioners involved in the development of new services for children and families. Every Child Matters: Change for Children guidance on participation in multi-agency working comments that 'Engaging with parents and carers is resource intensive – but not engaging them can be wasteful, because families are unlikely to take up any service provision that they feel has been imposed on them'. Further, Garbers et al comment that 'labelling them [parents] as 'hard to reach' can be simplistic, and sometimes a way of avoiding confronting and undertaking the necessary tasks' (Garbers et al, 2006: 295).

THE INVOLVEMENT OF FATHERS

This section of the chapter discusses some of the findings of an evaluation of the involvement of fathers in a Round Five Sure Start Local Programme.

The policy context

Engaging fathers has emerged onto the practice agenda in many child welfare agencies such as Sure Start (Lloyd et al, 2003). Government attempts to support involved fathering through the Supporting Families Agenda (Home Office, 1998) and the formation of the cross-Government Ministerial Group on the Family have been continued in the Government's child-centred family policy (Every Child Matters, 2003 and subsequent Children Act 2004) and its formation of a Child and Family Directorate. The National Framework for the Assessment of Children in Need and their Families (Statutory Guidance 2000) requires that fathers be included in assessments, as does the Common Assessment Framework. The Childcare Bill will require local authorities to provide relevant information to both parents, and the Equality Bill will require all public services to ensure access to services by both mothers and fathers, and the delivery of different services to each gender, when their needs are different.

The National Service Framework (NSF) for Children, Young People and Maternity Services (2004) specifically requires primary care trusts, local authority and children's services to provide targeted information to all fathers and to gain skills, through training, to work with fathers. The NSF states: 'The National Service Framework supports a cultural shift in all service provision, to include fathers in all aspects of a child's well-being'. A Fatherhood Quality Mark (developed by Fathers Direct) was launched in April 2005, to be awarded to services meeting the new standards in the NSF.

There is a strong emphasis on involving fathers in Children's Centres, and 'increasing the involvement of fathers' has been written into the core offer for these centres. Further, the Sure

Start Children's Centre Practice Guidance (2005) notes the need to personalise services for fathers, male carers and other male relatives, and states that 'All Sure Start Children's Centre services should be responsive to the level of local need to support fathers in their relationship with their partner and in their role as a parent' (Sure Start, 2005:53).

Such changes are being made within a context where 'British fatherhood is . . in the process of reconstruction and transformation' (O'Brien, 2004:12) with changes in employment and family structure and the growing multi-ethnic and multi-faith character of contemporary Britain 'creating new socio-economic and cultural contexts for negotiating what it means to be a father' (ibid.).

There is general consensus that involving fathers in family support services is desirable, whilst also acknowledging potential damage in some situations (Burgess, 2002). However, fathers are traditionally considered to be a 'hard to reach' group (Daniel and Taylor, 2001; DfES, 2002), and there has been a recognition that many services are not reaching fathers effectively (Ghate et al., 2000).

In addition to service use, there has also been an expectation for Sure Start local programmes to promote the participation of parents in the design and running of the programme. A National Evaluation of Sure Start (NESS) report, 'Early Experiences of Implementing Sure Start' (2002), based on a survey of 118 Round One and Two programme managers, noted that programmes found the involvement of fathers in management to be a challenging task. It did find, however, that programmes were taking some steps to actively involve fathers more generally in the programme, with a view to more substantial involvement.

Purpose of the evaluation

The purpose of the evaluation was to understand what contact this Sure Start Local Programme had with fathers and how this could be extended. The specific research questions were:

1. What contact is Sure Start having with fathers and what is being offered to them?

2. What difference does the involvement of fathers in Sure Start make to them and their families?
3. How could the Programme work to further engage fathers?

Conceptualising father involvement

The evaluation adopted the overall approach used by the National Evaluation of Sure Start (NESS) in its study of fathers in Sure Start (Lloyd et al., 2003). As they state, research on the involvement of fathers within families most often operates within the construct of father involvement developed in America in the 1980s (Pleck, 1997, drawing on Lamb et al., 1985, 1987). This typology includes:

- 'Engagement' – direct interaction with the child, in the form of caretaking, or play or leisure;
- 'Accessibility' or availability to the child – the father's potential availability for interaction by being present or available;
- 'Responsibility' for the care of the child, as distinct from the performance of care – includes making sure the child is taken care of and arranging for resources to be available for the child.

As in the national evaluation, in this study 'father involvement in Sure Start is operationally defined as fathers' participation in Sure Start local programme activities such as attendance at group sessions, meetings with a professional or involvement in a management group. That is, father involvement is being explored in terms of service use and service planning. These themes map onto engagement/accessibility on the one hand (being a service user) and responsibility on the other (involvement in service planning' (Lloyd et al., 2003:18).

Method

The evaluation was planned by the University local evaluation team and staff representatives from the Sure Start Local Programme. The methods were as follows:

1. Interviews with current/past members of the Dads' Group were carried out by a University evaluator and members of the Sure Start staff, with responses recorded in written note form on the interview schedule and coded to avoid identification (n=7, plus 4 follow up interviews).

2. Questionnaires devised by the evaluation working group were distributed by staff, mothers and members of the Dads' Group to fathers/male carers in the community and were completed face-to-face. Sure Start staff approached fathers/male carers they came into contact with during the course of their work in a given month to inform them about the study and to ask whether they would like to take part. Thirty-one questionnaires were completed with fathers/male carers.

3. Sure Start staff monitored their contact with fathers over a given four-week period, and completed a follow-up questionnaire reflecting on this contact and ideas for future work with fathers and factors that would help their own professional development in this respect.

4. Collation and analysis of existing consultation forms.

All data were analysed by these staff and the local evaluators together. The Statistical Package for Social Sciences (SPSS) was used to analyse the staff monitoring sheets on their contact with fathers and also the questionnaires carried out with fathers/male carers in the community to provide quantitative information on numbers of fathers accessing services and types of services used and qualitative information on the impact of Sure Start and ideas for the future. The dads' group interviews and staff reflection forms were content analysed to identify themes and patterns in the data.

Background literature

Some impacts of fathers' involvement in childcare and the family

There is growing evidence that promoting fathers' greater involvement in childcare can enhance developmental outcomes for children (Ghate et. al., 2000). Flouri and Buchanan (2003) found that early father involvement with a child was associated with continuing involvement with that child throughout childhood and adolescence.

Lewis and Warin (2001) highlight the positive contribution that men make to families and give some indications of the importance of fathers' involvement in the early years of parenthood. For example, mothers report that fathers are their main source of emotional support after the birth, and state that their ability to cope with a new baby is related to their partner's ability to do likewise. When fathers have sufficient knowledge about the benefits of breastfeeding this can act to encourage mothers to breastfeed (Earle, 2000). One of the best predictors of a mother's success at breastfeeding has been her perception of her partner's support (Whelan and Lupton, 1998, in Lewis and Warin, 2001).

Lamb and Tamis-LeMonda (2004) state that:

'Sensitive fathering – responding to, talking to, ... teaching and encouraging their children to learn – predicts children's cognitive and linguistic achievements just as sensitive mothering does (Lamb and Tamis-LeMonda, 2004:4).

The modern family is changing, with fathers with young children in dual earner families doing eight times more childcare than thirty years ago, and the ways in which parents share childcare and earning roles are very diverse (O'Brien, 2005). Fathers' involvement with their children under five is now two hours a day compared to fifteen minutes a day in the mid-1970s (ibid.). However, 'How fathers spend their time with their young children is more important to the father-child relationship than how often they are with them'. (Lewis and Warin, 2001:5).

Fathers' Use (or Non-Use) of Support Services

There is increasing awareness of the female-domination or mother-centredness of services and the need to engage fathers in service provision (e.g. Whalley, 1997; Ghate et al., 2000; O'Brien, 2004) and, indeed, of the potential problems of not including them (e.g. with regard to abusive behaviour) (Ryan, 2000; Collett, 2001; Burgess, 2002), whilst also still a juggling with constructions of father as 'risk' and father as 'resource' (Featherstone, 2001; Lloyd et al., 2003). The challenge for family support practitioners in general, O'Brien (2004) suggests, is 'to provide a gender-collaborative framework which is sensitive to the preferences of mothers and fathers but also produces the best outcomes for children' (O'Brien, 2004: 28).

It is widely acknowledged that it is much more difficult to encourage fathers to participate in parenting support than mothers, and that men are reluctant seekers of help (e.g. Singh and Newburn, 2000). A survey in the UK (NFPI/MORI, 1999) found that fathers were both less likely to admit to problems (43% compared with 54% of mothers) and less likely to have approached sources of help than were mothers. Quarterly monitoring of calls to the Parentline Plus helpline (July to September 2002) showed that only 12% of callers were fathers (O'Brien, 2004). It has been suggested that explanations for the low visibility of fathers in help-seeking settings include individual psychological characteristics and social and institutional factors (Moorman and Ball, 2001; O'Brien, 2004). The latter may include the attitude of staff and the suitability of activities (e.g. Ghate et al., 2000).

Lewis (2000) suggests that fathers feel under dual pressure, both to earn the major income to support the family and to contribute to the care of children. Fathers who work long hours and share childcare with their partners are more likely than others to feel dissatisfaction with their lives and report feeling stressed (ibid.). Men's own needs require greater recognition and support, as it has been found that around 10% of fathers experience problems such as depression in the postnatal period (Singh and Newburn, 2000). There is evidence that fathers want and need more information about the transition to fatherhood. They need to know more about what is happening to their partner and how they can help; about the impact that having a baby will have on their lives; and to have access to ideas about new roles in the family (ibid.). There is also a need for services, e.g. family centres, to engage with fathers as 'men' as well as 'fathers' (Ghate et al., 2000).

Impacts of Services and Interventions

O'Brien (2004:26) states that 'the empirical base on which to judge the efficacy of father involvement in family support services is still small and in need of further development'.

It has been found that fathers who have participated in baby-care courses take on more care of their babies than fathers who have not. They keep closer to their babies, engage in more face-to-face interaction with them, smile and look at them more and talk to them more (Lewis and Warin, 2001).

Lloyd et al (2003) state that short term early interventions with fathers have provided little evidence that they increase paternal involvement with children or more skilled interventions by fathers (e.g. Belsky, 1985). However, longer term interventions show different results and the evidence suggests that once they become involved with their babies men's involvement shows considerable stability, at least over the first three years (e.g. Lamb et al., 1988) and, as they point out, 'Sure Start provides possibilities for more sustained support for men as fathers' (Lloyd et al., 2003:7).

In America, the Head Start early intervention programme has found that men have reported higher levels of confidence in their parenting skills and greater involvement in child care and interaction. Six months after the intervention men continued to be more supportive of their children's educational development and their children seemed better prepared on education-readiness measures.

Findings

This section summarises findings relating to the three research questions of this study:

- What contact is Sure Start having with fathers and what is being offered to them?
- What difference does the involvement of fathers in Sure Start make to them and their families?
- How could the Programme work towards further engaging fathers?

How Staff are Working with Fathers

There was early commitment from team members to working with fathers, involving consultation and events and leading to the establishment of the dads' group. Subsequently a fathers' worker was appointed and took over leadership of the group, supported by the Toddler Power worker and crèche workers, and has worked to further develop the group and support individuals within it, and to promote the further involvement of fathers.

Figures for a snapshot four-week period in 2005 showed that the programme was reaching a large number of fathers (52), either individually (the majority, 27), with their partner, with their child or with both, although only five staff reported any contact with fathers that month. As a result of the contact, fathers were receiving information and support (e.g. on employment services and rights, tax credits, budgeting, childcare), treatment for their health/well-being, knowledge regarding their baby's development (weight), training (including football training) and self development, and one was involved in a consultation meeting regarding volunteers. Some internal referrals were made as a result of the contact, e.g. to the Health team, and some fathers were referred or signposted to other agencies such as Job Linkage and childcare settings.

Data from staff and paternal questionnaires indicated that fathers were accessing services that relate to all five Sure Start objectives, particularly Objective Five, Strengthening families and communities, for example through capacity building and personal development, volunteer training, signposting to work-related training and support/signposting/referral with regard to allowances, budgeting, job hunting and employment rights. Work related to Objective One (Improving availability, accessibility, affordability and quality of childcare) consisted of providing information on local childcare provision, Objective Two (Improving learning) some contact at toddler groups and crèche, Objective Three (Improving social and emotional development), behaviour management support, complementary therapies and family therapy, Objective Four (Improving health), children's health and development (baby clinic, HV visits, Paediatrician, 1st Aid course) and men's health and fitness. Data from the fathers' questionnaire show that each of the 28 Sure Start services listed had been accessed by between one and fourteen of the 31 fathers.

The impact of fathers' involvement on themselves and their families

Using Sure Start services

The fathers using Sure Start services noted that Sure Start was making a difference to them and hence their families in the following ways:

Support for Families and Parents

- opportunities for socialising, meeting new people
- reduction in stress (e.g. through massage, learning to relax and cope)
- help in finding a job/claiming tax credits
- support with paperwork e.g. claim forms
- increase in confidence through participating in groups and courses
- increased help and information on health, counselling and forthcoming events
- gaining skills e.g. through training to be a volunteer, Learn2Drive and Food Hygiene courses

Support for good quality play, learning and childcare experiences for children

- increased opportunities for undertaking activities with children (e.g. trips/events) and for children to interact with peers
- partner passing on knowledge and information from courses and both parents following up on activities at home to enhance developing skills, e.g. threading, colour recognition
- gaining information on childcare provision

Primary and community health care

- ease of access to baby clinics for weighing baby and raising any additional concerns
- access to the safety loan scheme
- increasing awareness of men's health issues through a Sure Start health visitor

The Dad's and Kid's Group

The group is run weekly for an hour and a half. Activities are provided for fathers and children to undertake together. Crèche workers are available so that fathers have the option of time out to talk to other staff or participate in training or planning events. 'Chatterbox' Bags are loaned to fathers in the group to encourage parental involvement in their children's learning. Information on courses is provided and these have been taken up by one or more fathers, e.g. Basic Food Hygiene, Common Childhood Illnesses, Learn2Drive, Community Sports Leader. Some of the fathers were also involved in a five-a-side football team that had been set up through the group. The fathers' worker was regarded as approachable, helpful and supportive, a good organiser, who also related well to their children and is very popular with them. Research into the role of father development workers (FDWs) within fathers' groups (Chawla-Duggan, 2006) has suggested that there were two main purposes behind the groups and the role of the FDW. These were, firstly, to raise confidence and responsibility among fathers and, secondly, to improve and influence children's learning. The findings of this small study contribute to knowledge of the impact of fathers' groups on fathers' relationship with their child, their own lives and family life.

Impact on father and child

Two fathers reported that coming to the group had brought about a change in how they felt about their relationship with their child, in one case through worrying less about the reactions of others:

> 'I have a brilliant relationship with my kids and now I don't fear what I do or how I do it or even where I do it, like playing in parks and carrying on at kids' parties'.

'It does [change what I do with my child] because she now understands she can come to me and I will play with her toys with her, she also will understand that if she does not understand something, dad will help her to understand'.

One father reported that he did different activities with his child, such as painting, one that he knew more about his child's preferences in play:

I didn't really do anything before – I used to kick a football, but I didn't really know what he liked himself, now we do painting, gluing and all sorts of messy play'.

One commented that he had learned from the other fathers:

'I've found that getting to know the dads and getting to know how they get closer to their children helps me in ways to get closer to my daughter (such as kicking a ball with her, playing cookery with her).'

Five fathers reported greater involvement with their child as a result of the dads' group. One commented that, although he had always played an active part in his child's life, he now felt more confident as a dad and it had helped him develop the relationship he wanted with his child, whereby he was able to spend quality time with him, which had been difficult for his own father due to long working hours. Other comments included:

'The difference has been unreal. For so long I've done nothing with my children and now it's like letting the kid out in me around my children. Every time my kids learn something new I feel so proud'.

'Well, I never got to spend as much time with my daughter as I would like to as she is always with her mum, so going to the dads' group is my time with her. It helps her to understand that dad is there too'.

'I am getting to know and understand my girls'.

Impact on fathers' own life

Some fathers also reported that their involvement in the group had helped develop skills that could be important in the future. For example, all members of the group had been involved in the organisation and running of the group's first birthday party including food preparation and risk assessment, and this had contributed to a record of achievement. Five-a-side football training was also potentially helping provide a pathway into a related job in sport. For one father, regular attendance at the group and joining in with activities had *'given me the confidence to meet and talk with other people'*. The group had provided an opportunity to *'talk to other men about anything – football, our kids'*. Some fathers met outside the group and took their children out together e.g. to the park. One felt that he fitted in more as a father.

Impact on family life

For some it had made a difference to family life, for example through becoming able to handle their children's behaviour or through a more equal sharing with their partner.

> *'[Before] I done nothing with my kids, which meant my wife done everything. Now I do a lot so she has time to herself, making it an all-round better atmosphere'.*

In one case where the father reported already shared roles and responsibilities with his partner and mutual support in their handling of their child, he still felt that the group had increased his confidence and made him really value the part he played in his child's life. One considered that *'these sorts of places will help relationships between parents and children and help people see dads and kids playing together as normal'*.

For individual fathers, the most important aspects of the group were reported to be the social aspect and opportunity to relax and *'just be a dad'*, the opportunity for going on trips, talking to and learning from other fathers and engaging in activities with their child, gaining ideas for activities to carry out at home and seeing what their children *'were into'*, increasing their fitness and doing something they enjoyed doing through the 5-a-side, and involvement in the organisation of the group's first birthday event.

This small study makes a contribution to knowledge of this area in that 'Father groups are an under-researched area and we know little about how 'fathering' is supported in such groups' (Chawla-Duggin, 2006).

Promoting the involvement of fathers

Lloyd et al's study, 'Involving Fathers in Sure Start' (2003) identified individual challenges for SSLPs in involving fathers, including female-focused services, traditional conceptions of gender roles, and the peripheral notion of fatherhood. Strategies that helped promote the involvement of fathers included the existence of a dedicated fathers' worker; early identification of father engagement as a priority; adequate referral systems; provision of fun and practical activities; structured sessions; and provision of services specifically for men. Findings from the present study in relation to this topic are presented below.

Factors that have promoted involvement

The Sure Start Local Programme had shown commitment to developing strategies to involve fathers, initially through the initiative and commitment of a small group of workers and subsequently through the appointment of a fathers' worker, and with the support of programme management. Findings of this evaluation, linked to findings of other research, provide indications of what works in increasing the involvement of fathers.

An enabling organisational context

In this Sure Start Local Programme there was early identification of fathers as a priority, also cited by Lloyd et al (2003) as one of five components found in programmes with high provision for fathers. This has been supported by commitment to working with fathers at programme management level. Organisational support, i.e. how much support there is in the organisation for providing services to fathers/father figures is one indicator of father-friendliness in organisations (NPCL/NHSA, 2000). The SSLP management has provided organisational support through funding a fathers' worker to develop and implement activities that would promote the inclusion of fathers within this and one other Sure Start Programmes; to promote and support the views of fathers within Sure Start; to contribute to the development of Sure Start as a father friendly programme and to develop and implement activities that would support parents in returning to work. There were as yet no fathers on the Partnership board, although two fathers had trained as volunteers for the Programme.

Staffing

A dedicated fathers' worker provides father/male carer specific activities, building on the commitment and action of a group of staff across teams to work together to develop strategies for involving fathers. The fathers' worker has done much to raise the profile of father involvement. The local media has acknowledged the success of the programme and reported on two occasions about events organised for fathers in the area. One father has been interviewed by local radio on his experiences and involvement in Sure Start. At the same time, there is recognition that working with fathers is the responsibility of the whole team, who may in some cases need additional training and support. Staff are open and receptive to the idea of providing services to fathers and prepared to provide services to fathers.

Evidence from this study shows that fathers were using services that are relevant to their child's development and health, well-being and learning and to their own and their family's welfare and development (e.g. training, financial advice and support). Staff from all teams were therefore taking fathers into consideration.

The fathers' worker meets regularly with a local expert voluntary agency (Fathers Plus, Children North East). This is important for enabling cross learning, for example about the most effective strategies for engaging fathers.

Family

At family level, high paternal caring responsibilities have been seen as a factor promoting fathers' participation in Sure Start local programmes (Lloyd et al., 2003). All the fathers in the dads' group took a sharing role in the care of their child, most felt well prepared and all were involved in the birth of their child. They felt included and well supported by midwifery and health visiting services, and reported being involved with and supporting their partners in the decision about how to feed the baby, in the general care of their child and in playing together, although this was an area in which some of them felt less confident before they attended the dads' group.

Female partner facilitation and support are important in promoting and supporting involvement, both with their children and in Sure Start. Research (Cook, 2005) has shown that the expectations of both parents are substantial predictors of fathers' instrumental involvement in the care of their child (e.g. feeding, bathing, changing). Mothers' 'gatekeeping' can hinder father involvement (Allen and Hawkins, 1999). The fathers interviewed for this study all reported that they and their partner had talked about how they would cope with a new baby, the roles they would both have and the way their lives would change. In some cases this had been facilitated by their attendance at antenatal classes. As one commented, for some parents-to-be, talking about these issues one-to-one with a health visitor before the birth could be beneficial. These fathers' partners were all involved in Sure Start in one or more ways and, as the National Evaluation report on Involving Fathers in Sure Start states, 'Maternal facilitation can act to promote father involvement in Sure Start by reinterpreting or communicating its relevance to partners' (Lloyd et al., 2003:48). Working with both parents together can emphasise the collaborative nature of parenting (ibid.), other than in situations where this would not be advisable or possible.

Strategies to get men involved

'Hook' activities are important to gain men's interest, and the introduction of five-a-side football training and matches has been important in this respect. Fathers have noted the importance of activities that appeal to men and introducing more such hook activities to encourage the involvement of new fathers.

Many of the fathers in this study were accessing Sure Start for practical help and support, e.g. regarding benefits, allowances, budgeting, job hunting, funding and employment rights. In some cases this led on to greater involvement with Sure Start, including the dads' group. Attracting fathers through practical services, such as housing and benefits support was also found to be successful in Sure Start Plus work with teenage parents (Sawtell et al, 2005). The findings in this SSLP are also consistent with this work in that it can be important to establish a relationship through a one-to-one service before inviting men to a fathers' group or fatherhood programmes (ibid.). Using mothers as potentially important, initial sources of information about what services offer can also be important when attempting to access fathers (as also found in Lloyd et al, 2003; Sawtell et al, 2005).

Strategies to keep men involved

The Programme undertakes on-going consultations with fathers. It is important that strategies are user led to promote and maintain involvement and build on men's interests. Fathers noted that things need to be directly relevant to their/their family's needs – *'I won't use a service if it doesn't directly benefit me or my child'*. Again, practical help and support are important.

Working towards Further Engagement with Fathers

The following were identified as ways in which this SSLP could work towards further engagement with fathers, which could also apply to other children's centres seeking to develop work in this area.

Staff training and support

Several staff had not received any training on work with fathers. The National Service Framework (NSF) for Children, Young People and Maternity Services (2004) specifically requires primary care trusts, local authority and children's services to gain skills, through training, to work with fathers. Staff also suggested being invited to any groups where fathers are present (e.g. to promote services) and receiving guidance from the fathers' worker and other staff who have worked with fathers through the sharing of expertise, advice and information. It was recommended that the Programme should re-examine the training needs of staff and ways in which the expertise of individual staff can be shared with the team to ensure ongoing programme wide commitment to father involvement (Lloyd et al., 2003) and to promote reflection on the extent to which fathers are being considered in all aspects of the child's well-being (DH/DfES, 2004).

Further development of activities and support for fathers

It was identified that, for the future, it would be important to continue to develop activities for fathers according to their stated interests, and to take into account possible gaps identified by staff, i.e. men's depression (also identified by Singh and Newburn, 2000). There are also key points at which it could be beneficial to engage fathers, such as pre-natally and in hospital at the birth of their child. The fathers' worker has recently started attending antenatal Parentcraft classes, Health drop-ins and baby clinics. These fathers reported that they would welcome:

•   more activities for fathers and children together. Fathers showed a particular interest in dads' and child's sports, gymnastics and swimming and other physical activities such as soft play, also Play with a Purpose and Messy Play.
•   opportunities to learn about and increase men's and family health and fitness (e.g. weight, diet, exercise; gym, training sessions)
•   parenting support for fathers, including courses and support when *'feeling down'* and after hours telephone contact.
•   activities to enable fathers to socialise with each other e.g. paintball, go-karting, nights out, trips
•   opportunities for personal development and courses to develop work-related skills (e.g. driving, health and safety at work), and to enable them to support their children's future learning (computer).

There was also a high demand for employment information and advice, including help looking for work. The knowledge, ability and capacity to work with fathers on practical issues including financial and employment issues are important for the future, both in their own right and as a potential 'hook' into other services.

Clearly, fathers are not a homogeneous group, and these general suggestions do not reduce the need to be sensitive to different groups of fathers (e.g. lone fathers, sole carers) and fathers' diversity of needs and circumstances.

Continuing to use mothers as potentially important, initial sources of information about what services offer and encouraging maternal facilitation and support, for example discussing expectations before the birth, sharing their learning with their partners or joint attendance at groups and activities in some situations, could all further paternal involvement in Sure Start.

Publicity and advertising

The NSF (2004) requires primary care trusts, local authority and children's services to provide targeted information to all fathers. The Programme will need to maintain ongoing review of its information and publicity and how this is targeted at and provided to fathers. The fathers' worker and dads' group make efforts to encourage involvement in the dads' group, and this is also promoted by other staff. Men's suggestions for advertising activities for fathers included local shops, GP surgeries, the Jobcentre and other employment related offices, Housing Office, the local Sport Centre, nurseries and libraries. It was also suggested that the dads' club could promote a *'cooler image'*. Services should be marketed in a way that appeals to men and promotes fatherhood positively (as also noted in Sawtell et al, 2005) and celebrate becoming and being a father (Lloyd et al., 2003). Two men had trained as volunteers and could play an important role in peer support and as role models.

Accessibility

The Programme had altered the time of the dads' group but children's centres may need to be more flexible in the timing of activities, possibly including evenings and weekends, and in the location of activities.

Monitoring

The Sure Start monitoring forms had recently been amended to include data on numbers of fathers accessed. It is important that this information is collected rigorously and is reliable, as it will provide data for indicators of success with regard to increasing the involvement of fathers as required in the Children's Centre core offer.

Participation in service planning and decision-making in Sure Start

There had as yet been no fathers on the Sure Start Local Programme's Partnership board or subgroups. Whilst the NESS study on father involvement in Sure Start (Lloyd et al., 2003) found some involvement of fathers in management, all staff in the Rounds One and Two programmes involved agreed that mothers far outnumbered fathers and the most frequent score was zero.

Some fathers had been prepared to play an active role in the delivery of this Sure Start Local Programme, e.g. having undertaken training developed by Sure Start to enable parents to volunteer for the Programme and this could be further encouraged. For example, one father's volunteering involved promotion of the dads' group, community driving and general support. There had also been ongoing consultation of fathers, for example at Fun Days, and this should be continued. Greater participation at management level is still, however, an area for development.

Father friendliness

Finally, approximately one-third of the questionnaire respondents considered that Sure Start could be more welcoming to men. Therefore, in considering future developments and in light of the expectation that children's centres will increase the involvement of fathers, the use of a tool for monitoring the 'Father Friendliness' of organisations (NPCL/NHSA, 2000), which has also been used in training sessions in the UK through the organisational framework of Fathers Direct and Working With Men, could be considered by Sure Start children's centres.

4
Parental involvement and participation

IN THE PREVIOUS chapter, parental involvement in Sure Start was discussed mainly in terms of 'service use' and related issues regarding, for example, accessibility and acceptability, and targeting specific groups. Parental 'involvement' and 'participation' have also been central to the objectives and principles of Sure Start from the outset at another level. In 2002 Naomi Eisenstadt, the then Director of Sure Start, stated that probably the key Sure Start principle was that programmes must 'promote the participation of all local families in the design and working of the programme', so that any new services will be accessible and appropriate to their needs (Eisenstadt, 2002). Another key principle was that programmes must 'involve parents, grandparents and other carers in ways that build on their existing strengths' (DfES, 2002). The emphasis on parental involvement and participation has continued into the development of Sure Start Children's Centres.

This chapter draws on the findings of three evaluations of parental involvement in Sure Start, carried out in three local programmes (one trailblazer, one Round Five and one Round Six local programme). In order to reflect their current progress with regard to parental involvement, and to enable the local programmes to share with and learn from each other, each evaluation focused on a different aspect of parental involvement. Selected findings from each evaluation are presented in this chapter to cover a range of themes relating to parental involvement and participation. These themes are:

I.   Types of Parental Involvement
II. Parents and Professionals Working Together: Changing Relationships and Boundaries and a Trajectory of Developing Empowerment
III. 'Effective' Participation

TYPES OF PARENTAL INVOLVEMENT

Section I of the previous chapter focused on issues relating to parental involvement in Sure Start as 'service use' and also referred to other types of parental involvement and participation. A further evaluation of parental involvement was carried out in a fifth wave Sure Start local programme. The aims of the evaluation were:

1.   To examine ways in which parents are involved in Sure Start Folde and ways in which this could be further developed.
2.   To examine the impact of parental involvement on parents.
3.   To explore the effectiveness of parental participation in Sure Start Folde.

The methods used were:

1.   Focus groups of involved parents.
     Two focus groups were held at Sure Start, the first with two parents and the second with four parents. Parents who were actively involved in Sure Start in one or more ways were invited (e.g. through 'Folde' Family Focus, La Leche breastfeeding peer support, volunteering). A crèche and refreshments were available. The groups were run by two members of the University of Sunderland local evaluation team and written notes were made during the session. Three of the participants had children of Sure Start age and one just over (5 years and older). Two were grandparents. They had been involved in Sure Start for between eighteen months and 3 years.

2. Staff questionnaire

    A questionnaire was distributed to all staff in order to ascertain their understanding of parental involvement, to examine ways in which parental involvement is encouraged, to seek examples of ways in which contact with parents had influenced their practice, to explore problems with or barriers to parental involvement and to explore how workers envisage parental involvement developing in the future. Twenty-one questionnaires were completed.

3. Desk analysis of:

    Sure Start Folde Delivery Plan (June 2002), Performance Plan (2005-2006) and Progress Against Quarterly Milestones (April-June and July-Sept 2005); minutes of 'Folde' Family Focus meetings and reports written for the Programme by the Community Development Worker (CDW); minutes of the Amalgamated Sub-Group.

4. Informal discussion with the Programme Manager

5. Following this, it was decided to undertake a second stage of evaluation to gain the views of a wider sample of parents/carers on their involvement in Sure Start Folde. A questionnaire was formulated by a researcher and one member of the Sure Start team and then taken to the full Sure Start team for comment and amendment. Opportunistic sampling was used. The final version was distributed by staff to users of their services over the period of one month. Forty-five questionnaires were returned.

The questionnaires were analysed using the Statistical Software Package for Social Sciences (SPSS). The focus group data was content analysed under themes emerging from the data.

Findings

The findings presented in this chapter relate in particular to the first research question. Selected findings are presented in order to discuss different types of parental involvement and implications for the future development of services.

The analysis of the data from parents/carers and professionals identified different types of parental involvement within Sure Start

'Folde'. This provided a framework for further analysis. The categories are:

1. Involvement as Service Users
    (including promotion of service use and partnership with parents regarding the care and development of their children)
2. Informing the ongoing delivery of the Programme – informal participation through service use
3. Involvement in supporting the delivery of Sure Start services as volunteers (e.g. La Leche breastfeeding peer support, Community Parents, other volunteers)
4. Involvement in decision-making and management re. Sure Start 'Folde' and City Wide.
5. Involvement in supporting/promoting wider community development ('Folde' Family Focus)

Achievements of the Programme were mapped onto these five categories. Staff and parental responses were analysed under emerging themes (i.e. parental perceptions of benefit/satisfaction; staff and parental perceptions of problems/barriers, and comments on/ suggestions for promoting parental involvement). These themes were coded according to the identified types of parental involvement and then mapped onto the framework of types of parental involvement.

Finally, the data were analysed against dimensions relating to the 'proficiency' of SSLPs identified by the National Evaluation of Sure Start (NESS, 2005a) and against the Sure Start Children's Centres: Practice Guidance (2005), in areas that related to parental involvement. The NESS Programme Variability Study set out to consider links between aspects of SSLP implementation and the level of effectiveness on child and parenting outcomes for 150 SSLPs included in its Impact Study (NESS, 2005b). Eighteen dimensions of implementation were developed and it was found that these, collectively, can differentiate between the most and least effective SSLPs on parenting and child outcomes. Specific findings also emerged, e.g. 'empowerment' was related to two of five parenting measures. The purpose of this final part of the analysis was to raise further questions for general consideration by the Programme to assist them in engaging in a process of continuous improvement. These five categories are now explored in more detail, and implications for services for children and families are discussed in the next section.

Involvement as Service Users

The percentage of children aged 0-5 seen by the Programme had increased, but was not yet at the SSLP average. The Programme had shown some evidence of developing strategies to promote service use, for example, whole staff 'Equality & Diversity' training to promote wider inclusion of families such as Asylum seekers. It had shown commitment to targeting particular groups, for example families with special needs (through the appointment of a Special Needs Support Worker and establishment of the 'Ups + Downs' Group [Downs Syndrome]) and through setting up a grandparents' group.

The outcomes of service use were not directly addressed in this evaluation. However, parents/carers did comment that staff were welcoming to parents, supported their decisions and thought of the best approach to suit individuals. Parents/carers had enjoyed acquiring knowledge and developing new skills (for example, parenting skills, a better perspective on the care of the child, and increased strategies for coping with behaviour); sharing ideas, passing on ideas and skills; getting out of the house, meeting people, making friends, and building up confidence. They commented on the accessibility of support and advice. However, parents and carers felt that there was still a lack of understanding of Sure Start and still a feeling of stigma attached to its use. They also commented on insufficient advertising, for example in GP surgeries and other agencies, and on a perceived lack of continuity as children reach 5 years of age, making it difficult for families with children under and over four. They suggested that '*a Community café might encourage people to come in without feeling they had to do anything*' and, along with staff, that more positive publicity was required and that the Programme should increase promotion in the antenatal period.

Informing the ongoing delivery of the Programme

There was evidence of changes to services and staff approaches to service delivery taking place as a result of ongoing contact and/or discussion with parents/carers, for example the content, timing, format/structure of courses, and groups being adapted to parents' individual needs. This is dependent on a conducive atmosphere, the approachability of staff and their commitment to continuous improvement.

The Programme had also shown commitment to consulting parents through a survey of a sample of service users to ascertain whether, and in what ways, they would like to be further involved in service use, service planning and service delivery. This consultation enabled staff in Sure Start 'Folde' to provide appropriate pathways for individual families through the Programme. Such individual consultation will help ensure that they are offered the services they want for themselves and their children, help provide opportunities for the development of social networks, enable parents to offer their skills and expertise in contributing to service delivery, and further develop their skills e.g. through training to be a Community Parent or other volunteer. The parents/carers also welcomed the suggestion of a 'Comments board' or 'Suggestions book/box' in the entrance to the building as an additional means for parents/carers to feed in ideas and suggestions.

Involvement in supporting the delivery of Sure Start services as volunteers

Parents were playing an increasing part in supporting the delivery of Children and Family services through their role as volunteers. For example, eight had been trained as Breastfeeding Peer Supporters, six trained as Community Parents, and two trained to run the regional Credit Union collection point at 'Folde'. Volunteers also undertook activities such as helping in the Sure Start playgroup, accompanying the Programme on trips, and distributing energy efficient light bulbs. The importance of social networks and peer or neighbour support has been highlighted as being crucial to establishing and maintaining a sense of community (Field, 2003). Through the evaluation questionnaire the Programme had encouraged parents to state what skills and experience they would like to offer the Programme and this was to be pursued. A volunteer pack was developed by the CDW and typed by volunteers.

Volunteers reported feeling well supported in their role and appreciated opportunities for informal contact with staff on and off the premises. They felt that they were consulted appropriately and their ideas taken forward. Their involvement was facilitated through the provision of a crèche, impromptu childcare and the flexibility of staff. They achieved greater recognition and increased self-esteem through gaining a Volunteers Award. At an individual level, there was, for example, greater awareness of *'how it is for other people, which makes you more open minded'* (Community Parent) and satisfaction through *'giving something back'.*

Staff reported that they would welcome more volunteers and expansion of their role, e.g. assisting in delivery of activities/events, undertaking training to enable them to run groups, empowering other parents to become involved in Sure Start. Volunteers noted that it can be daunting meeting a group and that it is important to start with something small. The evaluation found that a gradual approach appears to work best, supported by staff with whom parents have developed a relationship.

Involvement in decision-making and management re. Sure Start 'Folde' and City Wide.

Parents were involved in the development of Sure Start from the outset and there has been strong commitment to community development. 'Folde' Family Focus had become a constituted group with parent/grandparent officers and there was representation on the Partnership, the Citywide Parents' Group, the Citywide Community Parents Group and the Citywide Breastfeeding Strategy. Participants had gained skills to facilitate running and attending groups through Management Committee training, including increased confidence and assertiveness.

However, there was patchy attendance at Partnership meetings and over-reliance on a small group of parents/grandparents, *'always the same faces'.* It was reported to be difficult to involve new parents in an active role and insufficient parental input to help move things on. Findings from the evaluation suggested that this requires support from dedicated staff and adequate funding, also whole staff commitment. Parents reported that they need to be told clearly what their involvement will entail, what is expected of them, and what the aims and goals of groups and meetings are. They need good support so they are not *'thrown in at the deep end'* or *'left to their own devices'.* There should be areas for personal development, but *'without pressure'.*

In this particular local programme there was a 'gap' in parental participation, with no informal, 'low-key' group for parents. It sought to address this through establishing an informal parents' group and through informal coffee mornings to promote further involvement. This relates to the Sure Start Sixth wave guidance, which acknowledged that:

> 'For most programmes, it is a challenge to find more than a few parents who will agree to the commitment involved in being a member of a management board. Parental representation depends on nurturing a much wider pool of parents to be involved with the programme, as well as taking steps to minimise the burden of the role, and being careful not to overload and burn out those parents willing to become more closely involved' (2002:16).

In some cases parents in this study had become involved directly as a way to have a voice in Sure Start, and in other cases active involvement had been a gradual process leading on from the desire to socialise or from the use of services for general purposes or a specific need (e.g. family circumstances, breastfeeding support), leading to a desire to help others. The support and encouragement of individual members of the Sure Start team were an influential factor. For individuals, parental involvement is often a gradual process and is best fostered as such. This is an area in which all staff have a role to play.

Involvement in supporting/promoting wider community development ('Folde' Family Focus)

In the early stages of the Programme's development there were a number of subgroups, some with parental representation. The original Parental Involvement Group remained as 'Folde' Family Focus, which became a constituted group and was intended to access funding, strengthen community development, reach out to local organisations and be involved in the delivery of local activities related to families with children aged 0-4. This group met monthly with representatives from local services and projects (e.g. the City of [...] College, the local Community Development Project, the Welfare Rights Service, a housing association and the local church) to identify local needs within Sure Start and the local community. The group is co-ordinated by the Sure Start CDW, who supported it in becoming a constituted group with its own bank account and honoured officers. The group is also a fundraising group and helps fund activities in the community. The group had contributed through:

- the development of new initiatives in partnership with other agencies to fill gaps in provision in the local area (Triple F after school club for 5-11s)
- fostering links with training organisations, identifying, promoting and participating in training that could increase employability, or that could act as a stepping stone to further training (i.e. more recreational courses)
- fundraising, contributing to day trips, theatre groups, classes e.g. Arts and Crafts; organising community events.

Again, the issue of over-reliance on a small group of parents/ grandparents in such groups needs to be taken into consideration.

DISCUSSION

Involvement as Service Users

As noted in the previous chapter, facilitating access to services for children and families has been described as a universal challenge for policy makers and practitioners (Garbers et al., 2006).

Drawing on findings from the implementation module of the National Evaluation of Sure Start (NESS), Garbers et al suggest that it may be helpful to see access as a *continuum* and to consider this in relation to *different styles of parental service use*. The three (condensed from five) points on the continuum are: making initial contact, introduction to and take-up of a service, and autonomous and continuous take-up of a service. The three broad styles of service use identified, which the authors suggest are likely to apply to other services as well as SSLPs, are: parents who 'autonomously' take up services (autonomous), parents who may need more encouragement to take up services (facilitated), and parents who will take up services on specific individual conditions (conditional).

To get people engaged as service users, the Every Child Matters:

Change for Children guidance draws on evaluations of Sure Start, extended schools pathfinders and On Track to suggest, for example, make sure parents and carers know about the service; ensure the site is open, warm and welcoming (and that staff or linked practitioners can communicate in the languages spoken in the community); get the right people in community link roles; ensure that services meet the individual needs of the children, young people and families being served (including those with disabilities); show evidence of the way in which parental involvement has influenced the development and delivery of the service; link with other agencies and ask them to promote the service; and consider strategic use of local media to promote awareness of the service. The guidance also points out that the National Evaluation of Sure Start has highlighted the considerable challenges facing multi-agency services seeking to overcome unequal access to services for minority ethnic groups. It highlights effective practice in meeting the needs of a diverse community, such as managers of services sharing knowledge and experiences, the involvement of male workers and serious commitment to the involvement of fathers; and more diverse delivery patterns than during office hours only.

As described earlier in this chapter, indicators used in the NESS's Programme Variability Study (NESS, 2005b) could be used to help SSLPs and other children's services examine and improve practice with regard to service use. For example,

- Does the Programme have a well-articulated vision regarding parental involvement that is relevant to the community?
- To what extent is there a welcoming and inclusive ethos within the Programme?
- What strategies does the Programme have to improve/sustain use of services over time?
- What strategies are in place to identify new users?
- How will specific groups be targeted?
- Do communication systems reflect and respect the characteristics and languages of the community?
- In what ways do services accommodate the needs and preferences of a wide range of users (i.e., accessibility and availability e.g. venues, access points, opening times)?
- How does/will the Programme track which families are using its services and monitor trends?

Involvement In Service Delivery

Staff reported that they would welcome more volunteers and expansion of their role. Volunteers noted that it can be daunting meeting a group and that it is important to start with something small. The evaluation found that a gradual approach appears to work best, supported by staff with whom parents have developed a relationship.

Considering how best to develop and share the skills of the local community for the benefit of the local programme, the community and individuals (e.g. through developing employment skills) is an important area for the future development of services for children and families.

Consultation

The Programme had shown commitment to consulting parents through a survey of a sample of service users to ascertain whether, and in what ways, they would like to be further involved in service use, service planning and service delivery. At the same time, it is important that consultation extends to those who may not access the Centre and targets particular groups. Parents suggested that input via website/e-mail could be considered. The Sure Start Children's Centre Practice Guidance (2005) specifically mentions consulting expectant parents, parents of disabled children, minority ethnic parents and lone parents. It also notes that it is important to seek explicitly the views of fathers as well as mothers. The Sure Start Children's Centre Practice Guidance states that consultation can be a means to build the confidence of local parents – fathers and mothers, and to develop and share the skills of the local community. It can also be a means to enhance the professional skills of local workers; and build partnerships, especially with parents (Sure Start, 2005:14).

Decision-making and management

It will be important for Programmes to maintain and extend working groups of parents and professionals and a parents' forum. Every Child Matters documentation differentiates between 'general consultation'

('Important though this is') and 'involvement in real service planning and delivery', noting that 'consultation may reach many people, though sometimes not in any great depth' and that 'more information and input can be gained if community members are directly involved in service planning', e.g. through parent forums and parent representatives on working groups, and service delivery, described as involvement in governance e.g. partnership boards, interviewing staff, or working for the service, including as volunteers. (www.everychildmatters.gov.uk/parents/participationinmultiagencyworking)

Local Programmes and other services need to consider how best to facilitate effective participation in meetings. Issues such as the timing of meetings, childcare, preparation/training, understanding roles, use of jargon, ensuring members feel that their views are important need to be taken into consideration. 'Effective participation' is discussed in more detail in the third section of this chapter.

PARENTS AND PROFESSIONALS WORKING TOGETHER: CHANGING RELATIONSHIPS AND BOUNDARIES AND A TRAJECTORY OF DEVELOPING EMPOWERMENT

As parents/carers become involved in services for children and families there can be implications for parent/professional relationships. This section explores issues of changing relationships and boundaries with regard to parental participation in Sure Start, discusses notions of empowerment and proposes a model for a trajectory of developing contextual empowerment. A study was carried out in a trailblazer programme to investigate how its Parents' Committee was contributing to the Sure Start principles of 'involvement' and 'participation' (Morrow and Malin, 2004).

Aims and method

The aims of the study were to:

- determine how the Parents' Committee builds upon existing strengths of individuals or groups and promotes participation in the design and working of the programme
- compare staff and parental perspectives on the Committee
- examine the impact of the Committee on professional roles

The research was carried out over the period of one year by two university researchers, with backgrounds in early years education and social policy respectively, in collaboration with members of the local Sure Start programme team and the Parents' Committee. One researcher was involved in data collection and both were involved in planning the research and in data analysis.

The method consisted of:

- six focus groups with Sure Start staff to identify their understanding of the purpose and function of the Committee and of the nature and extent of parental involvement and participation, and their views of the Committee's impact on professional roles. The staff working directly with the Committee were interviewed as a separate group as they felt their presence in a group interview might influence the responses given.

- two group sessions with the Parents' Committee in which the researcher worked with the parents on constructing and refining a timeline of their involvement with the Committee, plotting significant events and discussing the impact of these events for themselves and for Sure Start. At the same time the researcher asked questions designed to further determine their views on what was important to them about the Committee, on the contribution being part of the Committee was making in terms of the principles described in the aims of this study and on the way in which they felt they related to Sure Start professionals.

Findings

Building on strengths and promoting participation

The parents/carers cited ways in which being on the Committee had contributed to building on strengths they already had, and to developing new skills and confidence and the ability to speak to peers and others, such as *'the bosses'*, which could be seen as empowering. Parents spoke of things that they could do now that they could not or did not do before. These included speaking out in a group, attending conferences and speaking at Network meetings, chairing the Parents' Committee meeting and taking the minutes, and representation on the Sure Start Partnership. For some there had been a development of self-esteem: *'Before I started I thought, 'I'm no-one''*, or a growing self-awareness and *'understanding that everybody's views are different'*. One mother described how, with Sure Start support, she had gradually gained confidence about leaving the house, and later joined the Parents' Committee. Through this, she had organised competitions, distributed leaflets to nurseries and schools, promoted Sure Start in the community, dressed up as characters at children's events organised by the Committee, spoken to parents at newly developing Sure Start programmes and at network meetings, been involved in health promotion activities (e.g. smoking cessation), been part of a working group organising a national visit to the programme and joined the Sure Start Partnership, representing the views of the Committee and taking some items for discussion by the full Committee. She reported that *'every one of these activities have boosted my confidence and skills as a person and parent'.* Some mothers noted that their Committee experience had opened up job opportunities and given them the confidence to apply for jobs. Several parents stressed friendship and support from others and wider benefits for the community were also identified. The Parents' Committee has *'given us a voice and helped give other parents a voice'* and *'helped the community by more parents getting to know each other'.*

Over time, new initiatives were being undertaken, such as bidding for funding for their own newsletter through the Single Regeneration Budget. Some parents were being recruited and trained to take part in job interview panels. The events parents were planning for the future were more ambitious and would be undertaken more independently than previously, with parents gradually taking on more of the decision-making about the organisation of activities and handling budgets that they requested for these. This demonstrates how their skills had developed and their confidence had grown. Staff support was valued, in that *'They're all for us ... they're there for support, and they've given us the confidence to do it'.*

Staff noted that the planning, organising and decision-making that the Committee undertook was mainly related to children's and family activities and felt that they tended to be most motivated by activities on a social level. These are clearly important because of their relation to children's social, emotional and intellectual development and the building of social networks. Furthermore, the staff who worked with the Committee suggested that the parents' organisation of particular events, such as their Christmas carol concert, provided evidence of the Sure Start principle of participation and suggested that this could be seen as *'like a rehearsal, training, practising and gaining skills'* for participation in other areas. More strategic decisions, and those regarding the management of the Programme, were seen by staff as taking place at Partnership or Group Lead level (the former being concerned with issues at a strategic level and meeting quarterly, the latter a management group dealing with operational issues, meeting monthly). There were currently three parental representatives on the Partnership, drawn from the Parents' Committee and this was at the early stages. One staff member expressed the hope that *'as they get used to the process and develop their own skills they'll be able to take more of an active role in the managerial running of Sure Start'*. Participation was seen as presenting challenges of a practical, achievable nature (such as the timing of meetings, fitting in with childcare, use of language/jargon) but also of adjusting to new ways of working – *'a learning process for professionals'*.

Impact on professional roles

Within Sure Start, parents and professionals had more direct, more informal, contact with each other than previously. The extent to which this relationship had changed varied according to professionals' previous background and experience together with the demands of their current role.

For professionals, it was *'a completely new way of working, probably for 99% of us who work here'*, which *'presented personal challenges and agency challenges'*. Staff stated that it was *'more human'*, *'you have a closer working relationship'* and *'we're more on a level with them – there's less of a barrier, a gap'*. For one person who worked with the Committee,

> *'one of the good things has been becoming a lot less precious about your professional status. People on the Parents' Committee respect you not because of your job role but because of their relationship with you – it's more real, more earned ... I think what I've got is more real, but it is like a loss of status in a way, but for me I think that's all right'.*

At the same time, sharing office and kitchen areas, for example, raised issues such as confidentiality. Meeting parents in different contexts, such as in the home and then in formal meetings involved different types of relationship. For some staff there had been very tight boundaries in their previous role where it was *'easy to adhere to what you did and didn't do'*, whereas now some felt they were having to *'juggle'* with regard to roles and boundaries and *'lines have become blurred'*. A tension was noted between meeting parents in a confidential, confiding context and in an informal context within the same setting, and it was felt that in certain circumstances parents might want to maintain a clearer boundary. Working within Sure Start sometimes meant meeting families on an ad hoc basis and staff were more available to be consulted on a variety of issues, such as suggestions for events, and this could present dilemmas. For example,

> '*by committing to one thing you're often committing other individuals to that thing, which is difficult, you have to be careful ... we all interlink a lot tighter here ... one decision you make has a bigger chance of having an effect on somebody else, so being caught on the spot like that can be difficult*'.

For some professionals, this was in contrast to their previous roles where, for example, for a member of staff trained and experienced as a secondary school teacher,

> '*... you just saw people at a certain point and then you went and did classes and you didn't see them. It was neater ... you feel more on call here ... I think the lines have become more blurred*'.

Within the Committee itself, developments over time meant that the dynamics of the meetings were changing, as parents started to take on the roles of Chairperson and minute taker and this had, in the words of one professional involved,

> '*shifted away from us being the kind of gatekeepers, like 'Everyone keep quiet now, because we need to move on' ... and the natural leaders in the group have started to think 'Oh, if they're not going to do it, we do it', where normally we would dive in and do it ourselves*'.

These developments, she felt,

> '*mean that parents no longer see it as 'them and us'. I think it's getting more that we're becoming part of the 'us', which can cause problems as well ... it's not easy ... and you have to do a lot of negotiating around where are the boundaries still*'.

The parents also spoke of changing relationships with staff. For example,

'I don't look at them as social workers and things ... you're just yourself. They treat you as a person. You're not frightened to say things'.

Changing relationships and boundaries are clearly an important feature of Sure Start, with implications of a different nature for professionals and parents. For professionals this requires explicit attention to dynamics of partnership working including how to support parents in different working relationships, e.g. how to promote respect in situations of inequality (Sennett, 2003).

Discussion of findings

The findings are discussed according to the main themes of personal development and changing relationships and boundaries. Finally, a tentative model of the trajectory of developing empowerment and the relationship between personal power and relationship power is presented.

Personal development

The Parents' Committee was clearly involving parents, albeit not grandparents or carers at that stage, in ways that built on their existing strengths and it was providing a forum in which parents were able to develop the confidence and skills to undertake the planning and organising of events, and gradually take on greater power and authority within the Committee. These examples suggest that, at least for some parents, with support and encouragement, they were able to undertake tasks that previously they might have asked professionals to do on their behalf. At the same time, it is important to point out that, as noted by Sure Start staff and in the literature (e.g. Farrell and Gilbert, 1996), not all parents will wish to be involved in a way that involves moving up a 'hierarchy', or they may enter at different points or progress at different rates. The staff stressed the importance of valuing and respecting diversity of commitment.

In the interviews, professionals spoke more about the 'bigger picture' in terms of government priorities and used terms such as empowerment. Clearly, notions of empowerment have implications for power relationships between parents (or service users) and professionals, as well as for personal development.

Empowerment was not a term used by the parents themselves. Several authors (Giddens, 1991; Adams, 1996; Pease, 2002) note an emphasis on empowerment as a process of helping people gain control over their own lives. For example, Adams (1996) defines it as 'the means by which individuals, groups and/or communities become able to take control of their circumstances and achieve their goals' (Adams, 1996: 5). In that sense, then, the parents were providing clear evidence of this through their words. What may not be clear is which of the many things they spoke of had brought that about. Was it, for example, the experience of being on the Committee and having to make decisions with other parents, was it to do with the informal contact they have with professionals because of that, or was it to do with the friendships, social networks and support they described? Are they all equally important? Is it possible to capture the essential ingredients of what was working in the Parents' Committee and replicate it in analogous forms with other parents? Certainly, both the concepts of 'situated cognition' (Boreham and Samurcay, 1999) and the 'contact hypothesis' (Hewstone and Brown, 1986) would suggest that the Parents' Committee was promoting the conditions for learning both the skills required to operate in such contexts and learning about the other people involved. 'Situated cognition' stresses the development of understanding at the point of use and the 'contact hypothesis' stresses the importance of interaction in meaningful contexts for breaking down stereotypes and generating mutual understanding.

Professionals clearly felt that parental participation was important and of potential benefit for Sure Start and the community, but it is also clearly a complex, gradual process that can operate at different levels (see, for example, Arnstein, 1969; Shemmings and Shemmings, 1995). Furthermore, whilst tokenism may be easily achieved, authentic participation may not. The latter suggests moving beyond the informing, consultation and placation depicted by Arnstein (1969) as degrees of tokenism, towards partnership, delegated power and ultimately control, at which levels citizens begin to share power through negotiation and ultimately have majority or full decision-making power (ibid.). Through collaboration with Sure Start staff and their developing knowledge, skills and attitudes, the Parents' Committee's decision-making with regard to activities and events for parents and children demonstrates that within the Committee they had a degree of power and the necessary mechanisms (structures and resources) by which such decision-making can flourish (Loxley, 1997).

Notions of effective participation were further explored in an evaluation of parental involvement in a Sixth Wave Sure Start local programme and the findings are presented in the third section of this chapter.

Changing relationships and boundaries

Biggs (2000: 367) states that user participation suggests 'an increasing permeability of boundaries between professionals and non-professionals'. This study has shown evidence of changes in and 'blurring' of boundaries between professionals and parents that seemed to be having a significant impact on the parents interviewed, and a varied but nonetheless notable impact on the professionals, for example through greater informal contact and access. Boundaries can, of course, be physical or psychological. At the same time, professionals in Sure Start were adapting to new ways of working with each other and with lead and other agencies, and creating new roles and identities within a multiprofessional setting. New situations arise, for example, opportunities present themselves unexpectedly for informal conversation, consultation or advice, and people are faced with deciding what to do about them. Biggs (2000) suggests that moves towards user participation and interprofessionalism might both reflect and contribute to a momentum 'away from old certainties and towards a situation that is more ambiguous and in many cases more ambivalent as well' (Biggs, 2000: 367). This has implications for the identities of professionals and parents, as individuals and in groups.

Staff interviews gave indications that there may be a tension for Sure Start between the community development aspect and the therapeutic or clinical intervention side. This may relate to the holding of different professional values (see, for example, Wilmot, 1995). The New Labour agenda suggests that complex, deep-rooted problems require joined-up solutions and emphasises a social model and a community-focused response (see, for example, DSS, 1999). The latter may be easier to 'map onto' if one's profession has a social or community-oriented focus rather than a more individualistic focus.

A trajectory of developing empowerment

Empowerment is a complex concept. The evidence of this study seems to suggest that there appear to be at least two important dimensions to consider:

1. *Personal Power*

   This is concerned with an individual's ability to satisfy his/her desires. It takes place at an individual level and involves greater awareness of one's own existing expertise and potential. Often, social networks enable this type of learning. Cooley (1918) refers to the 'looking glass self' and suggests that significant others give us feedback which creates the image we have of ourselves and of what we can do.

2. *Relationship Power*

   This is concerned with the ability to influence others and can operate at individual and group level. As people realise their own strength and potential, they renegotiate the power relationship with professionals. Parents (or service users) may take on more of the functions that professionals traditionally perform as they feel they have a contribution to make, and may contribute more equally to decision-making. For professionals, this may involve dilemmas or conflicts and a reappraisal of their role and contribution and how their expertise fits in.

Both of these types of power help to create what might be termed 'contextual power', which involves being able to influence one's context favourably. The empirical evidence in this study suggests that for some parents some level of personal power was being reached, and we suggest that this is a necessary, but not necessarily sufficient condition for increasing relationship power and contextual power. The dynamic relationship between personal and relationship empowerment is clearly a significant factor with implications for both parents and professionals. The former may be a necessary condition for participation, but on its own it may not be enough, as it is also dependent on power relationships with professionals, and on organisational context. It may also have implications for individuals, perhaps particularly in complex multi-agency settings, engaged in the continuing personal project of identity construction in 'communities of practice' (Wenger, 1998).

Thus, this study seems to suggest that for those people who seek to get a genuine form of contribution from parents and similar stakeholders, it might be helpful to consider the process in relation to these two dimensions: Personal power and Relationship power (Figure One).

Figure one. A tentative model of the trajectory of developing contextual empowerment

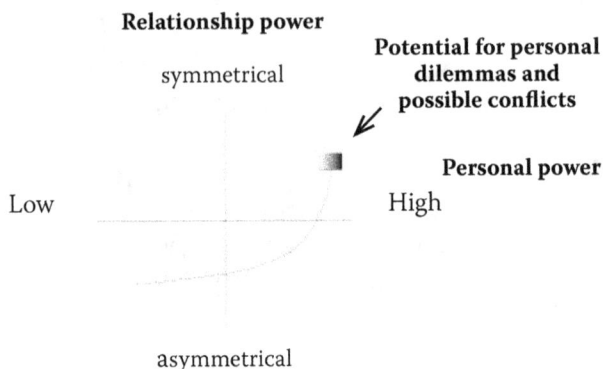

Relationship power

symmetrical

Potential for personal dilemmas and possible conflicts

Personal power

Low

High

asymmetrical

These do not develop at equal rates; the curve may contain high and low points according to the individual circumstances of people's lives. Further, as personal awareness becomes higher and power relationships become more symmetrical, there may be potential for personal dilemmas and conflicts, which manifest themselves in different ways. Surface behaviour manifestations (e.g. physical barriers, access to certain areas of the building) may give a revealing picture and provide indicators as to remaining psychological barriers and restrictions and the values professionals may still hold. This notion of potential dilemmas and conflicts also raises certain questions. For example, what happens as parents become more confident and capable and professionals have to redefine their role? Is this what professionals genuinely want? Do they have the skills to work in this way and how could such skills be developed? In a multi-agency project such as Sure Start this will have varying implications according to individuals' professional background, experience, sense of security and developing identity.

Pease (2002) considers that there is a paradox in being a professional and being committed to empowerment. Part of the definition of a profession implies possession of a specific knowledge base, expertise and the holding of an institutional position that places professionals in a position of power over others. He notes the potentially oppressive role of professional and scientific discourse and notes arguments for a dialogical rather than an authoritarian form of professional-client relationship. Furthermore, 'the tension inherent in the professional-client relationship is likely to undermine empowering interventions unless that relationship itself is reconstructed and the professional knowledge base upon which it rests is subjected to critical scrutiny' (Pease, 2002: 144). For a multi-agency project such as Sure Start the implications may be even more complex. In a separate family survey conducted in the same local Sure Start programme (reported in the previous chapter), reports given by parents not involved in the Committee of their relationships and interactions with professionals perhaps serve to demonstrate such a dialogical relationship in practice, and to demonstrate what this means to parents in terms of their feelings of exercising choice and maintaining control over associated aspects of their lives. For example, parents noted that Sure Start was *'not forced down your throat'*, that *'it's there for you to use as much or as little as you like'*, that *'they don't make you feel stupid'*, *'you feel on the same level'* and *'you're not seen as the problem but as part of the solution'*. Furthermore, there was evidence of consultation, choice and personal decision-making over proposed programmes or interventions, such that parents felt in control. This local Sure Start programme thus appeared to be empowering parents not only through highly visible means, such as through the Parents' Committee, but also through the nature of their professional approach and forms of interaction, enabling parents to feel they were active participants in the choices and decisions that they made with regard to parenting.

Conclusion

Involvement in the Parents' Committee had clearly contributed to the 'personal empowerment' of its members, has provided parents with opportunities to build on their strengths and develop practical skills, to establish strong social networks and to create new relationships with professionals. At the same time, changing relationships and changing boundaries have implications for power relationships and for the identity of professionals and parents. For those working in complex multi-agency settings, this may cause tensions and dilemmas and present a challenge that has implications for support and training and also for organisational restructuring (e.g. the modernisation of public services).

'EFFECTIVE' PARTICIPATION

This section reports on the findings of an evaluation of parental participation conducted in a Sixth Wave SSLP. It takes up the issue of 'effective' participation mentioned in the two previous sections of this chapter.

Background

This SSLP is a sixth wave local programme. Parental Involvement relates to one of Sure Start's key objectives at this time: 'strengthening families and communities: in particular, by involving families in building the community's capacity to sustain the programme and thereby create pathways out of poverty'. One of the targets under this objective was for 'All Sure Start programmes to have parent representation on the local programme board'. A key Sure Start principle is that 'all professionals with an interest in children and families should be sharing expertise and listening to local people on service priorities. This should be done by consultation and by day to day listening to parents'.

Eighteen months after approval, programmes were expected 'to have parents and community members represented on the main decision-making body and involved in a variety of ways in its management and consultation structure' (Sure Start, 2002:6). The guidance also refers to the intention that parents 'participate in' and do not 'merely attend' partnership meetings and the obligation this places on the organisational partners to see that they are easy to participate in. It notes a need for guidance, training and support. The Sixth wave guidance also suggested that programmes consider developing a parents' forum to encourage the involvement of parents and support them to take a more active role in the management; to help ensure that the voice of parents is strong and is not diluted by being one among many; and to develop a cadre of parents from which representation on the formal management groups can be later drawn.

Evaluation aims and method

The aims of the evaluation in this sixth wave SSLP were:

- To examine ways in which parents are involved in the SSLP, and ways in which this could be further developed.
- To explore the 'effectiveness' of parental participation in the SSLP and the impact on parents.

The evaluation was planned by the University local evaluation team, staff representatives and parents from the SSLP. Two initial focus groups were held at the Sure Start premises, the first with 8 parents and the second with 4 parents and were run by two members of the University local evaluation team. The purpose was to explore ways in which parents were involved and how this could be further developed. The same areas were also explored through a staff questionnaire and documentary analysis. These two initial focus groups were followed up by one further focus group at a different venue at a later date to explore notions of, and the extent of, effective participation (8 parents). This was run by one University evaluator and one member of the Sure Start team.

In order to explore 'effective' participation, documents such as the Sure Start sixth wave guidance and Every Child Matters guidance, and research literature (e.g. King et al., 1998; Halvorsen, 2003) were examined in order to explore notions of, and contributors to, effective parental/community participation. Issues drawn from the literature were categorised and this led to the establishment of five different domains to be explored. These domains are:

- Setting and organisation (e.g. style, timing, location of meetings);
- Aims/process (e.g. role of parent members; clarity regarding lines of communication and accountability);
- Preparation, training and support (e.g. capacity for effective participation);
- Co-operation and trust (e.g. learning from one another);
- Individual recognition/being valued (e.g. whether parents feel they are influencing events).

Themed questions were subsequently devised incorporating these five domains, in order to measure the degree to which parents felt included in decision-making processes and how this had been facilitated, i.e. whether, from the parents' perspective, effective participation had been achieved. The questions were used as a discussion tool with the second-stage focus group of eight involved parents/carers.

Findings

The findings were analysed under the five identified domains described above and relate to participants' experiences of participation in the Parents' Forum [referred to as the PF, rather than its given name, to respect anonymity], the Partnership and subgroups.

Setting and organisation (e.g. timing, location, style of meetings)

This relates to issues such as the time and venue of meetings, practical support (e.g. crèche and transport), the level of formality/informality in meetings, the use of jargon and acronyms, and support for people for whom English is a second or other language.

The PF had requested and achieved a change of time for Partnership and Capital group meetings. Whilst the timing of regular meetings was satisfactory, 'one-off' meetings were sometimes called at too short notice, and it was also pointed out that times were not suitable for parents who work, including many fathers. The PF has consistently been held at one location through the parents' choice, rather than responding to a Partnership suggestion for it to move round different locations. The Citywide Parents group was held in different Sure Start local programmes and this was considered a good opportunity to gain insight into other areas. The room used in the SSLP was not, however, considered conducive to participation, for example the positioning of the Chairperson and some workers on a platform was considered to inhibit participation and '*it feels like you're being judged*'. Small meetings, such as those with two to three parents and Sure Start staff (e.g. La Leche breastfeeding support group) were considered very 'child friendly' as they were held in a room with toys where parents felt their children were safe.

Practical support was provided for parents in terms of crèche, transport, resources and refreshments. However, there had been mixed experiences of childcare and a feeling of lack of consistency of venue and workers and stability, meaning that their children had to get used to different environments, workers and children. For longer events parents sometimes had to take their children out of nursery or pay extra to keep them there longer. The timing of childcare was not always satisfactory as it sometimes started at the same time as a meeting held in a different building, which meant that *'we miss the beginning and it looks as though our time-keeping's not good'*. Parents also had to leave the meeting early to get the transport to the crèche. The separate crèche location was also inconvenient when it was raining and in case of emergency. Parents felt that it would be preferable for Sure Start to have its own crèche facility and own crèche workers – *'local people who we can get to know and feel confident with'*. *'It is important to have the same workers, especially if the crèche is held at different places, as different workers and different venues can be unsettling for the children and put you off going'*.

The PF requested and received bags, and were also given folders for minutes and diaries, all of which were considered very useful. Parents were unaware of what resources were provided to parents in other Sure Start local programmes and felt that it would be useful to have a list of these to choose resources to suit changing needs, within a given budget.

The level of formality/informality varied between different meetings. The PF was considered to operate at a suitable level, enabling people to get to know each other. A social side to meetings was considered important. It was appreciated when food was provided (especially healthy options) as *'it helps informality and makes it more social'*. In subgroups it was reported that *'there are people from different areas and you don't know whether to say anything because you don't know if you're speaking out of turn'*, and that *'You sometimes feel intimidated and you feel they might pick up on us because we don't have the knowledge'*. It was a disadvantage that parents did not always know who people were. The 'set up' in the room was very formal, and people on the platform appeared to have a more formal role. Parents would welcome *'a cosier room where you can look at everybody, not sit in rows'*. It was suggested that people could have their names and organisations in front of them to make it easier to respond (*'not their job titles, though, that could be off-putting – for example, headmaster'*). Also, *'people should be forced to mix – there should be more informal get together, for example at the beginning of group meetings'*.

The use of jargon was seen to depend on the level of formality of the meeting and it was noted that, in some, it was easier to ask what things meant. Jargon was used particularly in Capital group meetings and *'you feel lost if you don't have the knowledge of what they're talking about'*. When parents got to know the workers in a group, such as the Citywide parents group, it became easier to understand the jargon used. Minutes of meetings also contained abbreviations and acronyms. It was suggested that at each meeting there could be a flipchart of abbreviations, acronyms and jargon used and that these could also be inserted into the parents' files.

Whilst it was recognised that the PF leaflet had been produced in different languages, it was also noted that people with English as a second language were not represented on the group or in other ways in Sure Start. Parents raised the issue of how, or whether, 'new to the area' families were encouraged to have a voice and felt that a dedicated worker with specialist knowledge of language and cultural/lifestyle norms would enable mutual learning as well as inclusion.

The implications of these findings are that the style of meeting rooms needs to be conducive to participation, and that, where possible, the crèche and meeting should be located within the same building to enable full participation in the meeting and enable immediate access in case of emergency or a child needing their parent's attention. For parents, consistency of staff and venue are important. An appropriate level of informality needs to be encouraged; jargon, acronyms and abbreviations need to be avoided or explained (e.g. flipchart, information for files), and steps need to be taken to help parents know who group members are (e.g. name and organisation on table) and to enable some social interaction at more formal meetings. These findings are significant with regard to 'Accessibility', a key factor in high-quality participation (King et al., 1998; Halvorsen, 2003).

Aims and process

Parents were clear about the purpose of the PF and noted that they had received explanation of the purpose of the Capital group. They were not all sure, however, about the purpose of the Partnership.

Parents expressed a dilemma over full commitment to groups. They felt it was *'not always easy to understand the purpose of a group unless you experience it'*, that *'it is important to have the opportunity to go to all meetings to put the whole jigsaw together'*, but also that *'it's not appropriate for all because of personal circumstances, and it also depends on how involved you want to be'*. It was felt that a system of having three parents volunteering to be on each subgroup would help parents get to know group members better and understand more about the aims of the group and how it operates.

Parents were clear about their role in the PF, which included encouraging new members, and were aware that it was *'very hard for people to 'go cold' and you need to build up their confidence'*. The PF had also helped them understand about their role in other groups, but they noted that they would otherwise have no awareness or understanding of parents' role in Sure Start groups. *'As a parent you could go to any activity and not know about anything else, you would think things just happen'*. Some parents reported that they had only just realised how much power the Partnership had and how important its role was and some did not feel that the process of Partnership meetings had been explained to them well. They felt it was very positive that a parent was now Chair of the Partnership and that it was important to avoid an appearance of Programme Managers running meetings, as this could be intimidating. It was reported that there were not always clear lines of communication. Parents did not always receive minutes beforehand or in enough time to make an informed contribution, and were unclear how to obtain information. It was stressed that *'communication needs to happen early in the process, then it would be more of a partnership, rather than complaining later when communication happens too late. The final decision might be the same, but we would have been part of the discussion of the pros and cons'*. It was not always clear how decisions had been arrived at and, whilst there was recognition that some decisions need to be placed in the hands of others, *'this still needs to be honest and transparent and they need to give the reasons behind their decisions and how and why they came to the decision, even if it's 'because the Government says''*. It was appreciated that the Parental Involvement Worker used her mobile phone to find immediate answers when she could, and was felt that it would be beneficial if other workers could do the same, and that it might be helpful for workers to have training on communication with parents. They did feel groups were committed to the involvement of parents, but also that it sometimes felt that it was 'because the Government says we have to'. In the PF there was a strong feeling that members of the Group built on each other's ideas in order to achieve the best possible outcome.

Parents reported that, for the future, they needed to know more about the purpose of the Partnership, what its authority is, why they meet, and how they are involved in decisions. They needed to know more about structures to help them understand their role within them. *'Participation can be daunting and it is time-taking to find out what links in with what'.* They felt that there should be a budget to enable 'parent Chairs' to have more training and confidence-building and to be offered pre-meetings to increase their knowledge and confidence in their role, *'so that the person with the most knowledge doesn't take over'.* Shadowing of the outgoing Chairperson for a few weeks was also suggested. They were in the process of developing leaflets and business cards about the PF and suggested that the Programme produces leaflets for all parents about the different groups, the purpose and structure of their meetings, how decisions are made and how parents can become involved. Parents reported that they need a greater understanding of what the Programme/Partnership has to achieve and greater involvement regarding targets so that they could use their local community knowledge to provide input and help the Programme work towards these. For example, *'We know women who breastfeed',* or *'If it's to do with more Health clinics, we could say it would be useful to do it this way'.*

Parents also felt they could support the Parental Involvement Worker's role in attending Sure Start sessions, outreach groups and toddler groups to enable families to give ideas informally that they could feed in to Sure Start on their behalf. More open days were also suggested, with the PF helping to publicise these in their local areas. The question was raised of whether it would be helpful for PF members to have some form of identification as parent workers (e.g. a 'top') so that they were recognised and other workers could signpost families to them to enable them to put their views across. They also stressed the importance of advertising Sure Start and celebrating its successes through a variety of means, e.g. on a website, through minutes, leaflets and the local press, and through information boards at, for example, libraries, GP surgeries and dentists.

Communication is key to effective participation. Parents need to be clear about the aims and purpose of management groups, their own and others' roles, and the decision-making powers and processes of the group. They also need to be well informed about the Programme's targets and objectives to understand the context in which decisions are made and to enable them to contribute to ways of achieving these. Communication with the wider community is also crucial for disseminating information and accessing the views of those who are unable, or do not wish, to attend meetings.

Preparation, training and support to parents

The PF was reported to have encouraged and supported parents in taking a more active role in the management of the SSLP. It had enabled members to learn skills in an informal setting, got them used to the processes of having a Chairperson and minute taking, and given them the confidence to speak out in a group. PF minutes were easy to understand and friendly and were a good preparation for more formal minutes. The Group was friendly, supportive and respectful. Members encouraged each other to try new things, recognised each other's skills and praised each other. Members felt that the Group was open and welcoming to new members, with parents bringing new parents into the meeting room from the crèche, rather than the worker. The Group contained a good mixture of people, with some wanting to stay within the PF and others wanting to go to other groups. There was a friendly, relaxed atmosphere and *'we are able to have a laugh when things get difficult, we don't let it get us down'.* There was a lot of support from the Parental Involvement Worker, who was *'proactive and positive',* for example in organising and reminding of meetings, organising training, and personal support. New PF members were prepared through Introduction Files, the meetings were made more informal and 'chatty' when new members attended, and Health and Safety issues were discussed.

The PF identified a need for Committee Skills training for participation in meetings. The Parental Involvement Worker liaised with the local College to find a tutor and an accredited course was run in partnership with three organisations. The Parental Involvement Worker and approximately eight parents completed the course. Other courses and training undertaken by parents (e.g. Speech and Language, Food Hygiene, Youth work, crèche course, Family Nurturing, Breastfeeding peer counselling, Domestic Violence, Behaviour Management) all *'indirectly help you have a voice because they give you more specialised knowledge and enable you to make a more informed decision'.* In addition, *'courses empower parents to help other parents'.*

Some parents did not always feel they knew what was expected of them as a member of a decision-making group and some were not aware of their rights at Partnership. Some did not feel they were given full information in good time, with the opportunity to clarify their understandings in advance of meetings. Parents stressed that it was very important to be well prepared as *'it can be frightening and intimidating to go to meetings'.* It was helpful when agendas were received beforehand at the PF so that members could take forward the views of those unable to attend.

These findings show the importance of parents being well prepared for meetings through receiving agendas, minutes and papers to be tabled in advance of the meeting to enable understanding and discussion. Training is clearly important, and will be key to involvement in Children's Centres. Parents felt that participation needed to be beneficial to 'both sides' and that training needed to be flexible and to recognise people's existing skills and experience. With a system of three volunteers for each subgroup these volunteers could be offered regular informal training specific to that group, e.g. members of the Capital group explaining how finances operate, jargon used, issues that are likely to come up, and how decisions are made. Parents suggested that, if feasible, it would be helpful for minutes to be placed on a website to refer back to. They also suggested a system for people to send in comments through the website, which would enable working mothers to contribute and possibly encourage more male participation.

Co-operation and trust

Parents felt that in all groups, particularly the PF, there was a climate of co-operation rather than competition. There was a climate of mutual trust rather than distrust, and of equality between team members in the PF and in meetings with health visitors, but some wondered whether the Partnership *'see us as there to complain and make life difficult'.* There was a feeling of *'less equality higher up'* and recognition that this was partly inevitable. One parent commented that, for those parents to whom this applied, *'I feel we would be listened to more if we came in our professional capacity'.* Parents' feeling of being 'at ease' within the group varied at 'different levels'. Meetings enabled them to learn from others with similar and dissimilar views, and this was *'enlightening'.* Parents felt able to learn from good and bad experiences and grow stronger.

Individual recognition and being valued

In most meetings parents felt safe expressing their ideas and opinions. This depended on their level of understanding of the topics under discussion. Members of the Breastfeeding support group were given *'lots of opportunities to do things our own way. The health visitors have listened to us and taken on our ideas and provided resources'.* They did feel that it was *'more detached further up – they sometimes see targets and finance and forget what it's like to be a parent'.* Nevertheless, they did feel that their comments were taken seriously and that they had effected change (e.g. times of subgroups, outdoor play facilities, development of Ducklings swimming sessions, type of community transport vehicle), although one person commented that *'sometimes it takes a lot of time and seems to be under duress'* and that although different viewpoints were listened to, different decisions were sometimes made and parents did not always understand why. Discussions were seen to be open, honest and thorough, with opportunity to voice opinions, but there was also a feeling that *'staff are dominant and it takes a long time to get through to people that we are equal'.* This relates to another key feature of high quality participation identified in the literature, i.e. that it is 'deliberative' (Warren, 1992; King et al., 1998; Halvorsen, 2003).

Some felt that their local knowledge, experience, contacts and expertise could be more fully utilised, for example in encouraging the involvement of more parents and working alongside staff in some areas.

Workers in multi-agency teams have very different professional backgrounds. These findings may indicate a need for training for professionals working in partnership with parents to increase understanding of community development and participation and ensure effective communication. Parents felt that the amount of support they received varied, and depended on personalities and professional role, for example *'how close they are to parents and their issues, like health visitors, or how long they have been away from working on the ground and the higher up they get'.*

It is important for parents to feel that they are important to the success of the group and their role is valued. These parents felt greatly valued by the Breastfeeding group and health visitors in particular and, of course, the Parental Involvement Worker. *'The workers on the ground are brilliant and value you and encourage you to be involved in the whole of Sure Start'.* It was considered important for professionals to openly and directly express their appreciation rather than pass this on through another worker, which was *'not good enough'.* Praise, and a feeling of doing something right, is important to parents and *'workers giving immediate praise and acknowledgement would increase our feeling of being valued'.* In any cases of criticism, parents would prefer to be taken to one side or *'have it come through somebody we feel comfortable with'.*

Features such as the opportunity to learn from others with similar and dissimilar views (McCool and Guthrie, 2001), believing decision-makers take citizens' comments seriously and that the resulting decisions reflect their consideration have been identified as contributing to participants' satisfaction. 'Satisfaction' is the third key feature of high-quality participation discussed by Halvorsen (2003). High quality participation 'contributes positively to effective, legitimate decision making' (Rabe, 1994; Stivers, 1990, cited in Halvorsen, 2003:536).

Given this importance of 'satisfaction', data from the introductory focus groups were also analysed to assess parental satisfaction through their reports on what they liked about being involved in this SSLP. This was:

- Learning, knowing what's going on, having a say
- Seeing positive outcomes, achievements and changes/ knowing you are making a difference in the area – *'[...] is a close knit community, you see people's lives change because of Sure Start, it's having a dramatic impact on people's lives'.*
- The high level of support and help they received, particularly from the Parental Involvement Worker and her Lead Agency, who had a strong belief in and commitment to parental involvement.
- The friendly environment
- Meeting people

This reinforced the findings, and also indicates the importance of professional commitment to parental involvement and of 'ethos'. The importance of the 'ethos' of Sure Start local programmes (SSLPs), i.e. where 'overall the SSLP has a welcoming and inclusive ethos' has been noted in the National Evaluation of Sure Start. A 'stronger ethos' was found to be related to higher maternal acceptance for families with a three-year old child (NESS, 2005b).

Parents generally felt that they had been listened and responded to and made to feel important, that some decisions had been taken on board and, if not, there had been good discussions and explanations. However, as previously described, there were still some ways in which some parents felt there could be improvement. These related to communication, e.g. regarding arrangements for meetings, the booking of crèche and transport; decision-making, e.g. issues regarding genuine discussion v. ratification; and the 'politics' of this and other organisations. This shows the need for continuous improvement as parental involvement develops over time.

Messages from the evaluation

Barriers to and facilitators of effective participation

Findings from this evaluation indicate effective participation in decision-making can be encouraged in each of the five areas identified for this study:

- Setting and organisation (e.g. style, timing, location of meetings);
- Aims/process (e.g. role of parent members; clarity regarding lines of communication and accountability);
- Preparation, training and support (e.g. capacity for effective participation);
- Co-operation and trust (e.g. learning from one another);
- Individual recognition/being valued (e.g. whether parents feel they are influencing events).

For Sure Start local programmes/children's centres seeking to increase parental participation it can also be useful to explore barriers to participation. The findings of the evaluation can be mapped onto the three-fold analysis of barriers identified by King et al (1998) as follows to show how the Programme had sought to overcome such barriers and ways in which they could be further addressed.

1. *Practical realities of daily life, e.g. transport, time constraints, family structure, number of family members in the labour force, childcare and economic disadvantages. Demands of daily life get in the way.*

    The Programme has sought to address this through, for example, allowing changes to times of meetings and providing transport and crèche facilities. Parents noted the importance of, for example, consistency of childcare and encouraging different methods of participation for those unable to attend meetings for any of the above reasons, e.g. via a website.

2. *Administrative processes, e.g. how information is managed, controlled and manipulated, whether the processes limit people's capacity to participate.*

    Parents noted the importance of being clear about the aims and purpose of management groups and their own and others' roles. They also wanted to be well informed about the Programme's targets and objectives to understand the context in which decisions are made and to enable them to contribute to ways of achieving these. It is important that parents are well prepared for meetings through receiving agendas, minutes and papers to be tabled in advance of the meeting to enable understanding and discussion.

3. *Techniques used in participatory processes, e.g. the structure of meetings can prohibit meaningful exchange; timing can mean that participation is often held late in the process, when decisions are already made; the process of conducting meetings.*

    Parents stressed the need for transparency regarding the decision-making powers and processes of the group and for involvement in discussions from the beginning. Training is also clearly important, for example with regard to committee skills, and will be key to involvement in Children's Centres. Parents felt that participation needed to be beneficial to 'both sides' and that training needed to be flexible and to recognise people's existing skills and experience.

As King et al note, these barriers cannot be seen in isolation from each other, and 'authenticity' cannot be achieved by addressing problems in only one area, i.e. 'To move towards authentic models, all three components of public participation – the administrative structures and processes, the administrators, and the citizens – must be addressed' (King et al., 1998:323). For example, 'empowering citizens means designing processes where citizens know that their participation has the potential to have an impact, where a representative range of citizens are included, and where there are visible outcomes' (ibid.) and 'citizen empowerment in the absence of administrative transformation is problematic' (ibid.). Administrative (or organisational) transformation may require changing institutionalised habits and practices (ibid:325). Re-educating administrators means changing their roles from expert managers towards that of cooperative participants or partners, and involves shifts at the personal level with regard to inter/intrapersonal skills, redefining the role of expertise, and changes to education and training (ibid.). This has implications for staff training and professional development. It also links to notions of empowerment as discussed in earlier sections of this chapter.

Consultation and direct involvement

This *direct involvement* was the focus of this study. Parents and staff also recognised the importance of ongoing consultation in the wider community. There was evidence of this taking place, for example through the PIW going to toddler groups, and the interest of the PF in contributing to this. Parents noted that, whilst the PF leaflet had been produced in different languages, people with English as a second language were not represented on the group or in other ways in Sure Start. Parents raised the issue of how, or whether, 'new to the area' families were encouraged to have a voice and felt that a dedicated worker with specialist knowledge of language and cultural/lifestyle norms would enable mutual learning as well as inclusion.

As stated earlier, the Sure Start Children's Centre Practice Guidance also specifically mentions consulting expectant parents, parents of disabled children, minority ethnic parents and lone parents. It also notes that it is important to seek explicitly the views of fathers as well as mothers. Finally, an area that has not been discussed in this evaluation, is consultation with children under five themselves.

As a result of recent training, the Programme was exploring the notion of developing community dialogue and a culture of dialogue involving 'community conversation' (West-Burnham and Otero). West-Burnham and Otero note that finding ways to bridge community and organisation can mean transforming relationships with the community and may involve changing attitudes, relationships and the deployment of resources. Two strategies for doing this are building relational trust (involving respect, competence, personal regard, integrity) and promoting and practising dialogue as a vehicle through which to interact with the community. One aspect of this dialogue is 'community conversation', 'a vehicle for people to express and share the diverse views that they hold, to negotiate and reaffirm directions and vision and to develop social capital' (ibid.). Effective dialogue skills are important at all levels of the community/organisation and have the potential to increase capacity to learn from one another (ibid.).

Empowerment

The Sure Start Children's Centre Practice Guidance states that consultation can be a means to build the confidence of local parents – fathers and mothers, and to develop and share the skills of the local community. It can also be a means to enhance the professional skills of local workers; and build partnerships, especially with parents (Sure Start, 2005:14).

Empowerment was one of 18 domains rated on a 7-point scale by the National Evaluation of Sure Start (NESS), to examine the proficiency of implementation of SSLPs. Each domain is illustrated by a 'statement of proficiency'. For the 'empowerment' domain, the statement is 'SSLP has procedures to create an environment that will empower users and service providers' (NESS, 2005:9). Empowerment can have outcomes for families and children. NESS have found that empowerment is related to two of five parenting measures (9-month-old maternal acceptance and 3-year-old home learning environment), which 'implies that strengthening SSLP activities that are relevant to *empowerment* may provide a means of improving their effectiveness for helping parents. Should this be the case then it is likely to later lead to better outcomes for children because both maternal acceptance and the home learning environment have been found to predict better child outcomes' (NESS, 2005: iv). In the context of their report, empowerment refers to 'specific procedures within SSLPs, for example, parents being involved in the planning of services and represented on the board; training offered to both paid and voluntary staff; services will include self-help groups; and there is mutual respect for parents, staff and others' (ibid.).

These findings also have implications for professional roles. Professionals need to have a positive view of, and approach to, parental participation and this needs to be evident to parents, so they don't feel like it's a token gesture or they are perceived as a '*bolshy*' group. Workers in multi-agency teams have very different professional backgrounds. As noted by the parents in this evaluation, the findings may indicate a need for training for professionals working in partnership with parents to increase understanding of community development and participation and ensure effective communication. NESS incorporated community development training for staff and evidence of mutual respect for contributions of all parties in their ratings regarding SSLPs' intention to empower users and service providers (NESS, 2005b). This raises the question of how far management of programmes supports parental involvement. Clarke (2006) raises the question of how Sure Start fundamentally conceptualises parents, suggesting that they are seen as both competent and incompetent. On the one hand, she suggests, 'parental involvement in the management of the programme and its local 'ownership' implies that parents are capable, reflective and aware of their own and their children's needs and able to articulate these needs effectively' (Clarke, 2006: 717). On the other hand, she suggests, 'the targets for the programme are built on an assumption of deficits in parenting and parental ignorance, with some parents at least who are 'hard to reach', unable or unwilling to acknowledge their needs and requiring outreach work to draw them in' (ibid.).

PARENTAL INVOLVEMENT: IMPLICATIONS FOR CHILDREN'S CENTRE DEVELOPMENT AND MULTI-AGENCY SERVICES

Findings from these three evaluations of parental involvement in Sure Start have implications for the development of services for children and families, both with regard to service use and with regard to consultation and decision-making. The Sure Start local programmes involved in these evaluations have become part of either Phase 1 or Phase 2 of the Citywide Children's Centre developments. National guidance indicates that the active involvement of parents/carers and the local community is to continue. The Phase 2 Planning Guidance (July 2005) states that:

> 'The intention is that children's centres services become permanent mainstream community services, which are developed and delivered with the active involvement of parents/carers and the local community' (Sure Start 2005:4).

The Phase 2 guidance also states that there must be: consultation and information sharing with parents/carers, including fathers, on what services are needed, and systems to get user feedback on services, and ongoing arrangements in place to ensure parents/carers have a voice.

These statements are reinforced in the Children's Centre Practice Guidance (2005), which states that wide consultation with parents and other local people is essential, and 'should be a continuous process which will support decision-making and shape the development of the children's centre' (Sure Start, 2005: 14). As well as being an important part of ensuring that services offered are what people want and need, the Guidance states that '[consultation] can also be a means to:

- build the confidence of local parents – fathers and mothers;
- develop and share the skills of the local community;
- enhance the professional skills of local workers; and
- build partnerships, especially with parents (ibid.)'.

Working groups of parents and professionals and parents' forums are still seen as means of ensuring that consultation and involving parents are an ongoing process.

*

This chapter has raised issues with regard to different types of parental involvement and their relationship to service use, service delivery and service planning; changing relationships between parents and professionals through parental involvement; and effective participation of parents/carers in decision-making groups. All these issues are relevant to future developments in the light of statements in *Every Child Matters: Change for Children* documentation, such as 'Parents, carers and families are important partners in the development and delivery of multi-agency services' (available at www.everychildmatters.gov. uk/parents/participationinmultiagencyworking/).

5
Interprofessionalism, multi-skilling and mainstreaming

THIS CHAPTER PRESENTS findings from three small-scale research studies examining the impact of changing professional roles within Sure Start programmes focusing upon interprofessionalism – different disciplines working together in new ways; multi-skilling – broadening and diversifying professional roles; and mainstreaming – altering the behaviour and role of mainstream service professionals. The first study considers how different models of interprofessional working have evolved within a Sure Start 'trailblazer' programme; the second study focuses upon health visiting and demonstrates how as a profession health visitors have taken a proactive role towards adapting to Sure Start and the third considers the process and outcome of establishing an interdisciplinary mechanism within two Sure Start programmes for assessing needs of children and families requiring support. All three studies provide evidence of programmes moving towards a more integrated approach of service delivery.

STUDY 1: MODELS OF INTERPROFESSIONAL WORKING WITHIN A SURE START 'TRAILBLAZER' PROGRAMME

Aim and method:

The aim of this study is to describe and evaluate interprofessional work within a Sure Start 'trailblazer' programme including assessing how far the setting of national programme objectives that emphasised 'working together in new ways that cut across old professional and agency boundaries' (DfEE, 1999:6) has helped to create interprofessional working. This is a qualitative single case-study design exploring relationships which shape and form the basis of interprofessional work undertaken by a Sure Start team located together in one building. Twenty-six team-members agreed to be interviewed individually regarding their involvement in interprofessional work, how this may contribute to Sure Start targets/objectives and factors which were seen to either help or hinder this type of activity. They were asked to describe how their practice had changed since being part of Sure Start focusing upon their role in interprofessional activity. The staff group included representatives from health visiting, clinical psychology, social work, community paediatrics, nursery nursing, early-years learning and family therapy. Interviews were open-ended and designed to explore informants' accounts of interprofessional work. They were audio-taped/transcribed and content analysis was used to search for *examples* of interprofessional working based around definitions of *multi-, inter-, trans-disciplinary* collaboration (Orelove & Sobsey 1991; Lacey 2003). The form of content analysis involved extracting information of reported experiences of individual involvement in interprofessional work to provide a rounded account of each activity.

Results

The following provides the most embedded examples of interprofessional working that have evolved from within the programme.

These examples are described and then analysed under the three separate categories of *multi-disciplinary, inter-disciplinary* and *trans-disciplinary* ways of working. Firstly, *multi-disciplinary* work is where two or more professionals from different disciplines work together or co-exist alongside each other but separately from each other. An example from the programme surrounds the subject of child protection and providing family support, the latter supplying the conceptual model upon which Sure Start is founded. Relevant Sure Start targets include reducing the number of children on the at-risk register; and achieving an increase in the proportion of babies and young children with normal levels of personal, social and emotional development for their age.

Multi-disciplinary activity

Description

The programme offers group work activity led by a health visitor, social worker or psychologist focusing upon families with children with behaviour problems and includes a nurturing programme, a domestic violence forum and whole-team training on child protection, domestic violence and anti-oppressive, anti-discriminatory practice. The nurturing programme is aimed to '*just sort of build on these parents, their self-esteem and to help them through their problems, their difficulties*' (health visitor). A social worker and health visitor work with teenage mothers on their housing needs although activities are conducted separately. Health visitors work with psychologists and child care centre staff in identifying problems of post-natal depression in young mothers yet individual professional input is differentiated and given separately. There is a whole-team training on e.g. breastfeeding, post-natal depression and sleeping patterns enabling all staff to keep up-to-date and make them feel better informed when talking to parents; and this was highlighted as facilitating interprofessional working – 'giving a clear focus on targets/objectives' (programme manager). There are links with the PCT and midwifery regarding vulnerability assessment to enable information-sharing on pregnant women at risk of depression and introduction of home visits in the antenatal period. Spending more time with families has meant increased sensitivity to the issue of child protection resulting in more referrals to mainstream services – *'health visitors maintain close links with health visitors from other GP practices'* (health visitor). The focus of the Sure Start objective of reducing the number of children on the at risk register produces a tension in deciding how best to deploy valuable staff resources. A social worker expressed her dilemma over the bland target of de-registration where child adoption may be preferable as her motive was supporting families and helping to change their behaviour e.g. drug/alcohol abuse, in order that the child would have a suitable environment in which to flourish.

A Sure Start target is to achieve 75% of families reporting improvements in family support. However, a social worker expressed concern over how families might choose to report this information:

'A woman who came with a housing issue had a heroin addiction. I do think that the addiction and the psychological distress that she experienced had a profound impact on whether she got her finances and housing sorted out. In order to help her with housing I need to help her with other things and she needs to say that she wants to change. Ultimately I can only do it on a voluntary basis if we can agree a shared agenda.'

The term 'family support' was contentious in a practical way as, according to one health visitor: *'it raised feelings earlier among parents that (Sure Start) was just getting loads of volunteers to do all the unpaid work'.* This may have been in response to the recruitment of community parents (volunteers) given training to act as mentors providing emotional and sometimes practical support to other parents as part of the overall programme.

Analysis

In the above example the effectiveness of doing multi-disciplinary work may be impeded by professionals giving different emphasis to either child protection or providing family support. This stems in part from a confusion regarding local interpretation of national policy, individuals giving priority to different targets and different management hierarchies pursuing objectives different from Sure Start producing conflicting loyalty (e.g. Johnson et al, 2003). Whereas de-registering the number of children may be a Sure Start target and increasing family support a means towards achieving this, some professionals take the view that parental willingness to change their own behaviour or to engage with Sure Start ought to be a condition of receiving other kinds of support. The term 'family support' has become associated with the 1989 Children Act which empowered local authorities to provide support for families with children 'in need'. Since then there has been a plethora of reports teasing out the implications of family support and its connection with other social policy measures (Penn & Gough, 2002). These include family support as a contribution to better parenting (Lloyd, 1999); as a service response to cases of child abuse (Thoburn et al, 2000); as a service to children in need (Tunstill & Aldgate, 2000); and as part of a debate about the value of home-based versus centre-based family support (Buchanan & Hudson, 1998). Penn & Gough (op.cit) conclude that social work and health services tend to operate within a model of family support narrowly focused on emotional support and behavioural change, rather than a preferred needs-based model which considers income maintenance, childcare, leisure and education. The Children Act provided the platform for the Department of Health to attempt to shift the emphasis in child protection work more towards family support (Frost, Johnson, Stein & Wallis, 2000). The over-riding concerns of the Children Act 1989 and Children Act 2004 are the definition and execution of the two tasks of promoting and safeguarding their welfare. While the detail of policy may change in respect both of measuring the relevant outcomes; and establishing the appropriate balance to be struck between the two tasks, the central duties are perennial and cross-cultural.

Inter-disciplinary work

Inter-disciplinary work is where professionals share information and decide on education/health/social care programmes together but where these are implemented separately by individual disciplines. An example of this type of activity that emerged from the analysis of the Sure Start programme concerns the process of child and family referral and assessment, namely the Referral and Allocation project.

Relevant Sure Start targets include involving families in building the community's capacity to create pathways out of poverty, and increasing the number of families reporting personal evidence of an improvement in the quality of services.

Description

The Referral and Allocation Project (later renamed Request for Services project) sought to develop through regular meetings an inter-disciplinary focus on discussing the needs of families who had been referred, or had referred themselves, to Sure Start and on suggesting ways in which support or advice could be offered and accessed in order to meet their needs. As different professionals were appointed to the programme and took up work with families, it gradually became evident that referrals were being made to Sure Start from a variety of sources and that different systems were in operation for handling referrals. Staff had come to Sure Start with different experiences of allocation, assessment, planning and review systems, or no experience at all. A working group identified that there was no clear referral process, a lack of co-ordination and restricted information-sharing and opportunity for creative use of knowledge and skills or rethinking of professional boundaries. As a result of the project professionals reported greater understanding of each other's roles although some expressed personal and professional discomfort e.g. that meetings could feel *'threatening and intimidating which had sometimes led to my not engaging'* (early years worker). Another referred to feeling 'under the microscope'; *'it has taken a long time to become used to dealing with a mixed group of people but become easier over time'* (family therapist).

Responses indicated that this inter-disciplinary project demonstrated a feeling of collective responsibility where individual staff felt that the meetings were contributing to their professional development through case discussion that would aid their future practice, teaching and learning. However there were still areas of difficulty. For example, some team members were not seeing the meetings as a priority. There were also expressions of professional anxiety related to how far individuals felt able to disagree with and challenge other professionals, as well as anxiety in relation to issues of hierarchy. It was felt that individual perceptions of hierarchy were influencing the conduct of the meetings in terms of staff looking to particular individuals for answers and of the ensuing impact on those individuals who perceived this as increased pressure. There was reference to pressures of 'bearing the load' while waiting for meetings to discuss cases or 'holding' families who did not engage with other professionals. Some staff expressed anxiety over justifying time spent in meetings that might be reducing time spent on 'face-to-face' work. Many staff were not used to dealing with complex cases, hence discussion of one case was sometimes leading to worry over other cases or past cases. The timing of the meeting left no time for people to talk to their colleagues about personal-impact issues. Some staff felt that the nature of their work was leading to them *getting closer'* (social worker) to clients, that 'f*amilies are offloading more' and that 'professional distance is no longer there'* (social worker). Individual staff recognised that they were struggling with the tension between traditional practice and different models of working. For instance in their previous posts, psychologists and social workers had commonly responded to external referrals, for example mental health and child protection, but were now finding themselves having to respond to wider family and community concerns brought to their attention by colleagues within the Sure Start programme. Difficulty was expressed in obtaining information to provide a complete picture when a range of agencies is involved e.g. obtaining information from minutes of meetings, not having health visitor colleagues on the same site, more children with more complex problems being referred and needing multi-disciplinary assessment.

Analysis

Inter-disciplinary work focuses upon professionals deciding on the form of intervention together but working separately accountable subsequently to the shared goal-forming process. Menzies Lyth's (1988) psychodynamic model as applied to teamwork within organisations suggests that a team is influenced by a number of interacting factors in developing a structure, culture and mode of functioning. These include not only the primary task (in the case of Sure Start to improve the health and wellbeing of families and young children); the technologies required (for Sure Start these would be the people and systems) but also 'the needs of the members of the team for social and psychological satisfaction, and above all, for support in the task of dealing with anxiety' (p50). The Request for Services project interpreted the encountered resistance as being due to the meeting generating different ways of working, for example, piecing together information from different sources which would lead to an increased workload for individuals and greater worry.

The outcome of each family assessment identified a lead professional to take responsibility for managing interventions most commonly in areas of family therapy and paediatric assessment/support, which suggested that professional hierarchy has at least some bearing on the decision-making process. Where professionals from different disciplines decide on what lies in the best interests of a child/family a clash of values may result and resulting decisions are usually governed by available resources e.g. expertise, professional and personal commitment. The issue of power-relationships was an emerging theme, with some members of staff feeling unable to voice their opinion for fear of being ridiculed or not having the authority to express their views, raising issues about the tension between responsibility and authority on the one hand and flexible working and creativity on the other. The evidence tends to support findings from other studies (e.g. Robinson & Cottrell, 2005; Harker et al, 2004) showing the tendency for a lack of understanding of others' methods of working, culture and background and that there is a need to develop relationships beforehand.

Trans-disciplinary work

Trans-disciplinary work is where sharing or transferring information and skills across traditional disciplinary boundaries enables one, two or more members to be primary workers supported by others working as consultants. An example from within this Sure Start programme is the Infant Programme (IP) managed by the consultant psychologist and delivered through teamwork involving health visitors, psychologist, family therapist and nursery nurses. Relevant Sure Start targets here included Sure Start visiting all families with newborn babies within the first two months of their child's life; for parenting support and information to be made available; and supporting the development of good relationships between parents and children enabling early identification of difficulties.

Description

The IP involved a health visitor taking a video-recording of participating mothers with their baby very early on 8, 10 or 12 weeks from birth. The IP is about:

'ensuring that family, parents and children are securely attached from day one basically. We offer a video of mum and baby about 9-10 weeks of age and we bring them back with permission to one of the psychologists and we watch the video and analyse it and then discuss how we're going to give mum some help on understanding her baby's development. Then we take it back to the home and share that with them and they do weekly videos to see if there are changes.' (health visitor)

The videotapes are examined to consider bonding relationships with mother and baby, and intervention is offered based around an assumption that such early bonding is vital to prevention of later problems in child development and family relationships. A control group of mothers was selected for evaluating effects of this intervention and an action research study conducted by a psychologist focused on measuring its impact. To support a solution-focused approach the Brazleton Neo-natal Assessment Scale was used by psychologists, health visitors and midwives to discuss the content of videos.

Health visitors asserted that the benefits of their IP training were not only confined to those mothers who agreed to be videoed. The consultant psychologist claimed a sufficient evidence-base to justify the concentration of professional input on the early months of a child's life and on effort to enhance mother-baby bonding at this stage of the cycle. He stated that this represented a new way of working, as a psychologist employed within the NHS would not normally be allowed to intervene in mother-child relations to the same intensity or to the exclusion of other types of intervention; that it was more difficult to change behaviour as a child grew older; and that the IP enabled professionals to be influential in preventing later mental ill-health in children. Health visitors provided a Crittenden CARE-Index screening (Crittenden, 2001) for planning intervention home visits with the psychologists. This examined adult-infant patterns of interaction by Sure Start staff and was used as an evaluation tool. The consultant psychologist led a reflective practice group to monitor the IP so that contributing professionals:

'can bring any aspect of our work that's troubling us to do with infant and maternal mental health and (he) gives us a lot of helpful information, research-based information.' (health visitor)

The project involved '*whole-team meetings, team building days, professional support/supervision and case-discussion*' which facilitated interprofessional working – '*I now have regular clinical supervision*' (health visitor); '*good support from my line-manager*' *(nursery nurse);* '*co-location of staff eases information–sharing*' (community paediatrician).

Analysis

The purpose of a *trans-disciplinary* approach is to encourage professionals to work together under common aims and systems, regardless of their discipline or status. The important features are information-sharing and skill transfer involving a problem-solving approach drawing on evidence gathered from a range of professionals. Training in techniques is cascaded through observation of colleagues as well as delivered directly during formal courses (Lacey, 2001:115-118). The role of the consultant(s)- in this example, the psychologist - is to encourage and enable team members to work out for themselves the best ways of working together, rather than by providing solutions to problems. Providing groups for parent teaching and parent involvement on the subject of sleep patterns, feeding and infant massage similarly involves a *trans-disciplinary* approach involving: psychologist, health visitor, nursery nurse. In this example, nursery nurses take on tasks traditionally confined to health visitors - child surveillance, parent teaching and mother-baby assessment, supported by peer/health visitor supervision. They work alongside health visitors in undertaking part of routine assessments with children, and other developmental assessments including sleep or speech programmes to free up time to do more intensive work. Health visitors in this example demonstrate 'skill mix, offering multiple forms of service delivery- outreach, individual support in the home, group-work' (DH, 1998) ; and 'multi-skilling including a more family and community-oriented model and holistic approach to working with families' (DfES, 2006).

Discussion

Findings demonstrate that there were examples of different models of interprofessional working present in this Sure Start programme and that if similar programmes look at interprofessionalism in the light of these models it might help them develop their practice.

The findings from this study raise questions in three main areas. Firstly the question arises as to whether interprofessional working helped achieve Sure Start targets, whether the existence of targets drives interprofessional working or whether there is no explicit evidence of a connection. Imposing externally-defined targets on professional working arrangements may have a counterbalancing effect when this affects a professional's capacity to offer discretionary judgement. Government setting targets and defining outcomes for caring professionals places this Sure Start programme within a quagmire of policy debate regarding tension between discourses of managerialism and professionalism still ongoing within the public sector in the UK since the New Right political attack on the welfare professions, which began in the late eighties and continued under New Labour. In the case of Sure Start, government policy sets the parameters, which focused on results/ outcomes, maintenance of standards, changing the working culture towards improving productivity, efficiency, incentivising contractual arrangements towards predictability, stability and regulation (e.g. Clarke & Newman, 1997).

Secondly there is a question of how interprofessionality impacts on roles, identities, status and power of individuals. The Request for Services project, which was characterised as interdisciplinary, portrays a process of professionals from different disciplines making a collective judgement where individuals possess different power and authority. The corollary of this is that some experience personal/professional discomfort, feel intimidated, undervalued hence leading to lower engagement and resultant ownership of the process. The discomfort may stem from failure to clarify terminology and professionals feeling inhibited to ask for clarification about meanings because of perceived hierarchies within the room or because they do not wish to be considered awkward or pedantic (Salmon & Rapport, 2005). Some considered the process time-consuming as they would have made a direct referral anyway- it had *'not added anything'* with regard to the family under discussion: *'it is a paper exercise, the main thing is to involve the people who are going to be directly involved'*.

Type of Interprofessional Working

Multidisciplinary

Definition Two or more professionals from different disciplines work/co-exist alongside each other on the same issue but working separately from each other

Example Different professionals working towards family support and child protection objectives

Interdisciplinary

Definition Professionals share information and decide on education/health/ social care programmes together but these are implemented separately by individual disciplines who are accountable to shared goals and objectives

Example Different professionals offering a forum for child/family referral and Request for Services

Transdisciplinary

Definition Professionals share or transfer information and skills across traditional disciplinary boundaries enabling one or more members to be primary workers supported by others working as consultants; the purpose being to work under common aims/systems regardless of discipline/status; encourage information-sharing and skill transfer involving a problem-solving approach

Example Different professionals providing a programme to promote mother-baby bonding development and family relationships (Orelove & Sobsey, 1991; Lacey, 2001)

Interprofessionality

Definition Emerges from a preoccupation of professionals to reconcile their differences & involves continuous interaction & knowledge-sharing between professionals organised to solve or explore a variety of education & care issues while seeking to optimise user/family participation (D'Amour & Oandasan, 2005).

Example In this Sure Start programme the following were identified by professionals as aiding interprofessionality: working practices including whole team-meetings & team-building days; professional support/clinical supervision & case discussion; co-location of staff & ease of communications/information-sharing; focus on targets/objectives.

The example of transdisciplinary activity, the Infant Programme, offers role convergence in a primarily health-based team where redistribution of roles and role-blurring poses less of a problem. Both the psychologist and community paediatrician acted as teacher/mentor to other practitioners regarding the technology and philosophy of the IP e.g. morale development in mother-child attachments and giving information on childhood illnesses and as role models in providing integrated supervision. In this way Sure Start professionals obtained support/supervision by crossing professional boundaries. Supervisory relationships are considered a prerequisite to good interprofessional working, especially in the psycho-dynamic context. The term 'supervision' may for some professionals conjure up ideas of discipline and criticism and imply more managerial than clinical connotations (Faugier, 1996), although few empirical studies exist that establish outcomes of clinical supervision (Sloan, 1999); the example of transdisciplinary activity reported in this study suggests that an integrated supervision approach is strengthened by regular whole-team meetings, professional support, case-discussion and information-sharing.

Thirdly, the example of multi-disciplinary activity highlights the fact that different professionals can work alongside each other serving a particular family but from a value base, which places a different emphasis on goals of family support, child protection, and children's rights. Professionals e.g. health visitors, social workers may work alongside each other but hold different views on the right balance in providing family support such as determining what action is in the best interests of the child and the family as a whole despite operating within a common programme such as Sure Start. According to Smith (2005:94):

> 'to develop effective partnership, effort must be put into providing preventive services, which should complement the child protection function, rather than being seen as opposed or irrelevant to it.'

The principles of family support should therefore inform child protection processes, rather than being seen as conflicting with them.

The Sure Start model is based principally upon a 'birth family defender' approach articulated by Fox Harding (1997) implying a belief in a positive role for state intervention to promote the well-being of families – 'adequate levels of support, both financial and in respect of other forms of family assistance, are sufficient, according to this view, to enable families to thrive independently. Children's upbringing is best promoted in this way, based on the notion of partnership between service providers and parents'. One method of providing family support was through recruiting community parents who would act as a volunteer/mentor to a family to offer support in circumstances where it is felt there was a need and where parents themselves were willing to accept this type of help. The approach is important because it helps to maintain a focus on family strengths as well as problems and presented less opportunity for value conflict.

Conclusion

This study shows how different types of interprofessional work and the experience of Sure Start have helped to re-shape the roles of several professionals e.g. health visitor, social worker and nursery nurse. This is in contrast to another study (Edgley & Avis, 2006) which showed that most mainstream professionals did not feel that collaboration with Sure Start had fostered innovation in their own working practices. To determine how an understanding of different dimensions of interprofessional work might support integrated services, it is relevant to define the latter term which, according to *Every Child Matters*, 'act as a service hub for the community by bringing together a range of services, usually under one roof, whose practitioners then work in a multi-agency way'. Integrated working comprises a way of improving outcomes for children and families and involves delivery of integrated frontline services supported by more integrated processes which include: the Common Assessment Framework (CAF), the Lead Professional and better information-sharing. The CAF consists of three elements grouped into the themes of development of the child, parents and carers, and family and environment and is intended to provide a process to assess the additional needs of a child or young person and to give a holistic view that considers strengths as well as needs.

The above study which describes and analyses interprofessional working offers evidence of *how* the examples given provide a foundation for more integrated services. One example concerns the *inter-disciplinary* Referral and Allocation project which encompasses a process for child/ family referral and assessment and combines improved information-sharing among different disciplines, holistic assessment and nomination of a lead professional to act as a single point of contact who is able to support the child/family in making choices and in navigating their way through the system. A second example concerns the *trans-disciplinary* Infant Programme which identifies a psychologist as a lead professional/mentor who draws upon the experience and skills of health visitors and nursery nurses in order to develop and evaluate a specialist project around mother-baby bonding. This project involves information-sharing and transference of skills where one or more practitioners take a lead role to ensure that interventions are coordinated, coherent and achieve intended outcomes. Lastly the Children's Workforce Development Council (CWDC) has been established to support the implementation of integrated working and is consulting on the role function of the Lead Professional (ECM Factsheet, February 2007). This is in the context of the development of a 'core' early-years worker signalled as an important condition for a common and integrated approach to the work (DfES, 2003). The ECM Outcomes Framework based on targets and indicators, and designed to be transparent in the way that it makes the connection between resources (inputs) and activities and outcomes, is intended to offer practice guidance towards integrated provision.

STUDY 2: AN INTEGRATED MODEL TO PROVIDE HEALTH VISITING SERVICES

Aim and method

Two neighbouring Sure Start Local Programmes (SSLPs) had health teams both of whom acknowledged that Sure Start had presented challenges for the health visiting service, including fragmentation of caseloads, increased training opportunities to Sure Start staff and uncertainty around the Sure Start agenda which had led to negative attitudes that needed to be addressed. They decided to work together to develop a vision for health visiting, namely 'Sure Start for All' which would adopt a 'collaborative, integrated and inclusive approach' in order to ensure equal access to services, equal workload for all health visitors, and the opportunity for all staff to deliver the Sure Start and Public Health Agenda (DH, 1998; 1999). The intention was to encourage specialisation and a more integrated and transparent approach within health visiting. The research questions of this participatory evaluation were:

1. How has the approach been developed and how successful has this been?
2. What barriers have there been and how could any remaining barriers be overcome?
3. What are the achievements of the approach?
4. What are the benefits for the local community?

   'Improving health' has been one of the principal objectives of Sure Start from the outset, and remains so for children's centres. Child and family health services are a key part of the children's centre core provision relating to Every Child Matters (ECM) outcomes: 'Be healthy' and 'Stay safe' and the National Service Framework Standards 1, 2, 3 and 5. The evaluation was planned as a group by the University local evaluation team and six representatives of the Health teams from the two SSLPs. The methods were:

1. Documentary analysis, eg 'Sure Start for All- an integrated health care model', internal reports and minutes of meetings.
2. Semi-structured interviews with the health visiting team (n=17)
3. Semi-structured interviews/written questionnaires with partner agencies and other professionals; voluntary agencies (n=7)
4. Interviews/questionnaires with parents/carers (n=51)

The documentary analysis and interviews with the health visiting team were undertaken by a University researcher and the interviews with partner agencies, other professionals and voluntary agencies and with parents/carers were undertaken by the staff representatives, who interviewed each other's clients, rather than their own, to reduce bias. The staff representatives also distributed written questionnaires to parents/carers they encountered during the course of their practice and these were collected in sealed envelopes to ensure confidentiality. All data were anonymous.

Results

Development of the integrated model

Prior to the emergence of the two SSLPs there were ten GP attached health visitors. In addition, three health visitors had a cross-boundary caseload, ie families living in the Sure Start area, but with a GP outside the area. It was agreed that one SSLP would appoint a further three health visitors, that the other would appoint two, and that two nursery nurses would also be appointed to each programme. It was noted by some individual health visitors that, as the first Sure Start programme in the city was set up, there was some initial friction, and some tension with regard to levels of experience and the amount of training that was to be offered to Sure Start health visitors, which led to feelings of exclusion. It was felt that change had been brought about through the influence of personalities. Historically, Sure Start health visitors had worked reduced caseloads from within the programme base in many areas, undertaking routine child surveillance as well as delivering the Sure Start agenda. In some areas Sure Start health visitors work independent of GP health visitors with separate baby clinics, hearing tests etc. However, the two SSLPs considered that 'many lessons have been learned from this approach, which has led to inequity and fragmentation of caseloads, some health visitors becoming deskilled in some areas, whilst others have an abundance of training opportunities. This leads not only to some staff feeling isolated but raised issues around poor communication and lack of contact for some parents with the health visitor' (Lowery, 2004). A consultation process was undertaken by the health visiting team and the following aims emerged: equal provision for all clients; equality of training; equity of workload/caseload; partnership with other agencies; develop joint objectives and equal access to incentives. It was decided that the first stage of the change would be equal division of caseloads within teams attached to GP practices but working in geographical patches. This would mean that each full-time health visitor would have approximately 174 children on their caseload. In some areas corporate caseloads would operate.

Multi-skilling was recognised as a further aim; hence as part of the change process staff undertook a skills analysis in order to plan further training and skills development. It was anticipated that all staff would be included in the training and, although only the health team participated in the skills analysis, the training would be extended to mainstream staff, partner agencies and parents. For example, a parent who completed the first Positive Parenting course continued to offer peer support to other parents on subsequent courses and then took part in the Training for Trainers course alongside staff from Sure Start and other professionals and worked as a volunteer for the programme. Another course was 'Working with Fathers' and this was offered to team members, mainstream services and community/voluntary agencies. Staff were also trained in infant massage and La Leche breastfeeding peer support, and it was anticipated that all staff would have the opportunity to deliver services across the area. For example, a request to the health co-ordinator to deliver Positive Parenting to a group of young parents was passed to the Domestic Violence support worker and the Play and Learning Co-ordinator. The aim was to give team members from other teams the opportunity to undertake service delivery, 'which in turn ensures equity and shared workload to all' (Lowery, 2004). Services were established for families and, due to the widespread geographical nature of the area, some were rotated rather than centralised in one area. Examples of courses/events delivered in the early stages were Family Nurturing which was delivered in partnership with a local nursery with costings split between the two service providers; Promoting Body Image which was a 10-week course on how bodies function, the effect of disease and the benefits of healthy lifestyles delivered by Sure Start staff in partnership with Wearbridge Women in Need and the Healthy Living Centre; and No Smoking Day Event which looked at accident prevention and safety in the home. Sure Start provided some 'incentives' e.g. toilet bag, first aid kit, Bookstart which were tailored to match targets set by Sure Start and these were made available for all clients on the health visitors' caseload irrespective of whether they lived in the Sure Start area.

Views of professionals

Interviews were carried out with 13 health visitors, including the Sure Start Health Co-ordinator (8 mainstream and 5 employed through Sure Start) and 4 nursery nurses (1 mainstream and 3 employed through Sure Start). All eight mainstream health visitors but only three of the Sure Start health visitors had worked in the area prior to Sure Start. None of the nursery nurses had previously worked in the area in a comparable capacity but had worked, for example, in a nursery. The majority of health visitors considered that having reduced caseloads had been a significant contributory factor enabling them to become more involved in the Sure Start agenda and existing public health work. Helping work towards Sure Start targets, such as an increased emphasis on working with teenage parents, had increased workload now considered to be less 'task-oriented' with more emphasis on identifying needs and having necessary training and resources to address these needs. Teams were considered to be much more diverse than previously and greatly enhanced by the employment of nursery nurses, particularly as they were achieving a higher level of expertise through their additional training. They were able to adopt a *'much more varied approach to the job of providing health care and a wider range of services.'* Delivering the Sure Start agenda was facilitated by ease of referral and access to a range of other workers, for example the community psychiatric nurse (CPN), psychologist, paediatrician and domestic violence outreach worker, and to a range of groups for families. The Sure Start library for health professionals and parents helped all *'use the same research and evidence-based information and sing from the same hymn sheet'*. Difficulties regarding different expectations of management and different systems (eg holidays, appraisals) were gradually being overcome to achieve greater sharing of roles and responsibilities and greater crossover regardless of employer.

Staff referred to 'team inclusivity' meaning ensuring that people's skills and training were recognised and their strengths were used appropriately. Training was open to mainstream and Sure Start health visiting teams and enabled staff to see how their work linked to targets. Training has been shared between the team so that there is a small group of specialists in a number of areas, such as Infant Massage and Family Nurturing, enabling effective use of expertise. Some groups are run jointly by a health visitor and nursery nurse. Effective communication and information sharing, for example through team meetings, is increasing knowledge of team members' areas of expertise, and facilitating the use of each other's skills and knowledge and targeted seeking of advice. Through joint training and a larger workforce, health visitors and nursery nurses are able to run courses together across geographical boundaries. Because there were *'more people there to help you, more bodies to deliver courses and cover for each other'* there was generally considered to be a *'more willing workforce'*. It was reported that, *'before, we were very much in separate, tiny teams and we only contacted each other when we had to, such as for clinic cover or when we were off sick. I think we can actually call ourselves a team now'*. The opportunity to carry out joint visits with nursery nurses was making these visits easier for health visitors and families, as communication was eased through the nursery nurse playing with the children. Nursery nurses have also carried out joint visits with, for example, a domestic violence support worker and community development worker. In the latter case this was to provide a 'bridge' for a parent considering accessing training that is providing relevant information and support. Health visitors, and nursery nurses, also acted as *'an informal support network to each other discussing cases and frustrations'* and there were opportunities to seek each other's advice and 'run ideas' past each other. Team meetings were enabling staff to keep up to date with new developments and share information. Colleagues were easy to contact by telephone or e-mail.

For both Sure Start and mainstream health visitors, Sure Start had provided greater opportunities for working with other professionals, such as a psychologist, domestic violence support workers, early years workers and community workers, which supported them in addressing social, psychological, physical and environmental issues and the impact of these on people's lives. Shared location at Sure Start enabled easier access and it was easier to leave messages. It was also felt that families were more willing to attend appointments when they got to know the names of the workers involved and did not have to go through a hospital route or travel distances. Joint visits were undertaken with, for example, a psychologist or the community paediatrician. One health visitor reported joint working with a community development worker with a client who was suffering from depression, having to give up work due to an unplanned pregnancy. Working in a multi-disciplinary way provided a wider resource and opportunities to '*look at who is the best person to do the job*'; also opportunities for informal case discussion, for example with a psychologist, community paediatrician or family support worker, and '*ideas for ways forward*'.

> '*We've got a community paediatrician that we didn't have before, and that's a real boon, because there is easy, direct access, a quick response for families and immediate feedback to us. Because there are more members of staff there are more people to toss ideas around with if there is a tricky situation.*'

Liaison with other agencies was also enabling wider input into groups and courses, for example Connexions worker attending Bright Stars group to discuss benefits and support for helping young people back into work, such as funding for childcare; a local training centre delivering sessions to the Bright Stars group on areas of interest identified by group members , for example issues regarding drugs and alcohol; dental hygienist from the primary care trust and complementary therapists from a local project attending the Stay and Play Babes group; worker from 'The Place' attending Bumps to Babes to inform and encourage use of services available to young parents. An example was provided of a Community Development Worker being invited to the Stay and Play Babes group to help parents follow up an idea for organising weekly walks. Attending groups and activities as part of their induction enabled new Sure Start workers to be more fully informed of what they could offer families.

Working with other agencies, such as dental health, meant that health visitors felt that they had become a much better informed service through being able to offer more information on children's oral health, enhanced by Sure Start funded dental packs. Providing services in a variety of venues and community projects delivering different services enabled *'two-way signposting'*, for example a Common Childhood Illness course was run in a venue delivering a Basic Skills course and the health visitor was able to gain information from the course leader in order to signpost one of the mothers on her course to this service.

Staff reported particularly close links with Leisure Services, facilitated in part by some similarity of targets, e.g. regarding 'wellness', and Leisure Services working closely with the NHS regarding heart disease prevention. They had worked together, for example, in organising and running Ducklings swimming sessions and other courses, and by the health team 'tapping into' Funzone activities for older children. Training provided by Sure Start to Leisure Services on working with fathers was enabling joint delivery of Dads and Kids sessions at the Leisure Centre. Strong links had also developed with Wearbridge Women in Need, a Barnados centre, community access points, the Health Development Unit and the Police. These were reported to be enabling better use of expertise and access to venues that were better used by the community.

Work had become more satisfying as the service the health team could offer families was considered to have improved through the availability of a wider range of resources (group and/or individual support), greater integration with the community and other agencies, and improved communication, which made it easier to *'follow families through and address their problems through having more things to access'.*

Some staff also reported that *'moving away from a postcode lottery'* had made them feel *'easier'* and *'more comfortable'*. Training had enhanced professional development and there were opportunities and support *'to try new ideas'*, e.g. an antenatal coffee morning, with a core group responsible for setting up and organising, but with others 'on board' and willing to cover if and when needed. Improvements in job satisfaction and professional development are important as they have implications for the retention and recruitment of staff.

Health visitors and nursery nurses considered that they were able to offer a wider variety of support, a more rounded service and greater choice to families, through group work and individual support. One of the main areas of difference noted was with regard to postnatal depression, due to the availability of groups and non-threatening informal support, such as coffee mornings, which enabled issues to be raised gradually and informally and provided opportunities for a more *'casual'* route into further involvement, e.g. with a CPN. This also applied to domestic violence work. As one mainstream health visitor commented:

> *'You only had yourself to offer before, now you can offer different groups and community based services, which can help relieve difficulties and stop things escalating out of control, for example opportunities to meet other mums or to bond with their baby through Infant Massage, or address behaviour through Family Nurturing or nursery nurse intervention. Before you had limited time with a big caseload and could only offer brief one-to-one interventions'.*

It was felt that Sure Start had:

> *'engaged in all areas of concern we have as health visitors, for example through setting up groups for teenage parents and providing transport to enable them to continue their education'.*

Parental representation on Partnership and other similar groups was considered to be providing greater community input into the planning and implementation of services. Group provision gave more time for working in the home with families who do not wish to attend groups for whatever reason, for example having already established family and social networks. Groups are open to all families and not based on postcode. The Sure Start database of clients means that there is:

> *'a ready pool of clients to deliver services to. Before we put signs up but we never knew who would come, and we didn't have lists of what people wanted, now there is a database of people who are interested in things, for example there is a waiting list for Infant Massage'.*

The larger team, in which there were two or three staff able to offer the same course meant that there was cover available if needed and this, combined with access to more venues, crèche facilities and transport, meant that courses could be offered to satellite areas. The availability of cover also meant that staff could keep services running when colleagues were absent, thus *'not leaving families in the lurch'.* Some reported that the provision of services and groups in informal settings was helping health professionals develop a more relaxed, informal relationship with their clients, for example *'the barriers come down and they talk to me in different ways'*, as well as providing opportunities for social interaction for parents and children.

Health visitors commented that, whilst there was still some perception of Sure Start as a charity and as being related to Social Services that was impacting on uptake of services by some, over time this was reducing and Sure Start was becoming better known in the community, more talked about and more normalised. It was important that Sure Start was advertised clearly and that all workers made it clear that Sure Start was for everybody. It was, however, noted that very few ethnic minority families had accessed services. One person commented that, whilst work with fathers had developed, this was an area in which further progress should be made (e.g. engaging fathers in a positive role in their child's development and play) and that there could be further investigation about *'what works well'*. Work with children with disabilities was being developed through the establishment of a link worker and looking at how services can be adapted for those with special needs. It was acknowledged that some families were still 'hard to reach'.

Seven representatives from other agencies/organisations took part in a face-to-face interview or completed a written questionnaire, according to their availability. The purpose was to ascertain how they had worked with the health visiting team, whether this had made a difference to their service delivery and to communication and co-ordination between agencies, and whether, in their experience, there had been an improvement in health and family support services for families with children under four since Sure Start. The agencies/organisations represented were a domestic violence support organisation, two schools, Leisure Services, Connexions, general practice and midwifery. The health visiting team had made it easier to access Sure Start services, for example the CPN, psychologist, domestic violence worker, family support, early years, behaviour support, the safety scheme, and groups such as Family Nurturing, Bumps to Babes, Bright Stars and the Dads & Kids Group. It was commented that the team provided prompt advice and services, and that calls were always returned quickly. The delivery of services at outreach venues, for example baby clinic held on school premises, was facilitating access to other Sure Start services. Other agencies had worked with the health visiting team on child protection reviews and information sharing, care planning with families and on the joint development of groups.

Five of the seven respondents reported that there had been an improvement in communication and co-ordination between agencies since Sure Start, for example work with asylum seekers. One person commented on increased ease of information sharing. One commented that there was already good communication and co-ordination. At the same time, individuals commented as follows:

'Clear channels of communication, however more regular updates of service provision would be useful so we are better able to advise our clients, e.g. monthly newsletter'

'Good communication via Sure Start staff through Family Nurturing Programme, though not in other areas generally'

'Need regular newsletters from Sure Start with training for staff, forthcoming events for families etc'.

Health visitors acted as co-ordinators of support to families by making agencies more aware of the need for specific services for children under eight and of the importance of adult intervention which led to innovations in programme activities; also by filling gaps i.e. through the provision of specialist knowledge. It was suggested that there could be more publicity (e.g. adverts, fliers) in a wide range of venues and regular newsletters to agencies informing them of training opportunities, current services and forthcoming events for families. The health visiting team acknowledged that 'getting people to work together' had not been easy, but that the process has been supported well through regular meetings, individual and team appraisals, good training opportunities and opportunities to share good practice. Communication and relationships had improved over time and the work of the new Health Co-ordinator in particular was acknowledged. The close similarity of PCT and Sure Start objectives also provided a focus for working together. One person commented that Sure Start health visitors were more 'target driven' than mainstream and that this raised the question of how far services were genuinely community driven or client led.

Whilst the success of and high attendance at some groups was noted (with waiting lists for some e.g. Infant Massage), it was also noted that group work did not suit all, and that building up a relationship with families through home visiting can often be a more appropriate and productive method for supporting families, and that, in addition, this sometimes provided the opportunity for opportunistic work with friends and other family members who might not otherwise access services. The balancing of group and individual work can create a dilemma regarding the amount of time available for intensive support for the most vulnerable families.

Some felt that opportunities for working across different professional teams within Sure Start (e.g. joint input at particular events) were not always taken up and could be further developed. Links with community organisations and venues should be maintained and further developed, and extending links with a local training centre and other course providers was suggested. It was also suggested that there could be *'more creative thinking about offering groups, and offering non health-related groups, such as recreational groups where targets could be addressed indirectly with people there to offer expertise in informal settings'*. It was thought that working together was facilitated among Sure Start health visitors through the presence of targets and that this contrasted with how they worked with mainstream health visitors.

Views of families

Fifty-one parents (but no other carers) participated in a face-to-face interview or completed a written questionnaire. All were mothers and all were of White British ethnic origin. All local areas were represented, although 19 lived in a single area. The majority of respondents were aged between 30 and 39 years (49%) or between 20 and 29 years (43%). Two were aged 19 or under and two were aged 40-49 years. Respondents had between one and four children (30 had one child only and two had four children). Families had heard about Sure Start in one or more ways, the majority through their health visitor (73.5%). The most common other ways were through Sure Start itself, through a midwife or through friends or relatives. Individual respondents had also heard about Sure Start from their GP, a nursery nurse, leaflets, nursery, toddler group or work. The vast majority (84.3%) felt that they knew what Sure Start had to offer. For example, Sure Start was known: to provide advice, support and information on health and welfare issues and facilities, and on other services for families with children under four; to provide practical help with equipment, e.g. safety equipment scheme, sun cream, breast pumps; toy library and book library; and local access to baby milk;

to provide groups and courses (the most frequently mentioned being Baby Massage and Ducklings); to provide local, informal support e.g. Drop-Ins; to provide/support activities and facilities for children (e.g. crèche, toddler groups and playgroups; trips); and to support mothers with breastfeeding.

All but two of the mothers reported having received a visit/visits from a health visitor and 13 had been visited by a nursery nurse. In the latter case, this was for advice/support with their children's sleeping patterns and/or feeding, behaviour, toilet training, Portage, or a 2-year assessment. Six mothers reported accessing no additional services. The majority of mothers had accessed two or four additional services (31.4% and 29.4% of respondents respectively). The other service most commonly accessed by these families was the Safety Equipment scheme (37 families). Families also accessed a Baby Clinic (29 families), Infant Massage (23), Drop-in (18), Ducklings swimming sessions (14), Bosom Buddies (5), Family Nurturing (4), and Bumps to Babes, Common Childhood Illness course and Stay and Play Babes (3 each).

Some mothers reported that they did not use any/many additional services due to their unsuitable time (9 mothers, with one commenting that with a newborn baby it is easier to go to groups in the afternoon), transport difficulties (4), lack of knowledge of services (4), not wishing to access any services in which their child was not included (3), not wishing to go alone (2), disability of a family member (2, e.g. meaning attending a lot of appointments), depression (1), tending to see family or friends whilst on maternity leave (1), lack of availability of a crèche for their older child (1) or because the other services were not needed (1). Just over half (55%) of respondents reported that it was very easy to get advice and support about their child's health needs and development (marking the highest point on a scale from one down to five). Of those who commented, seven commented on the ease of access by telephone, for example:

> 'All I have to do is pick up the phone and speak to someone on the phone or to make an appointment for a home visit.'

> 'If the health team are not in they will always ring you back.'

or by calling into a clinic. One commented on the approachability of the health visiting team. One had found that *some of the health visitors are too busy to get in touch when asked to phone clients*.

66% of respondents reported that the health visiting team had helped them access other services. This included referrals to other professionals (e.g. counsellor; support for older child), accessing childcare, toddler groups and crèche facilities, and information on services that were subsequently taken up, e.g. safety equipment scheme, Bosom Buddies, Ducklings, toy library, drop-in and baby massage. 23.5% reported that no other services were needed. 76.5% of respondents had found the service they had received to be very relevant and 19.6% fairly relevant. One person had found it not very relevant ('though fun for the children'). Comments included:

'The service was exactly what I needed for the help and support we received from our health visitor.'

'Appropriate advice at the right time'.

'Just what I needed at the time'.

'Information relevant to babies' age and stage of development. Information from health visitor has prevented unnecessary trips to GP'.

'Good advice on weaning, given at an appropriate time'.

Over half (58.8%) of respondents reported that the advice and support they had received about bringing up their child had been very useful (marking the highest point on a scale from one down to five). The service had been useful in providing explanations and advice, ideas and information, through listening, through appropriate referral to specialist services, and through providing reassurance and confidence. One mother commented:

'I have been given advice and options, not pushed into things, not made to worry about the development of my baby'.

In some cases, the service provided helped in other unexpected ways or led onto other things. For example,

'I made friends with the other women who attended the group, we still meet on a regular basis and we joined a mother and toddler group together'.

Respondents reported that they and their children had benefited from the services provided by the health visiting team in the following ways: by acting on specific advice from professionals (e.g. regarding colic, breastfeeding, weaning); through opportunities for both parents and children to socialise and interact; by improved bonding with child/more time to bond; by increased understanding between mother and child; by increased relaxation for mother and child; by providing more and better ways of coping; practical help through safety equipment e.g. house more child friendly; and by the development of children's skills, e.g. through swimming sessions.

Summary and conclusion

Reduced caseloads for all health visitors by virtue of a larger workforce contributed to their capacity to deliver Sure Start and public health agendas. Working as a team across the area avoided a 'post code lottery' for Sure Start services; whereas links formed with outreach venues, crèche facilities and transport increased availability and accessibility of local support. Targeted services have been provided for specific groups, such as young parents, both in the home and through groups (Bright Stars and Bumps to Babes). The health visiting team provide multiple forms of service delivery (outreach, individual support in the home, and groups) based on activities emphasising health promotion. Staff reported that they have become able to adopt a more family and community oriented model and a more 'holistic' approach to working with families. Greater emphasis on prevention is in evidence through, e.g. offering Family Nurturing and Infant Massage courses at outreach venues and in the home, and through the availability of safety equipment for all and 'incentives' such as bath and room thermometers and first aid kits.

The diversity of the services available within and beyond the health visiting team has enabled the team to offer greater choice to families and a more varied approach according to needs and circumstances, e.g. group work, informal drop-ins, support in the home. Additional training has increased knowledge, skills and expertise and led to a more diverse workforce. Groups of staff have developed expertise in particular areas e.g. Infant Massage and are able to share ideas and good practice. Staff also show evidence of drawing on others' areas of expertise for the benefit of families. The increased availability of 'cover' through the larger workforce and the training of several staff in the same area of expertise have contributed to the smooth running of services e.g. delivering courses. Joint working between mainstream and Sure Start health visiting teams ensures good knowledge of Sure Start services and work with families is facilitated by ease of referral both through ongoing contact with a range of professionals and through the Request for Services project. Joint visits take place with other professionals e.g. psychologist, community paediatrician, and there are welcome opportunities for informal case discussion.

The employment of nursery nurses has made a positive contribution to the working of the team, e.g. through sharing workload, providing interventions in the home e.g. sleep, behaviour, joint running of courses and joint visits to families. The training provided to nursery nurses as part of the team and their joint work with health visitors have increased their knowledge, skills and expertise and enhanced career possibilities. The networks formed with other agencies have led to joint initiation, planning and delivery of services targeted at specific groups e.g. fathers, young parents, have enhanced input into groups e.g. Stay and Play, and have made the team better informed.

The National Evaluation of Sure Start Impact Study (2005) found that there was some evidence that programmes led by health agencies had some advantages and a few more beneficial effects. One possible reason suggested was that health-led programmes found it easier to establish contact with families, or are better placed to start working with large numbers of children and families and/or are more experienced in data sharing, thereby facilitating service integration. They note that, 'In any event, data suggesting differential benefits of health-led services need to be fully integrated in the transformation of Sure Start Local Programmes to Children's Centres (NESS 2005, executive summary). Promoting public health is a core element in the expected service delivery of children's centres. The key role of health visitors is acknowledged.

'Evidence suggests that parents who would benefit most from intensive parenting support are best identified in the context of universal programmes such as routine health visiting, since this reduces stigma. Children's centres should offer services to all local families, and together with co-located health visitors and midwives, will be well placed to identify families with particular needs (disadvantaged families, parents with mental health difficulties or disabilities, or those with substance misuse problems) and to encourage them to access more intensive programmes of support' (Sure Start 2005:50).

STUDY 3: AN INTERDISCIPLINARY METHOD FOR ASSESSMENT, REFERRAL AND ALLOCATION OF SUPPORT TO CHILDREN AND FAMILIES (THE REQUEST FOR SERVICES PROJECT)

The Request for Services process was initiated and evaluated in a Sure Start local programme and was then known as the Referral and Allocation project. It sought to develop, through regular meetings, a whole-team interagency focus on discussing the needs of families who had been referred, or had referred themselves, to Sure Start and on suggesting ways in which support or advice could be offered and accessed in order to meet their needs. Following a subsequent cross-programme review and re-training of staff, the process was re-launched in late 2005 and became known in all programmes as Request for Services.

A further evaluation of Request for Services has subsequently taken place in two phases. The Phase One evaluation examined the process, outputs and outcomes of the Request for Services system in one Sure Start local programme and contains details of the aims and development of the system across the City. The evaluation was then replicated in four cluster areas (North, Coaldown, Central, North Washton) to gain a fuller picture of the process, outputs and outcomes of the system across the City and is reported here. The aims and method were consistent with those of the Phase One evaluation, with a larger target number of families and a longer time frame for monitoring data, examining figures across the City.

Study Aims

Process

← To describe the development of the Request for Services process

for families and young children
← To identify general characteristics of families referred
← To understand how the type of chosen intervention was decided, what happened and what was the result?
← To assess the contribution of external agencies to the overall process

Lead professional's role in intervention with families

← To evaluate the role and contribution of lead professionals in the process i.e. how professionals agree key actions to be taken and necessary resources/services required to meet desired outcomes for children and families
← To work with the key worker tracking the families and to identify the advantages/disadvantages of working in this way with families
← To assess how Request for Services has affected the way Sure Start works with families

Outcomes for children and families

← To track families through the system from initial referral i.e. through the meeting, action plan, review, identify changes in direction to an outcome (say) 6 months on (target $n=20$)
← To assess the impact on families e.g. are they satisfied with the way the issue has been dealt with, has it been resolved?

Method

The study had a quantitative and qualitative element.

1. Quantitative analysis of monitoring data for the period October 2005 – June 2006 e.g. number of families referred, range of key

workers involved, reasons for referral. Anonymous information was provided by the Sure Start Programmes.

2. Interviews with key professionals (the referrer and, in some cases, also the key worker) approximately three months after initial referral e.g. directly after 12 week review (*n*=24 interviews for 19 families. Some professionals were interviewed twice as they were involved with two of the families being tracked).

3. Interviews with parents approximately 3-5 months after initial referral (*n*=14). Five families from each of the four cluster areas were selected from the Programmes' monitoring data for the period December 2005 – June 2006 and tracked through the Request for Services process. Interviews were held with the family and their referrer/key worker separately.

Results

Outputs for the Period October 2005 to June 2006

Number of cases and intervention status

During this nine-month period 531 families were brought to Request for Services across the city. There were 65 families with a CIN/CINOP in the family. Only nine parents attended these meetings during this period, three from the Coaldown area and six from North Washton. No parents in the North or Central areas attended meetings. 125 cases (23.5.0%) were complete, including seventeen CIN/CINOP cases, and 383 (72%) were ongoing.

Uptake of support

66 families (12.4%), including thirteen families with a CIN/CINOP, either wholly refused (*n*=52) or part refused support (*n*=14). The highest number of refusals was in the Central area (35), and there were no refusals in North Washton.

Referrers

The majority of requests (322; 60.6%) were internal (including internal health visitor requests). Overall, the highest percentage of referrals was made by health visitors, with the highest percentages in Coaldown (37%) and Central (34%), and 17% in the North and 12% in North Washton. 145 other professionals made requests, the majority internal. The largest number of referrals from other internal professionals were made by a Speech and Language Nursery Nurse (n=12, in North and North Washton areas), other Nursery Nurses (n=10, in North, North Washton and Central), a Healthcare Assistant (n=7, Central only) and a Health Co-ordinator (n=6, Coaldown only). There were seventy external requests (excluding external health visitor requests), with the highest number in Coaldown (24) and the lowest in the North (9). The high number in Coaldown may be attributable to the fact that the system for making requests for funded childcare through Request for Services has been in place since the establishment of the Programme and has become well known, whilst in other areas it was only introduced in the financial year 2006-2007. North Washton and Central had 19 and 18 external referrals respectively. The majority of the total number of external referrals were from a member of the City's Social Work Team (n=34; 48.6%).

Key Workers

The majority of families had a health visitor as key worker (27.9%, n=148) or a CPN (21.7%, n=115, with the majority (100) in the Coaldown area where a CPN was employed by the Programme at that time). The next highest percentages were: paediatrician (12%, n=64), psychologist (9%, n=48, with the majority (44) in the Coaldown area), and social worker (6.4%, n=34). In 159 families the referrer and the key worker were the same and in the vast majority of cases (87%) this was a health visitor. In the case of the seventy external requests, a social worker was the key worker in the highest number of cases (n=12), followed by a Play and Learning Co-ordinator (n=9).

Reasons for Referral

The most common reasons for referral were for depression, including postnatal depression (15.6%, n=83), child's behaviour (12.4%, n=66), depression excluding postnatal depression (11%, n= 59), and medical concerns about the child, including height, weight and sleep (10.4%, n=55). 41 cases (7.7%) were referred for review.

In the 65 CIN/CINOP cases, the majority of reasons for referral were for parenting support and domestic violence (n=8 each).

Analysis by category of reason for referral shows that the majority of reasons related to the child's needs (n=215). 164 related to general issues, 147 to mental health issues, 108 to parents' needs, 69 to environmental factors and 19 to child protection.

Interventions identified

In the majority of cases multiple interventions were identified. The most commonly identified forms of intervention were psychology support (n=93) and paediatric assessment/support (n=92), followed by nursery/childcare referral (n=55, with the vast majority (49) in the Coaldown area) and CPN (n=47, again the majority in Coaldown). The full range of interventions identified demonstrates the range of support from different professions, representing, for example, Health, Psychology, Play and Learning, community and volunteer workers. Analysis by category of interventions identified shows that the majority of interventions related to mental health support (n=169), followed by specialist support for child from a member of the team (n=155) and parent/family support (n=113).

Cross-tabulation of reason for referral and interventions identified shows the range of interventions that has been offered. For example, with regard to depression, the following interventions were identified: psychology (the most frequent), CPN, family therapy, community parent support, antenatal support, community mental health team, play and learning support, nursery nurse support, parenting/family support and social worker support were all identified.

Cases referred outside of Sure Start

Fifty-four cases were referred outside of Sure Start. The vast majority of these were to Social Services.

Processes

Professionals' Views of the Process

Sixteen of the professionals reported that the Request for Services system was a better process than they would previously have been involved in, one that it was not, and two that it was better in some cases but not all.

Benefits of the Process

Benefits of the process reported by professionals were related to:

* *Easy and direct access to a range of professionals*
  It was noted that as a multi-agency team it was easier to get in touch with people than ringing and waiting for them to get back. Request for Services provides opportunities to 'sound out' ideas with practitioners from different professional backgrounds and for others to step in when a worker reaches a 'plateau' in their work with a family. External referrers found the documentation clear, and one commented that it had been helpful to have informal discussion with the Chair beforehand to help clarify the appropriateness of referrals. Meetings also present a good opportunity to arrange joint visits to families.

* *Quicker referral process*
  It was felt that referral through a G.P. (e.g. re mental health) would be a slower process, and noted that quicker referral enables earlier intervention. It was considered important for the referrer to have discussion(s) with the family prior to the meeting to gain an idea of the type of services likely to be preferred (e.g. group/individual).

* *Holistic approach*
  Request for Services provides opportunities for 'swapping ideas' amongst a range of professionals and enables input from workers who see families in different contexts (e.g. formal/informal; school/community). *'Pooling information from meeting families in different settings and in different relationships helps assessment of risk issues'*. It also helps clarify roles and responsibilities. It

Table 1
Request for Service Audit Summary, October 2005-March 2006

	Central	Washton	Coaldown	North
Chair's Role	Health Co-ordinators competent and effective in role.	Deputy Programme Manager – chairing generally good	Deputy Programme Manager with support from Health Co-ordinator	Deputy Programme Mgr & Health Co-ordinator – Deputy new in post and in chairing meetings
COMMENT: Training issues in effective chairing and questioning identified for chairs with little experience in role.				
Parental Involvement	No	No	No	No
COMMENT: Consideration needs to be given to the attendance of parents at meeting.				
External Professionals in Attendance	Yes – HV, Nursery teacher, special needs NN	Yes – HV's	Yes – HV's, Home School Partnership, Social Worker	Yes – HV's
COMMENT: Other partners to be encouraged to refer into RfS process. Consider awareness raising sessions for partners				
Number of families discussed	24	12	13	9
• Initial	1	0	4	2
• 1st Review	1	0	1	1
• Subsequent review	22	12	8	6
COMMENT: The average number of cases at each session = 7				

Table 1 (continued)

	Central	Washton	Coaldown	North
Time allocated to each case	5 minutes – time ran over in some cases	All cases 0-15 minutes	15 minutes new case 10 minutes review cases	6 cases 0-15 mins 2 cases 15-30 mins 1 case 30 – 45 mins

COMMENT: *The average time spent on each case 10-15 minutes.*

	Central	Washton	Coaldown	North
Pathway timescales case discussions	Achieved in all case discussion	Achieved in all case discussions	Achieved in all case discussions	2 cases delayed 1 week because of Christmas holidays

COMMENT: *Pathway timescales appear realistic and achievable*

Documentation:	Central	Washton	Coaldown	North
• Referral completed	1 not completed	All completed	All completed	All completed
• Genogram completed	Only 3 completed	None completed	7 completed	None completed
• Initial meeting completed	All completed	All completed	All completed	All completed
• Case Review	2 not completed	All completed	All completed	All completed
• Case Liaison	5 not completed	7 not completed	1 not completed	1 not completed

COMMENT: *Some liaison forms on computer not signed. Different case files in use, so no continuity. Membership needs clarification*

Administration:	Central	Washton	Coaldown	North
• Minute taking	Minute taker produced and circulated minutes.	Good no issues identified.	Good no issues identified	Minute taker typed and circulated minutes. Some issues arise when chair not available to check before circulation
• Booking/ Diarying	Future dates planned appropriately during meeting at end of case discussion.			

COMMENT: *Some differences between cluster areas. Training for minute takers to ensure effective practice across cluster areas.*

presents opportunities to think creatively about what to offer families in cases where some services have been refused. For external referrers it was reported to provide insight into *'the bigger picture'* and the range of services that can be offered.

- *Communication and Co-ordination*
  There was reported to be an improvement in communication and better co-ordinated support. One person commented that *'better co-ordination makes for a smoother, more manageable package of support'.* Both internal and external referrers commented on the value of review meetings, with the latter noting that they are a good way of sharing information on progress and whether families have accepted and used services. Pooling information from a range of sources usually gives workers, e.g. health visitors, a fuller picture of family situations (e.g. safety/domestic violence issues) and fuller information for Health records.

  Liaison between professionals, e.g. at review meetings, is enabling appropriate 'pacing' of activities, with some professionals 'standing back' while other work is taking place.

- *Efficiency*
  More than one Sure Start worker commented on the efficiency of the administrative support, for example in keeping records and keeping people informed. For both internal and external referrers, Request for Services meetings avoid the necessity for a large number of phone calls to different professionals. Individual external referrers commented that meetings *'streamline the process ... it can be fuzzy otherwise',* that meetings were very focused, and that it was an advantage to now be able to complete the review report online.

- *Service Implementation*
  The role of the key worker/lead professional ensures responsibility for making sure the family has full information and enables monitoring of processes. Going through Request for Services gives decision making *'more clout'* and formalises plans for families, outlining the role of each professional and accountability. It *'helps keep track of who is doing what and how the budget is being used'.*

- *Consistency*
  Monitoring uptake of services, telephone liaison, informal contact

and review enable consistent messages to be given by professionals, and enable reinforcement of approaches and activities provided by different members of the team (e.g. establishing routines).

- *Continuity*
  In one Programme it was reported that the attendance of a representative from commissioned childcare services aided continuity for families as Sure Start funded childcare is time-limited.

- *Supervision and support*
  Whilst not their primary function, Request for Services meetings also act as a form of supervision and support for professionals, both internal and external. Individual external referrers commented that Request for Services *'provides professional support through a team approach'*, *'helps anxiety in stressful situations'* (e.g. covering all the options), and *'sharing the load'*.

  Whilst some professionals felt unable to comment whether Request for Services was a better process for families than they would otherwise be involved in, others considered that it was facilitating access to services more quickly and in a user friendly, accessible and non-stigmatising way, and was providing a network of support and a choice of people to ring who offered different styles of working and different expertise. It was felt that there was greater opportunity to report back on discussions with, and new information provided by, families, ensuring that up-to-date information was available to other workers. Request for Services was felt to be helping avoid confusion for families through facilitating consistency of approach by those working with them.

Issues with Regard to Process

There were some issues for individual professionals regarding the Request for Services process that need to be acknowledged.

As in the previous evaluation, there was some concern over the membership of group – one professional referred to there being people present who did not need to be there. There was some tension with regard to full information sharing versus a 'need to know' basis, with some professionals feeling that not all issues are appropriate to be discussed in front of everybody. There were mixed views amongst external referrers on the timing of meetings including flexibility. There was some concern over the appropriateness of parental attendance at meetings in their current format. These expressed issues indicate a need for ongoing discussion and training, for example on the purpose of meetings and information sharing.

Impacts on families' contact with services and professionals

Of the nineteen families in this study, eleven of the referrals were internal and eight were external (of these, seven were from mainstream health visitors). Thirteen were referred by a health visitor, two by a family therapist, one by a psychologist, one by a social worker, one by a Health nursery nurse and one by a speech and language nursery nurse.

The Request for Services system has impacted on families' experience of contact with services in the following ways.

Accessing Services

The majority of families reported that they would not have gone looking for support themselves, or would not have known where to look. Two thought they would have gone to their GP and one that *'Social Services would have done something'.*

> *'I would have tried to plod on, but maybe not got anywhere'.*

> *'At the time I would probably have ended up moving in with my mam and dad. I would have tried to muddle on, now I realise I don't have to do everything on my own'.*

> *'You think you're alone and there's nothing out there'.*

Two felt that this system enabled quicker access to services (e.g. compared to hospital referral through GP) and welcomed the fact that it was community based.

> *'I would have been referred to Social Services for childcare support,*

although there would have been a longer wait for accessing this support. As well as the quicker timescale for providing the support, the fact that the planning meetings were held within my local community meant that the whole process was easier to handle – especially while I was in ill health'.

Two families compared their experience of being involved with Sure Start and the Request for Services process with their prior experience with other services. They referred to there being a much wider range of support available now.

'I was just given tablets before, that was it'.

They also referred to feeling more comfortable accessing services through Sure Start, despite some initial apprehension:

'I was quite shocked at how nice they were. It's not like the doctor's, they're full of chit-chat, down to earth and easy to talk to'.

All found Sure Start buildings accessible, although one suggested that one centre should have an entrance *'on the other side, on the main flat road, so it was easier for buggies and old people'*. At the time of the interview this parent also felt there should be more facilities for babies, e.g. baby station, heating up food, highchairs, but it is not known whether this has since been addressed. Two parents felt that Sure Start services should be better advertised.

Two also commented on their feelings as they were coming to the end of their support:

'I didn't feel on my own, like everything was finished and over, it's nice to know it's there in case and you can pick up the phone, and they get to know you well'.

'I've finished with [community parent] but I know the service is there if I need it – the option's there if I still need to speak. It was weekly at first, then fortnightly, then monthly, and it was my decision to try on my own and see how it works and I know it's still there if needed'.

Request for services meetings

Not all families were aware whether they had been invited to a meeting, and only two had attended (in one of these cases the maternal grandmother attended the initial meeting on the parent's behalf and the parent attended the reviews). On the whole, interviewees from the Coaldown and North Washton cluster areas seemed to have the fullest understanding of the procedures for referral, and of the existence and purpose of initial and review meetings. In these areas, one family reported not attending due to ill health, one due to childcare difficulties. Both felt fully informed about review meetings by their key worker:

> *'I know they have a meeting. [Key worker] tells me all about it and I know nothing is said there that has not already been said to me. [Key worker] always asks if it's OK to mention it in the meeting'.*

Those who had attended initial and/or review meetings reported as follows:

> *'There are regular meetings to see how I'm getting on, how [child] is doing, if there's anything anyone needs to discuss, or anything I need or want them to do, and it's good because everybody's together at the same time'.*

> *'There are regular meetings to see how things are going, if I need anything else, how much longer I'm going to need the services. A lot of different people not involved in the case offer alternatives – there are about eight different people – it's weird, you feel a bit under the microscope, they have high up backgrounds, and I'm not used to asking for help. If I can't go, [key worker] says this is what we talked about'.*

Communication between families and professionals

Informed decision-making

All parents felt that they had received full and clear information about the services they were being offered and the choices to be made. They also felt fully involved in the decision-making process, and several referred to not being rushed or pressured into taking up services.

> *'I felt that I was fully involved in the choices and decisions process'.*

'Everything was my decision what I wanted'.

'It's been me raising things and them suggesting options'.

Pacing and control

Sensitive timing and pacing of activity are important for uptake of services. Several parents reported that the services had been suggested at the right time, that they were able to take services up gradually and prioritise according to family circumstances and wishes, and felt in control.

> *'There was no pressure, it's as much or as little as I need, I can drop in or out as much as I want. I don't have to see [family support worker] if I don't want to'.*

> *'I feel in control, they get you well involved'.*

> *'I didn't feel pushed, I felt totally in control – [key worker] kept asking if I still wanted her to come. I was offered a choice of how often – they suggested fortnightly, but whatever I was comfortable with ... nothing was set in stone'.*

> *'We decided to leave the Family Nurturing course until next year'.*

Co-ordination of services

Liaison and communication

There was a feeling that professionals liaised and communicated with each other. This was appreciated as it meant not having to repeat information and provided consistency. For example,

> *'I didn't have to tell the same story over and over again, they all seemed to know what each other were doing, they're all kept in the loop, and I think that's a good thing'.*

> *'When [child] was having tantrums they all three said the same thing'.*

'It all seemed to fall into place, and I always know why they're coming. They all know the situation and seem to work together'.

'They all know the situation. If I say something to one they always make sure it gets passed on so I'm not repeating myself'.

The review meetings were considered a good forum for communication.

'Sure Start communication is better. The meetings are good. With the Hospital and the doctors and the physios before I felt I had to repeat myself all the time because they didn't seem to be talking to each other'.

'It's good that they're discussing things, it makes me feel I'm getting the best support and they're all working from the same book. They're all saying the same things to me and they're on the same wavelength'.

Providing a single point of contact

Parents commented that it was helpful to have the same person involved all through (i.e. a key worker).

'I prefer to have one person all through instead of a load of different people because you get to know them. She is the first one I phone'.

'It makes it easier to have consistency'.

'As I was introduced to the Request for Services process by [my health visitor] and she was the contact throughout the process, I felt that I was kept up to date with information and the process at all times. Things were explained to me every step of the way and as I had already built up a good relationship with [health visitor] I did not feel uneasy asking questions'.

It also benefited their children as they were able to develop a relationship with the worker.

Convenience of services

All families had received support in the home and all reported that this support was arranged to their convenience in that they were given a choice of times that enabled them to fit appointments around family routines, that everything was flexible, and that they felt that workers tried to fit in with them rather than the other way round. Parents appreciated being offered the option of whether to receive some services in the home or at Sure Start:

> *'I feel more comfortable at home, I get upset sometimes and they do have one-to-one rooms but it's good to have the choice – you don't have to walk out with red eyes'.*

Similarly, services taken up outside the home were also convenient in terms of location, time and transport. One parent reported being accompanied to appointments and found this helpful:

> *[Community parent] gets transport to the Hospital and comes with us, it's helpful, it saves money and I like it a lot better to have her come with me – I feel I've got support and if I don't understand she can tell us after. She's been to Court with me too'.*

Overall satisfaction

All families reported that they were happy with the way the issue(s) had been dealt with from first mention. All felt that they could approach Sure Start or other services again if they needed to, either directly or through their key worker, and in some cases following initial apprehension *('Now I could, it was hard to do the first step').*

> *'I have been very happy with the way the Request for Services process has been handled in my case and the process has included me every step of the way by providing me with a complete picture of what was happening and what to expect at meetings etc ... . I would have no hesitation in approaching Sure Start again if necessary and would be happy to approach the Sure Start programmes direct or via my health visitor, whichever was more appropriate at the time'.*

Outcomes for children and families

Nine cases were closed and ten were ongoing. In all nineteen cases, families and professionals were able to identify outcomes of the process for families. Outcomes related, for example, to:

- Integration into local services
- Crisis situation ameliorated through childcare support, reducing parental worry, providing a break for parent and other family members, and improving child's social situation; also through practical support
- Improved maternal mental health e.g. lessening of depression and stress
- Improved parenting skills, safer and more organised home environment, strategies for managing behaviour
- Skills and learning - improvements in personal and family situation through training and the development of skills
- Improved relationship between parent and child
- Child development e.g. learning to be independent, relate to other children; confidence; improved behaviour and better routines
- Social and emotional well-being e.g. more outgoing, attending groups, increased confidence, self-esteem and ability to cope, better family life through improvement in mood and greater ability to cope with family issues, better able to cope with own illness, made to feel positive.

Summary

Citywide Request for Services outputs
Oct 2005 - June 2006

During this nine-month period 531 families were brought to Request for Services across the City. There were 65 cases involving a CIN/CINOP. The majority of referrals were internal and the largest proportion of referrals was made by health visitors, with the highest proportion in Coaldown and Central. There were seventy external requests (excluding external health visitor requests), with the highest number in Coaldown and the lowest in the North cluster. The majority of external requests were from the Social Work team. There were only two self referrals. Sixty-six families refused or part refused support, including 13 families with a CIN/CINOP. The highest number of refusals was in the Central area, and there were no refusals in North Washton. The majority of key workers were health visitors, also a CPN; however there were other key workers from all teams within the Programme. The most common reasons for referral were depression, including postnatal depression, child's behaviour, depression excluding postnatal depression, and medical concerns about the child, including height, weight and sleep. In the majority of cases multiple interventions were identified. The most commonly identified forms of intervention were psychology support and paediatric assessment/support, followed by nursery/childcare referral and CPN. Fifty-four cases were referred out of Sure Start, the vast majority to Social Services. Only nine parents attended Request for Services meetings in this nine-month period, six from North Washton and three from Coaldown.

Professional views of the process and its impact on the delivery of services

Professionals identified benefits of the Request for Services approach as follows. It enables easy and direct access to a range of professionals and provides opportunities for 'sounding out' ideas, receiving input and new ideas from other professionals, and organising joint visits. It also provides professional support for both internal and external referrers. It enables a holistic approach and input from a range of professionals who see families in different contexts. External referrers found the referral process and documentation clear and there were individual comments that it was a more streamlined process with very focused meetings. It provides a quicker referral process thus enabling earlier intervention, particularly if initial discussions are held with the family to gain an idea of the type of services likely to be preferred. There was reported to be an improvement in communication and better co-ordinated support, with more appropriate pacing of activity. The efficiency of the admin support was noted. The role of the key worker ensures responsibility for making sure the family has full information and enables monitoring of processes. It enables consistent messages to be given to families by professionals and provides continuity of services.

As in the Phase One evaluation, there were individual concerns over the process. There was some concern over membership of the group and tension regarding information sharing, also concern over the appropriateness of parental attendance at meetings.

Parental views on the approach and their involvement

The majority of families reported that they would not have gone looking for support themselves or would not have known where to look. Benefits of the process related to the wide range and accessibility of support, including opportunities to re-access services once a particular type of support has ended; communication between families and professionals, including informed decision-making; appropriate timing and pacing of activities and feeling in control; co-ordination of services (good liaison and communication between professionals); providing a single point of contact (a main key worker) and convenience.

Outcomes for Children and Families

Nine cases were closed and ten were ongoing. In all nineteen cases, families and professionals were able to identify outcomes of the process for families. Outcomes related to e.g. integration into local services; amelioration of crisis situation through childcare and practical support; improved maternal mental health; improved parenting skills including strategies for managing behaviour; improvements in personal and family situation through training and the development of skills; improved relationship between parent and child; child development e.g. personal and social skills, improved behaviour; and social and emotional well-being e.g. increased confidence, self-esteem and ability to cope.

Conclusion

The Request for Services process has had positive outcomes for families and has been positively received by them. They felt comfortable accessing services and appreciated the wide range of support available. They felt that they had received full and clear information about the services being offered, were fully involved in the decision-making process and were not rushed or pressured into taking up services. They were able to take up services gradually and prioritise according to family circumstances and wishes, and felt in control. They felt that there was good liaison and communication between professionals, which meant not having to repeat information and provided consistency. It was helpful to have the same person (key worker) involved throughout the process. Services and appointments were arranged to suit their family routines and circumstances and there was flexibility in location as well as timing.

A key part of the reform of children's services is the integration of systems and processes so that the needs of children and families are met in a more appropriate way. For example,

> 'Children and families are supported most effectively when CAF *[Common Assessment Framework]*, the lead professional and information sharing procedures are planned and delivered in a co-ordinated way, to offer integrated support across the continuum of needs and services' (DfES 2006:7).

This study has shown that many of the proposed functions of, and principles underlying, the lead professional role are already in evidence in the Request for Services process. In addition, Request for Services is already incorporating the CAF pre-assessment checklist, which links to the Every Child Matters outcomes. Further work has been developed to ensure that the CAF and Lead Professional role are an integral part of the process. This will support integrated services based upon Every Child Matters outcomes. For the CAF, practice guidance will emerge in order to help identify (a) how best to engage with families to gain consent for multi-agency involvement; (b) how organisations and individual practitioners have utilised the CAF/Lead Professional process; and (c) how children, young people and families have been supported from multi-agency working. Having people from different organisations working together in an integrated way is an essential feature of children's centres, but it is also one of their greatest challenges, for example creating different models of governance and leadership.

FINDINGS FROM EVALUATING SURE START PLUS

6
Evaluating different models of delivering Sure Start Plus within five local authorities

What is Sure Start Plus?

It is 'now widely recognised that teenage pregnancy and early motherhood can be associated with poor educational achievement, poor physical and mental health, social isolation, poverty and related factors' (Health Development Agency, 2001). In addition, socioeconomic disadvantage can be both a cause and a consequence of teenage parenthood (Acheson, 1998).

The UK has the highest rate of live births to teenage women in Western Europe. The Social Exclusion Unit was asked by the Prime Minister in 1999 to work with other departments to 'develop an integrated strategy to cut rates of teenage parenthood, particularly under-age parenthood, towards the European average, and propose better solutions to combat the risk of social exclusion for vulnerable teenage parents and their children' (Social Exclusion Unit, 1999). This led to the launch of the Teenage Pregnancy Strategy in 1999. The Teenage Pregnancy Unit was based at the Department of Health.

Sure Start Plus forms part of the Government's Teenage Pregnancy Strategy and was originally the responsibility of the Sure Start Unit. It is a pilot programme that aims to reduce the risk of long-term social exclusion and poverty resulting from teenage pregnancy through co-ordinated support to pregnant teenagers and teenage parents under 18 years. It aims to improve health, education, and social outcomes for pregnant teenagers, teenage parents and their children.

Sure Start Plus was launched in April 2001 and there are 20 pilot sites covering 35 local authority areas. The 1999 Social Exclusion Unit report indicated that Sure Start Plus pilot programmes should be located in areas with:

- high rates of teenage pregnancy
- an existing Sure Start local programme
- a Health Action Zone (HAZ)

Sure Start Plus programmes were therefore based within former HAZ boundaries. Sites vary from those covering a single local authority to those spanning five authorities. Funding was initially for three years but was subsequently extended to five years.

Responsibility for Sure Start Plus was transferred from the Sure Start Unit to the Teenage Pregnancy Unit in April 2003. It is being managed as part of the overall delivery of the Teenage Pregnancy Strategy. In June 2003 the Teenage Pregnancy Unit was transferred from the Department of Health to the new Directorate for Children and Families within the Department of Education and Skills.

There are two main elements to what Sure Start Plus was designed to offer:

- personal support and advice for teenagers who discover that they are pregnant, so that they can make responsible and well-informed decisions according to their individual circumstances;
- co-ordination of a new support package for young parents, both mothers and fathers, tailored to individual needs, to help them with such matters as healthcare, parenting skills, education, childcare and housing.

In addition Sure Start Plus was intended to look at:

• reshaping existing services to make them more user-friendly and effective for teenagers, especially those who are pregnant;
• filling gaps in services, especially childcare.

Sure Start Plus has four main objectives: improving health, improving learning of teenage mothers and fathers and their children, strengthening families and communities, and improving social and emotional well-being. These objectives and their associated targets are shown in full in Appendix One at the end of this chapter.

Background literature

This section starts with some background regarding teenage pregnancy and parenthood. Following the introduction, points from existing literature are described under headings that reflect the main elements and objectives of Sure Start Plus.

Introduction

Rates of live births to teenage women are high throughout the post-industrialised world. The USA has the highest rate, and the UK has the highest rate in Western Europe (Social Exclusion Unit, 1999). Teenage pregnancy rates increase with deprivation levels and vulnerability, including those in care and those who have been excluded from school.

The phenomenon of teenage motherhood is of concern because 'teenage mothers are reported to be disadvantaged financially, educationally and cognitively, in both the short and long term' (Hanna, 2001: 456). Whilst 'many teenage mothers find strength and fulfillment in their motherhood role', this 'does not come without cost to themselves or their children, as many teenagers are considered unsuitable to be parents and do not have adequate support' (ibid.). As a group, teenage mothers are a fairly powerless group with high levels of disadvantage and social control and economic vulnerability (Rank, 2000). Teenage parents are 'more likely than their peers to live in poverty and unemployment and be trapped in it through lack of education, child care and encouragement' (Social Exclusion Unit, 1999: 6).

Decision-making on the outcome of the pregnancy

The likelihood of teenage pregnancies continuing to term is greater among groups experiencing socio-economic deprivation. Teenagers in more affluent environments are more likely to terminate the pregnancy (Social Exclusion Unit, 1999).

Research with women aged 17 and under (including 103 intensive interviews) has found that young women's decisions whether to continue with the pregnancy tended to depend on the economic and social context of their lives and personal relationships, rather than abstract moral views (Lee et al, 2004). Young women who perceived their lives as insecure were more likely to see motherhood as something that might 'change their life' in a positive way. Those with expectations that their future life would develop through education and employment were more likely to opt for abortion (ibid). In addition, there is a strong correlation between the proportion of under-18 pregnancies ending in abortion and the proportion of adult pregnancies ending in abortion, suggesting that local familial and/or cultural processes have an important impact (ibid.). Most young women perceived the outcome of pregnancy to be *their* decision and most had decided what they wanted to do before they booked an appointment with a referring doctor (ibid.).

Health

The Social Exclusion report states that 'the death rate for the babies of teenage mothers is sixty per cent higher than for babies of older mothers and they are more likely to have low birth weights, have childhood accidents and be admitted to hospital' (Social Exclusion Unit, 1999: 6). Statistics for stillbirths and infant deaths registered in England and Wales in 2003 show that the infant mortality rate was still highest among mothers under 20 (7.9 per 1, 000 live births), although less than fifty per cent higher than for the 30-34 age group, which had the lowest mortality rate of 4.3 per 1, 000 births (ONS, Winter 2004). Teenagers tend to access antenatal care relatively late (Botting et. al., 1998). A lower percentage of mothers under 20 breastfeed in comparison with mothers aged 20-24 and over (ibid.). Children of teenage mothers are more likely to have bad nutrition (ibid.).

Attitudes of services, and of older mothers, are an area of concern to young mothers. An Australian study undertaken with five young mothers (Hanna, 2001) reported that their main concern was not to be prejudged. They saw some personnel in the health system as too authoritarian and controlling. They felt conspicuous because of their youth and perceived older middle-class clients of health services as overtly displaying patronising attitudes towards them and this led to them not using health services.

Learning

Teenage mothers are more likely to have had problems at school before they became pregnant, and they are less likely to complete their education, have no qualifications by age 33, be in receipt of benefits and, if employed, be on lower incomes than their peers (SEU, 1999).

There is some evidence of poorer outcomes for children of teenage parents including developmental problems and delays, intellectual deficiencies, behaviour problems and lower school attainment (Wakschlag and Hans, 2000). However, there is also some evidence to show that some children of adolescent mothers do not differ from other children developmentally (Bucholz and Korn-Bursztyn, 1993).

Families and communities

There is a considerable body of evidence from British longitudinal studies that shows that girls from less advantaged backgrounds are more likely to become teenage mothers (Kiernan, 1980, 1995, 1997; Hobcraft, 1998; Hobcraft and Kiernan, 1999). A recent analysis (Rowlingson and McKay, 2005) shows that women from working class backgrounds are more likely to become lone mothers than women from middle class backgrounds. Teenage mothers have had little time to make long-term adjustments within their personal relationships and they rarely have the financial means to support themselves (Botting et. al., 1998). They are more likely to be lone parents (Kiernan, 1995), and more likely to find themselves in the middle of family conflict (SEU, 1999).

Ermisch's (2003) analysis of British Household Panel Survey data, 1991-2001, suggests that having a teen-birth, particularly when aged under 18, 'constrains a woman's opportunities in the 'marriage market' in the sense that she finds it more difficult to find and retain a partner, and she partners with more unemployment-prone and lower earning men' (Ermisch, 2003: 20). Teenager mothers are much less likely to be homeowners in later life and their living standard, as measured by equivalent household income, is about 20% lower (ibid: 20-21).

'In the longer term, their daughters have a higher chance of becoming teenage mothers themselves' (Social Exclusion Unit, 1999: 6).

Social and emotional well-being

Teenagers have a higher incidence of postnatal depression (Botting et. al., 1998; Liao, 2003). Liao's study found that whilst there is some evidence for long-term convergence in the level of mental health between teenage mothers and other mothers / teenage non-mothers, teenage mothers tend to have an elevated medium-term depression whereas the curves for the older mothers tend to be flatter (Liao, 2003), suggesting that more focused efforts should be given to helping teenage mothers, especially during the first three years postpartum (ibid.).

A study undertaken with mothers in Scotland several years after the birth of a child in their teenage years (de Jonge, 2001) found that some mothers had developed depression after the birth but had not received adequate treatment. They felt that people were watching them more closely and might take their baby away if they were not seen to be coping well, which makes it difficult for health professionals to detect signs of depression. In addition, they expected a condescending attitude from health professionals and were surprised if this was not the case. The majority of the women had not attended regular antenatal classes, as they felt inhibited to be with older mothers who were in stable relationships. They also highlighted a lack of information about services.

Support for young parents

It has been argued that 'a pathological view of young motherhood is a dangerous and counterproductive one if the desire is that young people should be valued, and given the opportunity to grow to be mature adults, working in the community' (Dawson, 1997). The needs of adolescent parents differ from those of older parents. Early parenthood involves a conflict between the young parent's developmental needs and the needs of their child (Wakschlag and Hans, 2000). Their developmental needs set them apart as a specific group, and the potential for negative outcomes for them and their children suggests the need for early interventions (Coren et. al., 2003: 80). For example, a review of parenting programmes indicates that 'parenting programmes are effective in improving a range of outcomes for both teenage parents and their infants including maternal sensitivity, identity, self-confidence and the infants' responsiveness to their parents' (ibid: 98).

Description of Sure Start Plus in the five local authorities

This region was announced as one of the 20 Sure Start Plus pilot programmes on 1 March 2000, and was formally launched in April 2001. It was selected due to the high rates of teenage pregnancy experienced in the region as well as the existence of the HAZ programme spanning three health authorities and five local authorities (source: Sure Start Plus Region's Mid Year Progress Report September 2001).

The Sure Start Unit identified this region as having the highest average number of teenage pregnancies per annum (under 18) when compared to the 19 other Sure Start Plus sites. Further analysis revealed that Authority S had the highest rate of conceptions for both the under 16 and the under 18 age groups (1996-1998 figures) (source: ibid.). Conception figures for England and this region between 1998 and 2002/2003 are presented in Appendix Two.

Sure Start Plus in this region funded six Sure Start Plus advisers, of whom two job-shared. The first adviser came into post in September

2001 and the last in January 2003. In one area the postholder's job title is 'Young Mothers' Outreach Worker' but the role is very closely equivalent to that of a Sure Start Plus adviser.

The Sure Start Plus partnership also allocated the Sure Start Plus grant across a network of pilot projects as outlined in Table 1. These programmes represent 'a combination of extensions to and reshaping of existing projects and new initiatives designed to improve the support services available to pregnant teenagers, teenage parents and all young people' (source: Sure Start Plus Region's Mid Year Progress Report, September 2001).

Evaluation study: Aims and method

Background

The evaluation of the Sure Start Plus project in this regional area (Authority S, Authority G, Authority SS, Authority NS, Authority N) was undertaken by researchers from the School of Health, Natural and Social Sciences, University of Sunderland. The evaluation was guided by a steering group, led most recently by the Regional Teenage Pregnancy Co-ordinator, with representatives from Teenage Pregnancy and Sure Start Plus itself. The research was originally commissioned and steered by the HAZ. It was requested that the main focus of the evaluation should be the role of the Sure Start Plus adviser and that there should be a strong emphasis on collecting the views of young people.

Aims of the Evaluation

Overall Aim

To evaluate the success of Sure Start Plus in this regional area in:

- providing personal support and advice for teenagers who discover

Table 1
Pilot programmes funded by Sure Start Plus in this Region

Authority N and Authority NS	
Project 1	Lead Midwife Project (Authority N)
Further Information	*Funding ongoing*
Project 2	Ashwell Young Mothers Unit (Authority N)
Further Information	*Additional full-time nursery nurse in childcare facility to allow young mothers to access courses at the Unit*
Project 3	Additional funding for Multi-agency support Project (Authority N)
Further Information	*Project has since closed*
Project 4	Riverview Young Single Parents Bridging Project (Authority NS)
Further Information	*Extension of amount of support offering education and training to young mothers (ongoing)*
Authority G and Authority SS	
Project 5	Aqua Housing Project (Authority G)
Further Information	*Additional support worker for young mothers in Eleanor House (ongoing)*
Project 6	Bedeford Centre Outreach work (Authority SS)
Further Information	*Outreach worker subsequently appointed to post of Sure Start Plus adviser*
Authority S	
Project 7	Young Parents Project (since renamed B2b+)
Further Information	*Appointment of Childcare Development worker, currently responsible for recruitment, selection, training and matching of volunteer mentors*
Project 8	Small Initiatives Fund
Further Information	*£9, 000 was allocated to cover crèche costs and immediate response costs e.g. beds, taxis*
Project 9	Lads and Dads programme
Further Information	Funding of research project re. working with young fathers
Regional Area	
Central Co-ordination	

they are pregnant, so that they can make responsible and well-informed decisions according to their individual circumstances

- co-ordinating support packages for young parents, both mothers and fathers, tailored to individual needs, to help them with such matters as healthcare, parenting skills, education, childcare, housing.

Key Objectives

To evaluate:

- How the role of Sure Start Plus Adviser has developed across this region
- The impact of Sure Start Plus on pregnant teenagers and young mothers and fathers
- Professional perceptions of impact of Sure Start Plus on mainstream

Method

1   One in-depth interview with each Sure Start Plus adviser, tape recorded and transcribed, plus informal discussions

2.   For pregnant teenagers and young parents:
- Individual or small group in-depth interviews with pregnant teenagers and young parents (total of 61 young people)
- Written questionnaires to current and past users of the service and, in one area, non-users. These were distributed by post or, in some cases, completed with the support of a familiar worker (total of 60 completed, 37 current or past users, 23 non-users).

The research with young people, which was seen by the evaluators and the steering group as a central aspect of the evaluation, was guided by two panels of young people brought together to discuss the research. The evaluator provided information on possible research methods and ethical considerations. The method was guided by their suggestions (for some partly informed by their previous experience as research participants). The panels advised that interviews would be the preferred method of data collection, and that young people should be given a choice of group or individual interviews. Some might not like to talk in front of others and might be concerned about confidentiality or feel under pressure in a group situation. Others might be too shy or lacking in confidence to talk to a researcher one-to-one. Those taking part in individual interviews should be offered a choice of venues as not all might want to be interviewed at home. Telephone interviews were not favoured by the panels. A written questionnaire was suggested for those who had had limited contact with Sure Start Plus, were no longer using the service or did not wish to be interviewed. It would be important for respondents to receive a full explanation of the research, to know what would happen to the information they gave, to know that participation was voluntary and they did not have to answer all questions, to know that their answers would be confidential, and for the interviewer to be friendly, make people feel comfortable and understand about issues facing young people. An incentive should be provided to encourage participation.

The panels gave input into the types of questions to ask to cover the range of support that was provided by advisers and issues that were important to them (e.g. attitudes, way services are put across, emotional as well as practical support) and the wording of individual questions, taking into account the sensitivity of the nature of the questions.

3. Semi-structured interviews with a range of professionals, other than Sure Start Plus advisers, working with young people in the five authorities. These included Teenage Pregnancy Co-ordinators, Chairs of Teenage Pregnancy Partnership Boards and representatives from Connexions, Housing, Education [Reintegration Officers], Midwifery and the EYDCP. The purpose was to explore how they had worked with Sure Start Plus and what difference this had made. Interviews were tape recorded and transcribed.

Results

The Role of the Sure Start Plus Adviser

Introduction

The role of the adviser is central to Sure Start Plus. There was some initial guidance with regard to the role (Sure Start Unit, 2000). For example, with regard to the two main elements of Sure Start Plus, it was not necessarily envisaged that the same person would fulfil both the advice functions i.e. that of supporting a newly-pregnant teenager to help her make the decision about whether or not to continue with the pregnancy, and that of providing an integrated support package. It was suggested that the first role might be more that of an advocate, whose role would be to listen and talk to young women, to give them confidence and assist them in accessing services. The second role was to support those teenagers who decide to keep their baby – in the later stages of pregnancy or the early stages of motherhood. This would involve assessing her individual needs, and those of the father and both their families, (including if the parent(s) decided to have the baby adopted) and co-ordinating an integrated support package of services to meet the needs identified. It was also stated that it would, however, be up to the partnership to decide the exact method of service provision to be offered in the light of local needs and knowledge of existing services. Partnerships were also free to decide on their preferred titles for either of these roles.

The skills, knowledge and experience required by Sure Start Plus Advisers were considered to be of the utmost importance in making the programme work effectively. 'Their key skill will be the ability to relate well to young people (i.e. to be on their wavelength), to be credible and down-to-earth, to be non-judgmental and supportive, and to be able to relate to different sections of the community' (Sure Start, 2000: 10).

The guidance also stated that Sure Start Plus advisers would be key to enhancing, streamlining and reshaping existing, effective services to ensure that robust and strategic support is provided to meet the needs and wishes of pregnant teenagers, teenage mothers and fathers and their families. This would be carried out by working closely with local authorities, local health systems, the education sector, and the voluntary and community sectors as well as young people themselves. Sure Start Plus advisers and co-ordinators would need to establish and maintain strong links with their HAZ, and HAZ partnerships and strategic programmes could provide the framework for activity to be taken forward and for any new and innovative ways of working to be mainstreamed.

Recruitment of advisers in this region

The complexity of the existing organisational structures across this region was considered to provide a key challenge in the development of the programme. Establishment of the Sure Start Plus pilot project occurred within an environment of organisational change. The modernisation of local health services, local authorities and the introduction of Local Strategic Partnerships required significant flexibility in the partnership approaches adopted by the Sure Start Plus programme. The emergence of Primary Care Trusts within each locality, the establishment of a Strategic Health Authority covering this and another area and the launch of the Connexions service were all considered to have a potential impact on the operation and implementation of the Sure Start Plus programme across this region. The restructuring of the Teenage Pregnancy function across localities would also impact on the implementation of the Sure Start Plus programme and subsequent partnership arrangements (source: Sure Start Plus Region's Mid Year Progress Report, September 2001).

This Progress Report highlighted several key challenges that the development of the Sure Start Plus programme in this region had presented since its formal launch in April 2001. These included timescales, particularly (as with several other time-limited funding programmes) working in partnership with several other programmes whose timescales and funding duration did not match (including the Health Action Zone). The local Connexions service was not due to be launched until January 2002, some nine months after Sure Start Plus, creating early difficulties in establishing a co-ordinated system of referral pathways. Making links with Sure Start and sharing information and learning were facilitated in this early stage by the development of strong working links with the Regional Development Officer for Sure Start. Recruitment of advisers and project workers provided a challenge with an increasing number of new services, or expansion of services, placing increasing demands on a relatively small skilled pool of labour and the additional impact of a relatively short-term contract (maximum three-years). The generation of roles, responsibilities and job descriptions was problematic when recruiting (originally) three advisers based on existing Health Authority boundaries, to fit with current structures and services. For each of the three areas a statutory body needed to be identified that was willing to become the employing organisation, and potential issues concerning different pay structures and bands needed to be addressed (source: ibid.).

The programme originally aimed to recruit three advisers, one for each of the health authorities. Due to reorganisation, this was subsequently amended to have advisers in each of the five local authority areas. These were all full-time posts. Six advisers (two of whom job-shared) came into post between September 2001 and January 2003. All were women. The two job-sharing advisers were considered to provide an important and relevant skill mix of youth work and midwifery. The job title 'Sure Start Plus adviser' was given to all, except in Authority G where the title was 'Young Women's Outreach worker/Sure Start Plus adviser'. They had backgrounds in e.g. counselling, midwifery, education, community and youth work, and social work. Employing organisations were Authority G Department of Learning and Culture, Barnardos (Authority N and Authority NS), Authority SS PCT and Authority S Social Services Department.

In two areas the adviser post was based in, and very closely integrated into, existing projects. In other areas the advisers were in professional bases. In Authority SS the postholder was based at the Health Promotion service and in Authority N and Authority NS in a multi-agency centre at a community school.

How the post has evolved in each area

In Authority S, the Sure Start Plus adviser was placed within an existing project for young parents, the Young Parents' Project, originally established in 1999, and over time these two elements became increasingly integrated, for example with joint referral. The overall project has subsequently been renamed by the young people as B2b+. It has involvement from other agencies including Authority S Teaching Primary Care Trust, the Education Authority and Social Services Department, Connexions, a Women's Group, a housing project, Children North East and an arts project, and has also gained funding from the NRF and ESF. The Learning Support

Service provides education for mothers-to-be/young mothers of statutory school age. A multi-agency initiative for young parents and young people leaving care is also based at the premises and its Partners include Sure Start Plus, Authority S's Leaving Care Service, the Connexions service in this region and an arts project. A range of courses is provided, including an antenatal course presented by the Sure Start Plus adviser, a health visitor and a midwife. Regular sessions are held by sexual health services, a health visitor and a Connexions Personal Adviser at the project and a young fathers' worker has been appointed to the project. The Sure Start Plus adviser has also undertaken training as a Connexions Personal Adviser. Young parents have access to a crèche, drop-in sessions, toy library, book library, safety loan scheme and computer suite. A Parents Committee is involved in consultation, planning and decision-making and parents are represented on management groups. One-to-one support is also provided at the project and in the home and the Sure Start Plus adviser has developed links and activity in four local Sure Start programmes, and the antenatal groups have been run in two of these programmes. Sure Start Plus funding has also provided for a Childcare Development Worker at the project, who has been involved in developing a volunteer mentoring project to extend the amount of one-to-one support that can be offered to young people. The Sure Start Plus adviser now manages and co-ordinates the B2b+ project as well as fulfilling her role as adviser. This is a very successful model, which is strategically well developed.

Authority G operates a successful outreach model. The Young Women's Outreach Worker/Sure Start Plus adviser is based at, and closely integrated into an existing project which was established in 1992 and offers support, information, advice and training to young women under 25, with crèche provision. A referral system has been established with the Hospital Maternity unit, and referrals are also received from other services in cases of particular need. The YWOW/SSPA makes initial contact and provides individual support (at the Project and in the home) and group support, and there is a range of other groups available enabling people to move on through the Project and also to access other services such as the Domiciliary Contraception Nurse, health visitor and pregnancy testing on site. There are also opportunities for joint work with individuals. Access to other services in the locality community centres and Sure Start local programmes is also encouraged and facilitated by the adviser, e.g. through accompanied visits. The outreach worker/adviser runs a weekly antenatal group at the Project that involves a midwife and health visitor and other relevant professionals and allows for input from the young women. Through the YWOW/SSPA's links with midwifery and the relationships she has built up with young people, young mothers are now involved in the maternity service liaison group. Sure Start Plus funding has also been used to fund a support worker at Aqua Housing (supported accommodation for young mothers).

In Authority N, the post of Sure Start Plus adviser has filled a gap in provision in the areas of the city (North and East) not already covered by a teenage pregnancy adviser. The adviser provides both group and individual support. Sure Start Plus funding also enabled the existing position of Lead Midwife Teenage Pregnancy to become a full-time post. Prior to this the post had been part-time, funded by the Local Implementation Fund through the Teenage Pregnancy Task Group and had had more of a strategic emphasis. Sure Start Plus funding enabled the extension of clinical work. The midwife post currently operates as a job-share.

As it was found that there was generally high attendance at 19-week scan clinics, the previous teenage pregnancy midwife established a weekly scan clinic for young women under 18 years old. In order to optimise the amount of services that can be received at one time this is also attended by the Sure Start Plus adviser, thus providing accessibility to the service and enabling the handling of issues such as housing and benefits, for example filling in forms together, phoning relevant agencies or providing information, and providing the opportunity for follow-up work. A tour of the maternity unit is also offered. A Connexions worker or reintegration officer can also be accessed at the clinic. The clinic has increased the percentage of young pregnant women reached by the specialist midwife and, hence, by Sure Start Plus. There are plans to introduce these scan clinics at an earlier stage in the pregnancy (12th week). There are also plans to develop a clinic to provide an opportunity for young people to discuss their options from positive pregnancy test.

A group for young parents/parents-to-be has been established in partnership with Sure Start in each of the two areas covered by the adviser and these groups are run on a weekly basis by the adviser in conjunction with the teenage pregnancy midwife, with timetabled input from, e.g. Sure Start, Connexions and a local college. Young people are encouraged to attend when they have got to know the adviser. Both the adviser and midwife regularly visit the city's Young

Mothers Unit, as do the teenage pregnancy adviser for the West of the city and a Connexions adviser. The Sure Start Plus midwife works alongside the community midwife and enables them to receive antenatal care without having to miss school. Her attendance at the Unit allows for informal relationships with young women for a longer period after the birth of their child. Sure Start Plus funding has been provided to the Unit for staffing in childcare.

This year the team have moved to a base closer to the city centre (also shared with Authority N Independence Network [Housing]), where there are facilities to meet young people, which had not been possible at their previous base, thus providing a more central and accessible service with a room for counselling by the Sure Start Plus Adviser, a trained counsellor. Authority N successfully operates a midwifery focus model, undertakes outreach work and has facilitated a co-ordinated approach to support for teenage pregnancies.

In Authority SS the adviser formed part of a multi-agency Teenage Pregnancy Team, which was made up of a partnership between the Health Care Trust and the Primary Care Trust. She is based in the Health Promotion service, as is the Teenage Pregnancy Co-ordinator. Key roles within the Team are the Options adviser, Sure Start Plus Adviser and the Pregnancy Service for Young Women. The Sure Start Plus Adviser has undertaken Smoking Cessation training to become a qualified Intermediate Adviser.

The work of the adviser has added value to the Authority's long-established (1983) Pregnancy Service for Young Women through attending weekly antenatal clinics and being able to offer, or signpost to, support on a range of issues beyond their maternity care. These clinics are also attended by the Options adviser, a liaison health visitor for teenage pregnancy and social worker as well as the midwives. There are close links with the Options adviser who informs newly pregnant young women of the options available to them with regard to the pregnancy and makes any necessary referrals and provides counselling and support. The Options adviser is part-funded by Sure Start Plus. A referral pathway flowchart ('I think she may be pregnant' poster) has been produced. This was distributed initially to 700 professionals from a range of agencies and organisations, which may have contact with young people.

The role of the adviser developed since her appointment in January 2003. Sure Start Plus came to be considered to be the lead for the supporting arm of the Teenage Pregnancy Strategy, with the adviser building on her earlier work to take a more strategic lead looking at service development, e.g. with the EYDCP, and how mainstream services can work to best support young parents and working to identify different funding streams for different service provision. The adviser also provides a supporting role to other workers in the field, e.g. in a supported accommodation project. She chairs a multi-agency working party forum that has been developed to ensure co-ordinated support for pregnant teenagers and teenage parents. The role still allows for support for young people and is supported by an additional full-time adviser funded through the Local Implementation Fund [although working under the title of Sure Start Plus adviser for consistency]. Due to her experience, the original Sure Start Plus adviser works with those young people who have more complex needs. The Authority SS model is a good example of Sure Start Plus as part of a multi-agency team and of how Sure Start Plus operates a strategic model for overall co-ordination of services for young people through pregnancy into parenthood.

Authority NS operates a successful midwifery model with outreach contribution. Two Sure Start Plus advisers were appointed on a job-share basis, one a midwife seconded two days a week from her Hospital midwifery role, the other with a background in community youth work and employed for the other part of the week as a young fathers' worker with a separate organisation. At the time of writing, the adviser post had become vacant as one adviser had changed role, as will be described below, and the other had taken up a new post. Sure Start Plus funding has also contributed to a project that provides support for young parents on training and education.

The advisers have provided individual and group support. One adviser ran a group with a health visitor in collaboration with a Sure Start local programme, and the midwife Sure Start Plus adviser runs a Young Mums group at another, supported by input from Sure Start workers, e.g. speech therapists, play worker, health visitor and other agencies, e.g. a dietician from the Health Promotion department.

Young parents have been involved in the development of services e.g. through visiting other projects with an adviser, fundraising in order to set up a toddler group, making a video about interaction with babies and young children and going into schools to talk about being a young parent.

The experience of the Sure Start Plus adviser also working in the mainstream midwifery service has subsequently led to a reshaping of this service, and she has taken on the newly introduced role of Lead Teenage Pregnancy Midwife. She sees all the young parents under

18 at the Hospital from the date of their first scan between seven and twelve weeks. This post is partly funded by Sure Start Plus and enables her to continue to support young parents for as long as they need it, in addition to their midwife's input for 28 days after the birth. She continues to run the weekly Young Mums group at Sure Start as before. The Sure Start Plus adviser still to be appointed will be present at her Hospital scan clinic times.

In summary
- A range of successful models of ways of working has been developed across this region, e.g. based on outreach work, midwifery.
- Sure Start Plus Advisers help to provide links among projects dealing with needs of young people.
- Sure Start Plus funding has been used to employ support workers e.g. Aqua Housing (Authority G); also to fill gaps in mainstream provision and to develop new services and resources e.g. leaflets, videos, CDs, peer mentors, which specifically highlight and meet young parents' needs.
- There are better links with midwifery services (i.e. Sure Start Plus has helped to involve midwifery more than previously in meeting the needs of young parents). There has also been reshaping of midwifery and both antenatal and postnatal care.
- Most one-to-one work done by Advisers has been related to financial benefits, housing and emotional support.
- Young parents have continued to seek advice from Sure Start Plus regarding accessing college and childcare.
- Advisers used an empowerment model, jointly agreeing a plan of work with the young person e.g. listening/gaining their trust.
- Developing relationships on a one-to-one level was important before asking the young person to join groups etc.
- Sure Start Plus Advisers have received an increasing number of referrals from different agencies over the three year period e.g. Connexions, Health Visitors, GPs, Social Services.
- All Sure Start Plus Advisers reported links with a plethora of agencies, e.g. Teenage Pregnancy Coordinator, Connexions, housing departments, Health Promotion Teams, a principal feature of which was information-sharing.
- Having links with different agencies was associated with creating integrated support packages for individual young people; a named person leading the process was viewed as a vital addition.
- Lack of clarity regarding the role of an Adviser from the outset

meant the need to carve out a role begun for instance by shadowing an existing Teenage Pregnancy Coordinator/Adviser.

- There was a significant need expressed to do more work with fathers and ethnic minority groups

- A possible tension has emerged between the strategic and operational role of Advisers, similarly a questioning of their capacity to undertake both aspects of the role i.e. between helping to plan services and offering services/support to individual young people.

The Views of Young People

The Views of Non-Users

Twenty-three questionnaires were completed with young people not known to use Sure Start Plus. These were completed in the presence of, and with the aid of, staff from the Hospital Social Work Department in one of the five local authority areas. The workers invited the young people to take part during the course of their work with them within a given month. It needs to be noted, therefore, that all these young people were receiving support from this Team.

Table 2
Demographic characteristics of respondents (*n*=23)

Age	15-18
Ethnicity	White British: 23
Pregnancy/parenthood status	Pregnant: 6 Mothers: 17
Age of children	5 weeks – 21 months
Special needs	Parents/parents-to-be: 0 Children: 1

- *Knowledge of Sure Start Plus*
  Of the 23 respondents, 10 had heard of the support offered by Sure Start Plus and 13 had not. Of the 13, 9 had, however, heard of the project for young people in which Sure Start Plus is based and into which it is integrated. Of the 10 who had heard of Sure Start Plus this was in all cases from the Hospital social work team, but some had also heard of it from other sources, i.e. school, Connexions, Reintegration Officer or midwife.

- *Reasons For Not Using Sure Start Plus*

  Some of the young people had accessed services (e.g. education classes) at the project for young people but had not used the service of the Sure Start Plus adviser directly. One was currently considering accessing the service.

  Of the ten respondents who had heard of the support but not used it, eight gave reasons why they did not use it. In the majority of cases (seven) it was because they were getting enough support from their family, and six of these respondents were also accessing other services. These ranged in number from one service (Hospital social work team) to six services (GP, midwife, health visitor, Hospital social work team, Sure Start, Connexions). In the eighth case the respondent reported using a number of other services (GP, midwife, health visitor, Hospital social work team, Sure Start). Two of the eight also said they had not yet needed any specific help, advice or information. More specific reasons given for not using the service were *'because of the area the support service is in'* and *'I didn't want to go until I had other things sorted out'* and *'I don't need it'.*

- *Services respondents would access if the need arose*

  Respondents named a number of services that they would access if they needed help, advice or information and all but one said they would talk to their family for one or more aspects. The numbers of responses for specific areas of support are given in Table 3 below. Some respondents named more than one source of support for a particular area (e.g. GP and family).

Would respondents Use Sure Start Plus for any of the above areas of support?

As well as naming the above sources of help, advice or information, 12 of the 23 respondents reported that they would consider getting in touch with Sure Start Plus. This was because:

'It would be another source of advice, help, support or information'.
'It is there to help people'.
'They have a lot of experience in dealing with problems'.
There are good facilities / things for mother and baby to do / crèche

Table 3
Support Young People would access if the need arose (*n*=23)

Area of help, advice or information
and numbers of responses for sources of support that would be used

Service	Family	Other	Don't know
Deciding whether to continue with a pregnancy			
GP (6)	17 (mainly mother)	Friend (1)	1
Contraception			
GP (16)			
Family Planning Clinic (4)			
SHOWT team (1)	3		
Antenatal care			
Midwife (13)			
GP (7)			
Hosp. social worker (2)			
Sure Start (1)	5		1
Own health			
GP (23)	5		
Baby's health			
GP (18)			
HV (5)			
Midwife (3)			
Hospital (2)			
Social worker (1)	5		
Looking after baby (e.g. feeding)			
HV (12)			
GP (2)			
Midwife (1)			
Social worker (1)			
Sure Start (1)	11		
Child's development, e.g. language, play			
HV (15)			
GP (4)			
Midwife (2)			
Sure Start (2)			
Hosp. Social worker (2)			
Hosp. Consultant (1)	5		1

Getting childcare
Hosp. Social worker (6)
Reintegration officer (2)
Connexions (2)
Sure Start (2)   10   2

Housing
Hosp. Social worker (15)
Housing Officer /council (6)
Housing Group (3)
YMCA outreach worker (1)   2

Benefits
Hosp. Social worker (12)
Benefits agency /
 * House / DWP (7)
Connexions (1)
Job Centre (1)
YMCA outreach worker (1)   5   1

Education or training
Connexions (10)
Hosp. Social worker (6)
College (2)
Existing project for young people (2)
School (1)
Social worker (1)   1   3

Getting a job
Job Centre (7)
Connexions (6)
Hosp. Social worker (4)   1   7

Emotional support
GP (4)   Friend (2)
Hosp. Social worker (2)   Partner (1)
                                                     17   Keep to myself   1

Relationship with family or partner
Hosp. Social work team (6)   11   Friend (2)
                                                             partner (1)
                                                             sort out with
                                                             those involved (1)   2

At the same time, one said she would only contact them about childcare and another that having a social worker was very helpful (easy to talk to).

Eight respondents reported that they would not consider using Sure Start Plus. In the majority of cases this was because they felt they already had enough support, would rather go to their family or stick with people they already know. In one case it was because she did not know enough about the service, and in another it was because of the area of the city in which the support was based. One reported 'no reason'.

The views of young people who had used Sure Start Plus

Introduction

Sixty-one interviews were carried out with young people at their home or at groups run by Sure Start Plus advisers. In the latter case, the adviser informed the group about the research a week prior to the attendance of the evaluator, and the evaluator asked for volunteers so that the respondents were not pre-selected by the advisers. The questionnaires were posted by the advisers to a random selection of current and recent users of the service. Thirty-seven questionnaires were returned. In one pupil referral unit the questionnaires were filled in with the support of a Reintegration Officer. Demographic characteristics of the total number of respondents (n = 98) are shown in Table 4.

Advice and Support in making a decision about pregnancy

This element of the role of Sure Start Plus has not been taken on as a central role of the adviser for the first pregnancy. This is partly because the referral systems that have been set up with midwives and hospitals and the points of contact that have been established mean that the young people have already taken the decision as to whether to continue with the pregnancy. In some areas Sure Start Plus advisers are able to liaise closely with an Options service that provides this support and refers into Sure Start Plus. In one area the Options adviser is part funded by Sure Start Plus. Nevertheless, respondents were asked about the support they had received when making a decision about the pregnancy.

A large majority of the respondents reported that they had received adequate advice and support in making decisions on what to do about the pregnancy, e.g. whether to continue with the pregnancy.

Table 4
Demographic characteristics of young people consulted through group/
individual interviews and questionnaires (*n*=98)

Age	14-15	10%
	16-17	34%
	18-19	52%
	20+	4%
Ethnicity	White British: 96	
	White South African: 1	
	Asian: 1	
Language other than English	0	
Pregnancy/parenthood status	Pregnant: 22	
	Mothers: 70 (of whom 3 also pregnant)	
	Fathers: 6	
Age of children	0-5 years	
No. of children in family	0-4	
Special needs	Parents/parents-to-be: 3	
	Children: 1	

One young woman had chosen termination (second pregnancy) and had received support from her Sure Start Plus adviser, who had accompanied her to the hospital, stayed with her throughout and also accompanied her to a counselling appointment at the hospital, to which she had referred her.

Support had been received from e.g. an existing project for young women/parents, social worker (in care), midwife, GP, specialist service/clinic. Five had received information or support from a Sure Start Plus adviser (usually for a second pregnancy, and often in conjunction with other services). For some, family and/or partners had been a good source of support, for others services had been helpful when family 'didn't want to know' or 'didn't want to talk about it'.

Young people had often received support from more than one source, e.g. GP and family, midwife and family, with some referring to up to five areas of support (family, GP, social worker, midwife, Sure Start Plus adviser).

In the majority of cases the advice and support received from outside the family, including Sure Start Plus advisers, had been helpful because:

- Options were explained in full
- Impartial advice was given and the young person felt able to make their own decision and that they would be supported in that decision
- There was clear information about advantages and disadvantages of different options
- Staff were helpful and friendly

For some there had been no decision to make, e.g. *'I didn't have to think about it at all, I just decided myself'*. Although the majority reported that they had made up their own mind, in some cases they would have liked more support in this e.g. *'Nobody asked me, so I just made up my own mind', 'It wasn't offered', 'My midwife never asked if I was happy about being pregnant – I would have liked to talk it over even though I had decided'*. Even when young women appear to have made up their own minds to continue with a pregnancy, they would still welcome the opportunity to 'chat', know that there was someone available to talk to and would welcome reassurance.

A big issue for several young women was telling their family and coping with their reactions, and in some cases there was a difference of opinion about the future of the pregnancy, which affected the young people to different extents.

'If I'd listened to my mam and dad I wouldn't have had him, I got no support from them but I did from my boyfriend's family and the doctor'.

"The GP asked what I wanted to do and I said I was keeping it, but my dad hated the idea and said get rid of it. Our heads were all over the place, we [pregnant young woman and partner] didn't know whether we were coming or going'.

'I'd had one abortion already and I didn't want another one. I felt like I was expected to get rid of it because they'd put a lot of money into me doing [vocational course], but I've proved them wrong and I'm still doing it'.

Talking to family was an area in which several young women would have welcomed more support, e.g. at a time when their *'heads were all over the place'*:

'I knew I wanted to carry on, but I didn't know how to tell my mam'.

'I didn't tell anyone because I knew my mam would go off it. I decided to have an abortion to make her feel better, but I couldn't do it'.
'I would have liked support in helping my mam understand how I felt about being pregnant'.

The pregnancy sometimes changed their relationship with their mother and their own sense of self and this was particularly difficult when there was a perceived lack of support:

'I found out through the GP that I was pregnant but I wasn't given any information about where I could go for help. I went to see the midwife. I would have liked more support – it put a dent in my relationship with my mum and a dent in my confidence as to who I was. I was very quiet then and had to be spoken to'.

A small minority (seven of the 98 respondents) did not feel they received adequate advice, support and information in making a decision about the pregnancy. For example,

'I just got lumbered with a load of leaflets to read through'.

'I needed help to decide, not be made to do something'.

They felt that there had not been enough information available on their options and the support available to them and felt there should have been more support workers, also workers who had been in the same position as themselves. One reported on a lack of friendliness at the hospital. One felt that there had been a lack of privacy at the walk-in centre she had attended and would have liked more discussion of the options and support in her decision handled in a more private way.

In summary, the findings suggest that most young people had received adequate advice, support and information on making a decision about the future of the pregnancy. Once they had made their mind up they would, however, have liked further opportunity to talk and, in some cases, receive reassurance about their decision. Newly pregnant young women would welcome more support in how to talk to their family about their situation.

About a quarter of the respondents said that they had made up their own mind (in six cases with their partner) or that they did not need to think about it. One reported that her pregnancy had been planned.

The young people had received advice, support and information from a range of services, often more than one. For about a third the decision had also been made with their family. Only five of the respondents had accessed a Sure Start Plus adviser for support, presumably because at this stage they were unaware of the service and it has not been a key part of their role. It may be helpful to have a quicker 'transition' into this service for those who need extra support in the early stages of pregnancy, and for services to consider how links between pregnancy testing services, including GPs, and Sure Start Plus could be further developed.

How young people had heard of Sure Start Plus

Of the total of 98 young people who were interviewed or filled in questionnaires, all but two had heard of the service offered by Sure Start Plus advisers. As the specific job title and name of the Sure Start Plus project would not necessarily be familiar to the young people, the names of the advisers were used when asking this question.

The majority of respondents had heard of Sure Start Plus from their midwife. The high number who had heard of it through school/pupil referral unit reflects the high level of support given by one unit to the research and their encouragement of young people to complete questionnaires. A substantial number of young people had heard of Sure Start Plus through existing projects for young women/young parents, through young mums' clinics and through their family/partner/friends.

Introduction to the Service

This section uses data collected in the 61 in-depth interviews. The majority of the young people interviewed felt that they had gained a clear picture of what the service could offer when they first heard about it or when they were first in contact with a Sure Start Plus adviser (69%). Some felt that it was not entirely clear at first, but that they found out much more about it as time went on or they talked to friends (21%). 10% reported 'don't know'.

The young people were asked what had made them decide to take up the service. In the largest number of cases (21%) it was because of the adviser's ability to help with one or more specific issues, e.g. support in accessing a nursery place because of the mother's concern over her child's speech, seeking asylum, or needing somewhere to live when experiencing problems with parents. The next most cited reason was the opportunity to meet other people in the same situation

(20%). This highlights the importance of group activities as well as one-to-one support. Young people were also incentivised to access the service because of the *range* of support that could be offered and the activities available.

Others commented that it was wanting someone to talk to, the potential for general support or they wanted to give it a try and see what she could offer. Some were acting on recommendation by a social worker or friend.

Eight young people reported being encouraged by the personal characteristics of the advisers themselves, mainly the way they spoke to them.

'It was different to what I expected – she was very friendly and not pushy – some are more formal'.

'She was very nice and approachable, responsive and easy to get on with'.

'She came across as very nice and warm'.

One or two commented on an initial apprehension or reluctance.

'The health visitor mentioned it to me and asked if it was all right to pass my name on to [adviser]. She came and told me about courses and things but I had depression and I didn't want to go on a course. She kept coming and I wouldn't open the door and she sent letters and I gave up in the end! She took me lots of places and helped me with my benefits. Now I'm nearly qualified and I'm doing another course and the Duke of Edinburgh award'.

What young people had most wanted help with when they were first in contact with Sure Start Plus

Some young people interviewed had wanted help in one specific area, others cited up to four areas The most significant area in which help, advice or information was needed was financial matters, i.e. benefits, allowances and grants. Housing was also a very significant area. A significant number also wanted social support (in terms of getting a break, getting out of the house and meeting other people in the same situation as themselves) and what they called general support. Once this specific help was sought and given, the majority of respondents continued to maintain a relationship with their adviser and accessed their support on a number of issues.

In summary

- Teenagers received advice on their pregnancy from a range of sources principally GPs, Midwifery and their own family.
- Sure Start Plus Advisers gave specialist advice including explaining options in full; also the service was felt by young people to be impartial.
- Most teenagers stated that they had received sufficient advice on making a decision to have/not have their baby. Midwives in particular were seen as helpful here.
- Most young people having heard of Sure Start Plus decided to use the service for dealing with a specific issue e.g. support in accessing a nursery place, housing needs, opportunity to meet other young parents.
- Some young people just wanted to discuss their position expressing a need for general support; and appreciated the friendly manner of Advisers.
- The main area in which help, advice or information was sought concerned financial matters i.e. benefits, allowances, grants, also housing, reduction of isolation and general support.

Use of Sure Start Plus

The amount of use of the service by those interviewed included, in one case, one-off use for a specific purpose, occasional use as needed (16%), frequent or regular use (52%) and recent return to the service after previous use (e.g. second child). All but four were still using the service. Of these four, one no longer needed the service as she was accessing other services (Sure Start and another community facility) and three no longer needed it but would contact the adviser again if the need arose.

Forty-eight young people were still using the service and intended to continue doing so. For some the type and amount of use had changed over time as their circumstances had changed, e.g. starting college. Seven did not know whether they would be using the service again.

Types of Support Given

The following sections use data from both the interviews and the questionnaires (*n*=98).

Young people reported that advisers had given a range of types of support, including telephone contact, home visits, outings and group work. Support had included:

- Information about or referral to other agencies (e.g. benefits, housing, psychologist, Sure Start)
- phoning or writing to agencies on their behalf
- help with filling in forms
- going over what they had been told by other agencies to discuss accuracy, next steps (including accompanying them to appeals)
- accompanying them to appointments, on hospital / college / nursery visits
- taking them shopping
- visiting them / them and their children in hospital
- support on emotional issues
- support with problematic relationships with the father of the child / (ex)partner (including dealing with solicitors, injunctions)
- help with rebuilding relationship with their mother, including after leaving care

In some areas group work was being run, either within an existing project for young women or in conjunction with Sure Start. For example, an antenatal group was run with a health visitor, midwife and nursery nurse.

Group work that included antenatal groups and young mums' groups had:

- provided the opportunity to meet other young people in a similar situation and form friendships
- involved relevant personnel, e.g. housing, refuge workers, drug counsellors, nutritionists, Sure Start, college and careers workers, to enable information sharing and broaden the range of expertise offered
- alleviated fears about the pregnancy and the birth
- developed young people's confidence and parenting skills *('I'm a good mam now, I think I do everything right')*
- provided the opportunity for their children to mix with others through crèche facilities
- given parents something to look forward to *('Life would be hell if I didn't have this [young mums' group]')*
- for some, made a difference to how they were with their children

('I'm different with her because I've got this to look forward to. I would start begrudging her. I appreciate her more because I've got a bit of life for myself as well'.)

The level of support varied according to individual need, e.g. from being given information and following it up themselves (e.g. a telephone number) to accompanying them to appointments (e.g. housing) and speaking on their behalf. The approach taken by the advisers corresponds to the 'empowerment, user-led model' identified in the National Evaluation of Sure Start Plus (Wiggins et al., 2003) and, as will be discussed in more detail later, there was evidence of several young people becoming increasingly able to deal with things themselves.

Views of the Service

* *Accessibility*

The majority found the service easy to use and felt happy to phone their adviser and felt they were well received. They appreciated being phoned *'just to see that I'm OK'*. This happened on a regular or occasional basis, depending on their level of need at the time. Having somebody who could help with a range of things was particularly helpful and made accessing support much easier.

'When I've phoned she's always interested and bubbly. She says, 'How are you? Would you like to meet? Would you like to go for a coffee?' If she can't help she finds somebody who knows the situation you're in and would get on the phone straight away'.

Two young women reported that it was difficult to contact their adviser because she was so busy. This was difficult when *'you phone and have ready what you want to say because you're all confused and jumbled, but in a couple of days it can be gone'.*

The provision of transport and crèches was facilitating access to groups, as was the personal encouragement of advisers, who phoned the young people on the day of their groups to check that they were coming.

* *Adviser support*

Talking to their Sure Start Plus adviser was a highly valued addition or alternative to talking to family or, in some cases, their health visitor, if this relationship was perceived by the young parent to be unsuccessful.

Advisers were non-judgmental and honest and were trusted to maintain confidentiality. They were often perceived to be different from family and other professionals in that the young people did not feel they were being *'told what to do'* and they valued feeling able to make their own decisions, with support.

> *'It's nice having someone to talk to who doesn't judge. There's stuff you can tell them you can't tell people at home'.*

> *'There's stuff your family would probably tell you off about or talk you out of, but [adviser] supports you more and sees your point of view, and gives you other options as well'.*

> *'I could tell her things I knew she wouldn't tell anyone else. You can't tell your friends everything. I'm only 19 and a lot of my friends were younger and I'm not speaking to my mum, but she [adviser] understood what I was going through'.*

Advisers were felt to be encouraging:

> *'She's always patting us on the back and saying this was good and that was good instead of putting us down'.*

In all cases young people felt that they were being treated as they would want to be treated. The perceived lack of formality and being treated as an adult or *'like an equal'* were particularly important. A very common comment was that their adviser was more like a friend than a worker. Several commented that *'you can have a laugh with her'*, but they also commented that advisers were serious when they had to be and would say if they felt something was wrong.

> *'She didn't patronise me'. 'She treated me like an adult not like a kid'.*

> *'When you talk to [adviser] it's like I can be myself and I don't have to change myself to be a different person in front of her'.*

> *'She's really understanding and you can have a laugh with her. You don't feel embarrassed and feel you shouldn't have said something. You're not worrying about what she thinks of you'.*

'If she was formal it would put me off, but I feel I can talk to her about things'.

Respondents appreciated advisers' commitment to (and persistence in) engaging with them (both in their initial encouragement to take up the service and through ongoing regular phone calls) and in the amount of time advisers were prepared to spend with them,

'I thought it would be quick little chats and over with, but she comes for 1½ to 2 hours'.

'She has never given up on us'.

At the same time, they appreciated that *'she doesn't pressure you into saying things if you don't want to'*, *'she doesn't hound you into doing things if you're not ready'*, and *'she doesn't nag on'.*

Sure Start Plus advisers were sometimes viewed in a different way to other professionals. *'With health visitors you're not relaxed. You can tell them stuff but there's always a niggle of doubt that they think you're a bad mother and you worry in case they get the wrong idea. You feel [adviser] is totally impartial, it's like she's making sure we're OK and keeping an eye on us'.*

Perceptions of impact

Analysis of the data showed that Sure Start Plus advisers and one person in a very closely linked role (Sure Start Plus midwife) were having an impact on young people in several areas. It should, however, be noted that, for many young people, these were not discrete areas, and Sure Start Plus had touched their lives in a number of ways. The main areas in which Sure Start Plus was having an impact were:

• *Material Quality of Life / Living conditions*
Several young people felt that they had been misinformed or 'fobbed off' when inquiring about e.g. benefits and maternity grants, and felt that their adviser's knowledge of their entitlements and 'the system' was invaluable and that they had 'more clout'. They felt it would have been much harder to tackle these issues on their own. Some were concerned about the perceived attitudes of those they spoke to.

'They tend to tell you anything on the phone. They lost my claim forms

and they think because you're young they probably think they don't have to try as hard. If an adult got on the phone and knew what they were talking about they wouldn't be like that. They think they can do what they want. They keep passing us on from one person to the next'.

For many, filling in these types of forms and *'speaking to people like that'* were things they had never had to do before.

'I asked her to sort out my benefits and she rang up for me and wrote a letter and my benefits got put up, but she said it still wasn't right so she rang again and they got put up again. I get fobbed off but she knows the ins and outs. I was told I couldn't get a maternity grant but she rang and I got that too'.

Similarly with housing,

'I was told I was too young to get a house because too many kids my age get them and it all goes wrong. She got me an appointment and came to the Civic Centre with me and helped me fill in the forms and I got a house'.

Advisers acted as advocates and made good links with the appropriate agencies that could help in the different authorities. Advisers had also supported young people in *'making the place habitable'*, e.g. in acquiring furniture and fittings, connecting services and tackling problems such as leaks in the house.

- *Personal and emotional issues / personal development*
Sure Start Plus advisers helped because *'You can sit and talk and have a good cry and she calms you down and relaxes you. I was able to talk about my relationship with my mum and I knew if I needed any more help this could be arranged. Not many people will sit down and just let you talk'.* They helped in gaining a perspective and understanding what was happening.

'I had a very immature outlook on things and I didn't know what I was getting myself into but [adviser] gave me a lot more support after I had decided to carry on [with the pregnancy] and made me realise what would happen and how your life revolves round them'.

Sure Start Plus advisers were often reported to have made young people's lives happier, to have increased their self-esteem and to have altered their perception of themselves and their views of the attitude of others. For example,

> *'I felt ashamed at first about being pregnant so young, but now I've made new friends and I don't feel so alone'.*

> *'She's helped us get a better light on what's happening. I thought my world was ending. I was pregnant, had nowhere to live, my mum didn't know how to handle it, I had no partner and his family weren't speaking to me. Through [adviser] I met other people in the same situation and she helped me understand I'm not the only one'.*

> *'She's helped me understand the way things are. At first I felt people were looking at us and giving us hacky looks, but now I don't get stressed about it and I think just let them, or I think they're looking at us because I've got a beautiful baby'.*

> *'She's [adviser] made me feel confident in myself so that even if people do think you're no good you know you are and you're a good mum. I don't think I'm a bad mum because I'm young. If they think that, then that's up to them'.*

A very commonly cited way in which young people felt they had benefited was through an increase in confidence. This was having an impact on their lives in many ways, and for some it seemed that this impact could have lasting significance in their lives and their relationship with, and attitude to, other professionals. Impacts included:

- *Confidence in their developing parenting skills*
  'People kept on saying don't do that, do it this way. She [adviser] helped me to do it the way I wanted to do it and helped me to stop them butting in as long as I wasn't harming her'.

- *Enabling them to access other venues/services and form friendships.*
  'I've started going up the [....] family centre. I was never that good round other people, but I got confidence from coming here and it's easier to make friends'.

  'I can talk to my neighbours now'.

Further,

> 'When I see a young lass like myself I always talk to them – it's made us more sociable'.

- Changing their relationship with, or attitude towards, other professionals and other sources of help
  'When I first had a health visitor I couldn't talk to her because of lack of confidence, but now I don't mind asking if I'm worried – it's a lot easier'.

> 'When [adviser] told us about things I wasn't getting (like milk tokens) it made me think I've got to start sticking up for myself and it made me think it's not a crime to get help if you need it – if you need the help it's there, so I'm not embarrassed about it now'.

> 'When I go to other services now I don't think they're just going to tell us I'm no good'.

- Empowering them to tackle issues themselves
  'She's made me more confident about phoning others ... anything formal or official I didn't like to phone . . . it's still hard but I do it'.

> 'Coming to the Civic Centre with me was brilliant. We went and got forms [for housing] and went back to my gran's to fill them in and then we took them back to the Civic Centre. I can read them properly now and understand them better so I can do them myself. I would go to the Civic Centre by myself now'.

> 'I'm a bit wiser now, I know how things work'.

This ability to tackle things themselves could be seen to be developing gradually over time.

> 'She always used to phone for me, but now, say I get a bill and I don't know what it's for, I ring her and she tells me who to phone'.

> 'It's made me more knowledgeable. If I didn't have [adviser], I would be, 'Where do I start?' But with her being there from the beginning she has started us off . . . and she's made me more confident about ringing places. I've got her to back me up. I'm more knowledgeable and sure of myself and I can still go back to her and say, 'They said this, and do this and that'.

It was good to know that support was still there if needed:
'Because I've been [to the Civic Centre] with someone who's held my hand I can go myself now. I know the layout and where reception is. I know that if there's still something I don't understand I can phone [adviser] and say I've got this problem what shall I do?'

- *Encouraging active participation in projects*

A small number of young women interviewed had gone on to more active participation in the groups or projects for young women/young parents that they had become involved in through their Sure Start Plus adviser. This included volunteering/welcoming people to the group, attending Teenage Sexual Health meetings, giving presentations, being on the Management Committee. This was reported to have led to a feeling of pride and greater confidence and happiness.

- *Socialisation*

This particularly applied to those who were attending groups and projects that were integrated into or part of other projects for young women / young parents, and to a smaller degree to those attending groups run by Sure Start Plus advisers at other venues, e.g. Sure Start, community centres.

Several young women talked about losing their friends when they became pregnant or had their child – *'some of my friends aren't talking to me now I'm pregnant'; 'they back off and lose interest when you've got kids'*. Some of them also had difficult family situations or were leaving care. Meeting other people in the same situation in a supportive environment was extremely important, and also provided them with opportunities to develop their skills and gain qualifications.

The social element was particularly important to those who had been depressed.

'I go out now so there's not so much to get depressed about, I'm not sitting in the house thinking about what's happened'.

- *Education, training and work*

Important aspects in this area were not only providing information about courses and childcare, but also the personal support provided that encouraged access, such as accompanying them on visits. For example,

'She asked me what I was planning to do in the next year and I said I

wanted to go to college to do Beauty Therapy, so she took me down and helped me get enrolled. She gave me a list of different nurseries and I chose [....] but it was full, so she phoned [....] nursery for me and that had spaces. I wouldn't have gone to the college – I would have felt daft, I'm shy and nervous about going new places. I was OK when I got there because there was a friend from school there'.

• **Health and Antenatal Care**

Only three young women had attended general antenatal classes. Whilst some said they would not have minded attending with older women, a larger proportion did not want to because of their perceptions of what it would be like.

'If I went to classes with the doctor you'll find there's older women who would look down at you and talk about you behind your back'.

For one who did go, it was not a positive experience:

'I went to antenatal classes at the doctor's and I felt people looking at me and judging me – I was only just 18 and I was the only young one, and I had to keep asking things'.

The others who had attended did not necessarily feel the same way.

The large majority had received antenatal care either in group or individual settings from a Sure Start Plus adviser or Sure Start Plus midwife. Groups included information and advice on contraception, usually provided by a specialist worker and individual advice was also provided by specialist workers and Sure Start Plus advisers/midwives. Contraceptive services were available in the projects for young parents from where two Sure Start Plus advisers worked.

Respondents reported very favourably on the presence of Sure Start Plus advisers in some areas at hospital clinics. It meant that they were less nervous about going to hospital for appointments. *'I was at the hospital yesterday and it made us feel ten times better because I knew who she was'.*

Those in areas with a Sure Start Plus midwife or adviser/midwife reported extremely positively on this aspect of the service. They felt that they had built up a very good relationship, had got to know them well and trusted them and had learned a great deal about the pregnancy and birth and the early care of their baby. This was achieved in a very informal manner, sometimes through games and videos, and in both group and individual settings.

- *Parenting and Child Development*

A small number of respondents felt that they did not have a good relationship with their health visitor. In such cases, the Sure Start Plus adviser had been used as a source of support, e.g. with regard to breastfeeding, reassurance about their baby's weight and bonding with their baby. One felt that her health visitor *'talks to my mam not me and tells her what's going on'*. For one person, the Sure Start Plus adviser had acted as an advocate in accessing a nursery place for a child with speech difficulties.

Some respondents reported feeling boosted as a parent by their adviser, e.g. through their praise and encouragement. They felt more confident because they did not feel alone and knew that help was available.

> *'She's praised me and made me feel I've done a good job. She says I'm doing the right thing with raising her and going the right way about it'.*

Work with Fathers / Male partners

In Authority SS, a Young Men and Boys worker has been appointed, and part of the remit will be to work with and support young fathers and the partners of teenage mothers in conjunction with the Sure Start Plus Advisers. In Authority NS, one of the advisers also worked part-time as a Young Fathers' worker, but has since taken up another post.

The project in Authority S, where the Sure Start Plus adviser has a dual role as adviser and manager, identified a gap in provision of support for young fathers and a bid was made to the European Social Fund (ESF) and the Neighbourhood Renewal Fund (NRF) to fund a dedicated worker to provide advice and support to young fathers. A Young Fathers' worker has been appointed, is based at the project and receives referrals from e.g. social services, the Hospital social work team, Leaving Care and girlfriends/partners. He works closely with the Sure Start Plus adviser/manager of the project and liaises with, for example, Connexions and provides advice on e.g. housing, benefits and budgeting. Group and one-to-one support are provided on issues such as domestic violence, positive parenting, communication, equal opportunities, masculinity and fatherhood. A CD has been made on which fathers talk about fatherhood, relationships and how they are coping. In some cases couples are worked with together. The young fathers' worker also attends antenatal classes.

Three interviews were carried out with fathers who had worked with the Young Fathers' worker in Authority S and the Sure Start Plus adviser/project manager. In all cases this was initially through their partners who were in contact with the Sure Start Plus adviser. The fathers had initially most wanted support on issues such as advice about being a dad and coping, getting a job, housing and decorating, benefits entitlements, asylum and child protection issues. Because of the shared base, these men had received support from both workers. For one man, meeting the Sure Start Plus adviser through his partner during pregnancy had encouraged him to attend antenatal classes and the Dads' group. He noted a significant difference between the support he had received with his previous child and the support he was currently receiving, which had led him to take a more active role in his child's daily care, had led to the formation of friendships, and had increased his confidence as a person and father. These benefits were also noted by the two other fathers interviewed. They felt that they would not have helped as much with their babies and would have been less confident without this support. *'I'm really glad they've been there to show me what to do'.* One commented that it had improved his relationship with his partner. Whilst they reported positively on the support of the Sure Start Plus adviser and felt they had a good relationship with her, particularly noting her praise and encouragement, they also considered that it was important for them to be able to talk to a man, particularly about relationships. *'It's good to have a male bond'.*

Two interviews were carried out with mother and partner together in another area, and one questionnaire was returned by a father. In addition, several mothers referred to the support their partners had or had not received. It was generally felt in this small sample that Sure Start Plus advisers were including fathers where possible and had provided good support both for specific needs such as employment and in their relationships, e.g. *'helping us understand how we both feel'* and *'helping us with each other's needs',* but that there was still generally a lack of support for young fathers/male partners.

In summary:
- Types of support given by Sure Start Plus Advisers included telephone contact, home visits, outings and organised group work with young parents, the last i.e. group work being frequently run in connection with Sure Start Programmes e.g. as an antenatal group including a health visitor, midwife and/or nursery nurse.
- Young women who contacted Advisers stated frequently that Advisers are accessible, helpful and non-judgemental.
- Young people mentioned gaps in services e.g. courses on parent classes, better advertising on what is available, more childcare, help in how to get back to work.
- Fathers interviewed felt that there was a lack of information for men on how to treat children and also expressed a need for emotional support. Those fathers who had had contact with a young fathers worker felt that they had gained e.g. increased self respect.
- Young women valued the information given to them by Advisers regarding financial benefits/entitlements and contrasted this with how they may have been dealt with previously.
- Young women valued highly the emotional support given to them by Advisers and the latters' ability to act as advocates for them.
- Young women appreciated Advisers' help in enabling them to join groups/projects and meeting others; also their providing of information about courses/childcare, and their support in hospital clinics.

Mainstream professionals' perspectives on the impact of Sure Start Plus

The following presents findings from interviews with different professionals (*n*=27) covering their *perception* of the impact of Sure Start Plus on mainstream provision for pregnant teenagers/young parents. Interviewees are from the five Sure Start Plus constituencies (see Diagram 1).

All 27 interviews were audiotaped/transcribed; analysis of transcripts suggests that Sure Start Plus has impacted in the following ways:

1. Raising awareness, networking and coordination;

Diagram 1

	Teenage Pregnancy Coordinator	Midwife	Connexions	Reintegration Officer	Housing	Chair of Partnership	Other Managers
Area							
G	◆	◆	◆		◆◆	◆	
N		◆	◆	◆	◆	◆	
NS		◆		◆		◆	◆
SS	◆	◆	◆		◆	◆	
S	◆		◆	◆		◆	◆◆
							◆◆
Total	3	4	4	3	4	5	5

2. Additionality e.g. supplying extra services and support to young parents;
3. Changing the role of mainstream professionals e.g. new ways of working.

The following expands upon each of the above themes supported by selected interview extracts:

Raising awareness, networking and coordination:

There is evidence that Sure Start Plus has raised awareness of the needs of young parents among different professionals and equivalently raised awareness among young parents of types of support available to them personally, thereby creating a positive image of Sure Start Plus and a *trickledown* effect i.e. young parents pass on/circulate information to other young parents.

The role of the Adviser has been constructive in engaging a response from mainstream professionals to the needs of pregnant teenagers and young parents. The Sure Start Plus Adviser's role has been linked to that of Connexions giving Sure Start Plus *'a strategic element'* enabling support for young people who have *'complex needs'*. Advisers appear effective in networking e.g. among midwives/health visitors *'swamped with finance, benefits, all the stuff they haven't got time for normally'*. The Programme itself therefore has enabled a strategic overview of the needs of young parents and created greater awareness and understanding of their needs through a database:

> *'We have a good database we bought in and we spent quite a lot of money on that out of the underspend when we didn't appoint a nursery officer. We bought a database so we could really track these young women and we can produce also the reports that are necessary to show how many young women have been worked with and what we've worked with them about, to help with the six-monthly monitoring that's required'.*

A further example of the drive towards a strategic approach involves work in each of the areas between Sure Start Plus and the Early Years Development and Childcare Partnership (EYDCP) agencies in planning for childcare facilities and childcare provision i.e. *'getting people to think about young parents in a different sort of way and not just lumping them in with a big group because it's often not necessarily the right way to do it'.* There is evidence from the interviews of Advisers liaising with housing departments and housing agencies encouraging referrals to them when the latter receive applications for help from young parents under the homeless legislation *'we're working on that at the moment on the basis of meeting the target that no young parent should be in an unsupported tenancy'.* Making information available to young parents about support services has led to *'a much more consistent and co-ordinated approach to support where if they have a problem they know where to ring and get support.'* Whereas Sure Start Plus targets theoretically provide a rationale for coordinated action in practice evidence illustrates that such coordination is related less to targets and more to broader areas of support and, as one manager acknowledged, *'targets can be a distraction . . . and that doesn't do justice to the amount of work that's undertaken by Sure Start Plus'.*
The argument was made that the Connexions Service may focus upon education targets and fail to interact with health targets (the converse applies) thus diminishing the resultant intended benefit to young people. The process of networking by a Sure Start Plus Adviser involves discretionary judgement – whether to refer or to work with the young person herself:

> *'If she can make a referral to an existing agency who will give that woman support, be that, in the young women's outreach project or in one of the community centres or with Sure Start or in needing care or whatever, then she will tie them in to the most appropriate agency. The young women that she tends to work with and follow through are the ones that either*

don't want to go to any of those agencies or the ones that don't kind of fit neatly into any categories.'

Sure Start Plus Advisers helped to strengthen links with other projects e.g. Aqua Housing/Young Women's Outreach/Sure Start enabling a clearer assessment of young parents' housing needs enabling them to supply information to Partnership Boards. Advisers inform midwives about availability of services in the area, e.g. training, parenting, housing benefits. Raising awareness/trust of support services cascades among young people themselves where one young parent recommends the Adviser to another young parent:

'Once they've met one person who has that understanding it gives them a trust in other professionals as well. The key difference with the teenage parents is that they are being introduced to somebody who is genuinely interested in them.'

Advisers have produced informational leaflets to introduce themselves to young parents, e.g. *'I am [Adviser]. I've been doing this job for so long and these are the sorts of things that have come up with other young women who are pregnant so if you want to contact me, I'll talk to you; I'm here to help you because you're a teenage parent.'* Sure Start Plus has raised the profile of young parents strategically by creating a local database; and among different professionals e.g. improving communications:

'I think Sure Start Plus has put teenage pregnancy on the political agenda; it's made us more politically aware. I used to be a midwife many years ago and I worked in the antenatal clinic so I had quite a lot to do with the young parents and I did realise that they were excluded, they weren't given the same opportunities as other people. It's up to them to access services but they don't for a number of reasons; like confidentiality. They don't understand quite often what the services are like because they're only young so there is a need for specialised services so the Teenage Pregnancy Strategy and Sure Start Plus have really put teenage parents on the map and said let's treat them with respect.'

In Authority S Sure Start Plus networks with a Leaving Care Project *'so it's not just young parents but also young people who aren't parents; the young parents have developed a CD as to how they feel about being young parents.'* Developing health promotional information has been part of Sure Start Plus strategy e.g. information packs, training; thereby extending requests from young parents for support and helping to break down prejudice. Sure Start Plus Advisers on receipt of information about a young parent have become able to offer individualised advice on support available based upon continual updating of their knowledge of community services.

Additionality

This is about Sure Start Plus creating or helping to create additional support services for pregnant teenagers/young parents either by direct funding or through the Sure Start Plus Adviser, or indeed both. There has been a conspicuous move in all five areas to create/enhance *specialist* provision for young parents through the Teenage Pregnancy Strategy, e.g. specialist support within Sure Start Programmes. Midwives in particular referred to this aspect of Sure Start Plus as *'filling gaps'* e.g. providing information on housing/benefits entitlement, individual counselling, pathways to education. Examples of extra funded services include specialist health visitors, an Options adviser trained in counselling, a specialist reintegration officer and a young fathers' worker. A key sentiment again expressed by individual midwives was that the Sure Start Plus Adviser *'takes the load off me'* so that they can concentrate on doing midwifery (and therefore not having to counsel young parents):

> *'At the time (prior to Sure Start Plus) I was doing everything myself, contacting Health Departments, sorting out benefits and had nobody else to offer any support so she was welcomed with open arms and she comes to clinic every Thursday. She's in the clinic every Thursday so she is there to see girls as they come through the door, they haven't got to make appointments to see her (from this) we have developed what we call now our Teenage Pregnancy Team (i.e. interdisciplinary)'.*

A development emerging over the two year period has been a separating out of the Adviser's function dividing between *strategic implementation* of the Programme e.g. networking, creating database, target-setting; and *performing a hands-on role* e.g. counselling young parents. The specialist advice/specialist clinic provided by a Sure Start Plus Adviser was welcomed by the midwives (and others) interviewed.

Additionally professionals viewed the Adviser as an advocate for young parents, as she offered a non-judgemental approach and acted as a valuable intermediary between young parents and clinical services:

> '*I have my clinic and I will ask her to be in one of the other little rooms so that if (the girls) have any issues and they can see the Adviser on the day then they will go and see her and it can get the ball rolling.*'

Additionality includes helping to make support services more effective e.g. by maximising the information/data sources they have at their disposal. From interviews with Connexions Officers/ Reintegration Officers the establishing of close working links with the Sure Start Plus Adviser enables the former to become better informed of the background/needs of individual young parents, and hence improve the quality of their services:

> '*(We have become) more knowledgeable about referral processes. One of the things the Teenage Pregnancy Coordinator has done is a flow-chart as to who to contact in which circumstances and for pregnancy testing and things like that so that the whole thing is much clearer than it used to be and I think Connexions staff are developing quite a clear view of what needs to be done and when and sort of basic knowledge really.*'

The distribution of confidential information across agencies is not a straightforward process as legal, administrative and ethical regulations of Primary Care Teams guide a process where personnel are understandably wary about sharing client-based information. The Sure Start Plus Adviser has acted as a lynchpin for other professionals/ agencies supplying information and advice *about individuals* when required and as a consequence developed a deservedly high profile within support services for pregnant teenagers/young parents. The provision of parenting training including groupwork, peer counselling has grown out of Sure Start Plus funding; occasionally linking with existing training e.g. APAUSE (acronym for Added Power and Understanding in Sex Education):

> '*Some of the ways that we have worked together is that (SSP) run quite a lot of courses certainly for girls that are outside of the Sure Start system (and we contact them and recommend such courses)*'.

One example of groupwork is a young mums/dads group set up

in Authority S reinforced by Sure Start Plus funding where there is now an additional focus on young parents who have been previously in care. Crèche facilities, payment for taxis, education opportunities are supported through Sure Start Plus. Some existed previously but were advanced not attenuated by the intervention of Sure Start Plus Advisers whose advice/support to young parents judging from interviews appears to make a strong overall impact. Different groups have been set up through Sure Start Plus:

> 'Within Authority NS there are two groups running on a regular basis . . . People come in and speak to the young people on different issues over the weeks, parenting skills, issues like that, and they're held in a Sure Start centre so the advantage of that is they have crèche facilities for the parents who already have children.'

Funding extra posts allows additionality to mainstream:

> 'Sure Start Plus provides funding for one of our nursery staff, currently doing NVQ level 2, a midwife, extension of crèche facilities.'

> 'Sure Start Plus has brought additional resources to the service as it exists. We did have midwifery input, we did have Adviser input prior to Sure Start Plus but what it's done is enhanced them. It's provided more contact time, more hands-on time that's important with this particular group because if they don't have a relationship with you they won't work with you and if you've only seen somebody once a fortnight it's very hard for them to build a relationship. So I think it's enhanced the services that we've had rather than change anything.'

Changing the role of mainstream professionals

Here the argument is that the introduction of Sure Start Plus has brought about change/adaptation of some individual professional roles, for instance within a housing agency in Authority N:

> 'I've done a lot of joint work with [Adviser] on teenage pregnancy and I think the biggest change for our organisation was the referrals we were getting from [Adviser] and also the referrals we could send back to her as well and the joint work we were doing and I think that was the biggest impact, the amount of referrals that were suddenly coming through.'

Aqua Housing in Authority G may be typical of how professionals in mainstream have been assisted by Sure Start Plus funding and the contribution of the Adviser in providing advice/support to young parents on housing and income benefits: *'we're hoping to move them on in steps so they'll move onto a managed tenancy.'* The Adviser has been responsive to requests from Aqua Housing in coordinating packages of individual support for young parents and Sure Start Plus funding has helped the running of this housing project, making staff accountable to Sure Start Plus objectives/targets.

By enabling midwives to concentrate on the needs of women who are *not* young parents constitutes a role shift for midwifery, i.e. towards a more unidimensional focus on midwifery skills, displacing their current position of needing to supply advice to pregnant teenagers/young parents. A general theme from the interviews is that through offering support dedicated to pregnant teenagers/young parents Sure Start Plus has allowed mainstream professionals to focus more on others' needs. At the same time Advisers enhance the impact of mainstream through helping to create a better appreciation of young parents' needs. Because of resource limitations, an Adviser links to a small number of young parents: *'in terms of the total number of teenage parents I think that we do not actually engage enough of them.'* Such statements suggest that the impact of Sure Start Plus is rather less than might at first appear and by inference its global impact on the work of mainstream health/education and other professionals.

A key focus of the Sure Start Plus Adviser's role is that of mentoring young parents which is by definition time-consuming, requiring skills in counselling and knowledge of areas such as housing, welfare benefits, training/education services and Sure Start facilities locally. If a teenage pregnancy strategy is to fulfil its objectives then coordination of professional support is a necessary part of a strategy where several agencies appear to have a role to play:

'The function of a Sure Start Plus group will be to provide a strategic framework for supporting parents for the teenage pregnancy action plan but also to work on the nitty-gritty issues of tracking these young people and ensuring the data-sharing among agencies and ensuring that young people are involved and sorting out issues such as benefits and housing, so we can get people together who understand these issues and can sort them out as well as providing more strategic input.'

Another manager observes Sure Start Plus as catalytic:

'Not only filling a gap in the system but also, by its presence pointing out other gaps in the system because I think if there hadn't been a Sure Start Plus Adviser I don't think we would have had a specialist teenage midwife or a specialist teenage pregnancy health visitor.'

Gaining inclusion is purportedly a goal of New Labour's approach towards teenage mothers. Kidger (2004: 291) argues that 'conceptualization of the route to social inclusion is problematic for young mothers in that it ignores the structural and contextual barriers to them gaining inclusion, it discounts full-time mothering as a valid option, and it neglects the social and moral elements of their exclusion'. The work of Sure Start Plus Advisers appears to help young parents in particular feel less excluded by mainstream health and other services (if indeed this was ever the case) through their professional approach and the personalised, individualised support they offer.

Working towards Sure Start Plus objectives

Improving health

From the period January - June 2003 to the period January – June 2004 there was an increase in the proportion of pregnant teenagers in contact with health services by the 14th week of pregnancy (from 15% to nearly 51%), which is one of the main health targets for Sure Start Plus.

Sure Start Plus is also enhancing the availability of information about pregnancy and the birth to young people, e.g. through funding specialist midwives or liaison with the midwifery service, including Adviser presence at the 19-week scan clinic (Authority N) and jointly run groups set up specifically for young people (e.g. Authority G, Authority N), sometimes in collaboration with Sure Start local programmes (e.g. Authority S), and through one-to-one work. Young mothers-to-be reported very favourably on the presence of Sure Start Plus Advisers in some areas at hospital clinics, for example in making them feel less nervous about attending hospital appointments. Young Mums' groups (postnatal) focus on health as well as other issues (e.g.

Authority N, Authority NS) and relevant personnel are invited to groups e.g. nutritionists and drugs counsellors. Young people reported that groups and one-to-one support had alleviated their fears about the pregnancy and the birth, developed their confidence and their parenting skills and, for some, made a difference to how they were with their children.

As found nationally, there was less evidence of impact on issues such as smoking and breastfeeding, and the monitoring data show a high proportion for whom this information is unknown. This may be due to difficulty collecting the data, to the relationship between Adviser and client being transitory or to priority being given to more immediate 'crisis' work and the needs-led approach. Some Advisers also commented that it was difficult challenging entrenched cultural and family attitudes towards breastfeeding. Sure Start Plus Advisers commented that it was difficult and sometimes inappropriate to address the issue of smoking early on, particularly when they were developing their initial relationship with young women, often at times of crisis, and that young people prioritised other issues as more critical than smoking. It was noted that the largest amount of one-to-one work was regarding benefits, housing and emotional support. In one area the Sure Start Plus Adviser has undertaken training to become a qualified intermediate smoking cessation adviser (Authority SS).

Contraception is being addressed e.g. through access to a Domiciliary Contraception Nurse and pregnancy testing on site (Authority G), regularly held sexual health sessions (Authority S) and through close links with a Young Women's Pregnancy Options Adviser who is part of the multi-agency Teenage Pregnancy Team and part-funded by Sure Start Plus (Authority SS). Some young women reported that they would have welcomed more support in how to talk to their family when they found out they were pregnant. They would also welcome further opportunity to talk after they had made the decision about the future of their pregnancy and, in some cases, receive reassurance about their decision.

Improving learning

In one area in particular (Authority SS), strong strategic links were established with the EYDCP in planning for childcare provision and facilities. In some areas close working links with Connexions advisers and reintegration officers have enhanced information sharing both with regard to referral procedures and the needs of individual young parents. In Authority S the Sure Start Plus Adviser has undertaken training as a Connexions personal adviser. In another, Sure Start Plus funding has extended the amount of support for education and training to young mothers in an existing project (Authority NS). There have also been reports of an increased number of referrals and an increased amount of joint working. College and careers workers have been invited to Young Mums' groups (e.g. Authority N, Authority NS).

In England, 29.7% of teenage parents were in education, training or work in 2002-04 (TPS, 2004). Figures for this region were higher than this in each of the two monitoring periods in 2003 (69% and 64%). This figure dropped to 45% in January – June 2004, but was still higher than the overall figure for England. There was, however, a number for whom the information was unknown, which may provide a skewed picture of participation (Rosato et al, 2004). Wiggins et al (2005) also suggest that Sure Start Plus figures may represent a looser definition of what constitutes a training course.

As with some of the health targets, issues regarding education, training and employment were in most, but not all, cases not the area of immediate concern when contact was established with a Sure Start Plus Adviser, and on the whole tended to be addressed as the relationship developed. Sure Start Plus Advisers have shown evidence of keeping themselves up to date with services, training and facilities available in their areas for signposting and referral. Young people reported that what had been important to them had been not only receiving information about courses and childcare, but also the personal support Advisers had provided that encouraged access, such as accompanying them on visits.

Advisers spoke less of contributing to improving the learning of children. This may be because the focus has been more on pregnancy and the early months of the child's life and because it is not an area commonly highlighted by young people. Nevertheless, children's play and learning have been addressed through courses and in Young Mums' groups in some areas, e.g. through inviting Sure Start workers, play workers and speech therapists to the group, and, in one area, through access to a Toy Library. Groups and training courses have also provided opportunities for children to mix with others and access play opportunities through crèche provision. In Authority N Sure Start Plus funding has been provided to the Young Mothers Unit for extra staffing in childcare.

Strengthening families and communities

The most significant way in which Sure Start Plus appears to be contributing to this objective is through increasing the availability and accessibility of parenting classes, decreasing social isolation, improving young people's housing situation and improving their financial situation e.g. through helping them access the appropriate benefits. Sure Start Plus has identified considerable unmet need in the latter two areas, which it has addressed through working closely with other agencies, organising training and supporting young people according to their needs and the individual level of support required. Advisers stressed the importance of having a 'named person' with whom to liaise, although it had not always been possible. Relevant personnel, e.g. housing and refuge workers, have been invited to Young Mums' groups to enable information sharing and broaden the range of expertise offered.

Through Sure Start Plus, some young mothers had gone on to roles of active participation, for example as part of the maternity service liaison group (Authority G), through volunteering and giving presentations, and being involved in the development of services, e.g. through visiting other projects with an Adviser, fundraising in order to set up a toddler group, making a video about interaction with babies and young children and going into schools to talk about being a young parent (Authority NS). In the Authority S project a Parents Committee is involved in consultation, planning and decision-making and parents are represented on management groups. This active participation was reported to have led to a feeling of pride and greater confidence and happiness. At a personal level, there was evidence of young women becoming increasingly able to tackle issues themselves (such as making telephone calls about housing and benefits) through the support of their Adviser.

Improving social and emotional development

There is no available data on postnatal depression in this study, however there was clear evidence from interviews with young mothers of Advisers providing support in this area. If social and emotional development is taken to include self-esteem, emotional well-being and confidence, Sure Start Plus Advisers can be seen to be having considerable impact on their client group.

For example, young women reported that Young Mums' groups had given them something to look forward to, and had provided the opportunity to meet other young people in a similar situation and form friendships. There was evidence that Sure Start Plus Advisers had helped them in gaining a perspective on their situation and understanding what was happening to them, had increased self esteem and altered their perception of themselves and their views of the attitude of others, also changing their attitude towards other professionals and sources of help, and had given them confidence to access other venues and services and approach other people.

In relation to all objectives, there is less evidence of impact on fathers, and the study has indicated the need for work with fathers to be further developed. In some areas this has been addressed through additional funding for a fathers' worker.

In relation to all four objectives, Sure Start Plus has raised awareness of young people's needs and has improved referral and care pathways to enhance a multi-agency co-ordinated approach and has facilitated access to other services (e.g. housing). It has created, or helped to create, additional specialist support services either through direct funding or through the Sure Start Plus Adviser or both.

Data obtained from the six-monthly monitoring process

Method

Sure Start Plus programmes collect statistics on the uptake of their services and the outcomes for service users. Copies of the monitoring forms for three periods (Jan-June 2003; July-Dec. 2003; Jan-June 2004) were submitted to the evaluators by each of the five programmes. The data were combined to present a picture of progress over the whole of this regional area. There were some initial problems with regard to data collection (e.g. problems of double counting, which may or may not have been resolved) and it is not known whether methods of data collection have remained the same over time, which may affect the reliability of the data. However, the data provided do give an indication of the progress of the Sure Start Plus programmes during this time.

For the first six-monthly period for which monitoring data is available (January 2003-June 2003) it has been possible to compare national and regional figures, and this information is presented in each of the sections on results below. The comparative data for this period is also presented in table form in Appendix Three. National data has been taken from the National Evaluation of Sure Start Plus Summary of Interim Findings (Rosato et al., 2004).

Results

Advice in Pregnancy

A total of 259 pregnant teenagers (under 18) were advised by Sure Start Plus programmes in this region in the year January – December 2003. This is from a total of 1, 168 under 18 conceptions (source: ONS and TPU 2005). The total of 259 advised therefore represents 22.17% of all under 18s who became pregnant in this region in 2003. The total number of pregnant teenagers advised in this region has increased over the three monitoring periods from 113 in the first period to 178 in the third period.

For the 18-month period January 2003 to June 2004 a total of 437 pregnant teenagers (under 18) were advised by Sure Start Plus. Of these, 86.5% were aged 16 to 17 years and 13.5% were aged under 16 years. Similarly, national data for the period January – June 2003 shows that the vast majority of pregnant teenagers advised nationally in this period were 16-17 years old rather than under 16. Of the total number of pregnant teenagers advised in January – June 2003, there was a smaller proportion advised under the age of 16 in this region than nationally and a higher proportion aged 16-17 years.

Of the total number advised in this region between January 2003 and June 2004, the majority (69%) were advised at or after the 14th week of pregnancy. However, the proportions of both those advised before the tenth week and those advised at or after ten weeks but before the 14th week have increased over the three periods (from just under 1%

to just over 7.5% before 10th week, and from 2% to nearly 11% 10-14 weeks), indicating that, over time, Sure Start Plus advisers are coming into contact with pregnant teenagers earlier in their pregnancy.

Table 5

Advice in Pregnancy: Number of Pregnant Teenagers advised by Sure Start Plus in three 6-monthly periods, Jan.2003-June 2004

No of Pregnancies	Suspected but not pregnant		Advised before week 10		Advised during weeks 10-13		Advised week 14 or after	
Age	<16	<18	<16	<18	<16	<18	<16	<18
Jan-June '03	1	0	1	3	0	9	16	83
July-Dec '03	1	0	1	8	10	20	10	96
Jan-June '04	0	1	5	28	4	43	10	87
Total	2	1	7	39	14	72	36	266

Note: *In this and all following tables where age is represented, the definitions of age groups used by Sure Start Plus are as follows:*
   Under 16s are those aged 15 and under
   Under 18s are those aged 16 and 17
   Under 20s are those aged 18 and 19.

Pregnancy outcomes

Pregnancy outcomes were recorded for a total of 281 young women who were advised by Sure Start Plus in the period January 2003 to June 2004.

Of these, 89% gave birth and kept their child; 3.5% had abortions, just over 4.5% had miscarriages and small proportions had stillbirths (2.5%) or had their children adopted (<1%). However, the outcome of the pregnancy was unknown for nearly a quarter (22%) of teenagers. This figure is the same as that in the National Evaluation findings for the January – June 2003 monitoring period (Rosato et al., 2004). They comment that this suggests that programmes are having difficulty collecting the data or that the nature of the relationship is transient (ibid.). It should be noted, however, that in the third monitoring period the proportion of unknown outcomes is considerably less than in the previous two periods.

A comparison of pregnancy outcomes for teenagers under 16 and those aged 16 to 17 (as advised by Sure Start Plus for January 2003 - June 2004) shows a higher proportion of miscarriages in the under 16 age group.

	Abortion	Miscarriage	Birth: Kept	Adopted	Stillbirth	Unknown
Under 18	9	10	233	1	6	74
Under 16	1	3	17	0	1	6

Both locally and nationally, with regard to pregnancy outcomes recorded between January and June 2003, the majority of young women gave birth and kept their child. The proportion was higher in this region (76% compared to 58% nationally), and there were lower proportions of abortions and stillbirths, no miscarriages and no cases of adoption. The proportion of unknown outcomes was slightly lower in this region than nationally.

Support packages for pregnant teenagers/teenage mothers and for teenage fathers/partners

Pregnant Teenagers/Teenage Mothers

At the beginning of this data-gathering period (January 2003) a total of 290 pregnant teenagers and teenage mothers under 20 had support packages in place. Of these, 94 were existing packages and 196 were new packages. A further 207 new packages were put in place in June – December 2003 and 245 in January – June 2004. Thus, between January 2003 and June 2004 a total of 648 new support packages have been put in place for pregnant teenagers and teenage mothers.

Table 6

Number of pregnant teenagers/teenage mothers for whom support packages are in place

	New				New and Existing			
Age	<16	<18	<20	Total	<16	<18	<20	Total
Jan-June '03	19	131	46	196	35	188	67	290
July-Dec '03	15	128	64	207	20	195	106	321
Jan-June '04	18	133	94	245	23	193	170	381
Total	52	392	204	648	78	576	343	992

When the total number of new and existing support packages (January 2003 – June 2004, n=992) are split by age group, it can be seen that just under 35% were in place for 18 to 19 year olds, 58% for 16 to 17 year olds and just under 8% for under 16 year olds.

For the period January – June 2003, nationally the majority of support packages in place were also newly set up. This region had a higher proportion of new support packages (69% compared to 63%) and a lower proportion of support packages already in existence. Both nationally and locally, the highest proportion of support packages was for 16 and 17 year olds (66% in this region, 59% national) and the smallest proportion for under 16 year olds (13% In this region, 11% national).

Teenage fathers/partners
At the beginning of this data gathering period (January 2003) a total of 16 teenage fathers/partners under 20 had support packages in place. Of these, one was an existing package and 15 were new packages. A further 15 new packages were put in place in June – December 2003 and 14 in January – June 2004. Thus, between January 2003 and June 2004 a total of 44 new support packages have been put in place for teenage fathers/partners.

When the total number of new support packages (January 2003 – June 2004, n=44) is split by age group, it can be seen that 45.5% were in place for 18 to 19 year olds, just over 52% for 16 to 17 year olds and just over 2% for under 16 year olds.

Table 7: Number of teenage fathers/partners for whom support packages are in place

	New				New and Existing			
Age	<16	<18	<20	Total	<16	<18	<20	Total
Jan-June '03	0	12	3	15	0	13	3	16
July-Dec '03	0	2	13	15	0	12	20	32
Jan-June '04	1	9	4	14	1	14	5	20
Total	1	23	20	44	1	39	28	68

Support Packages Overall
When the total numbers of new support packages are compared by gender, this shows that nearly 94% were put in place for pregnant teenagers/teenage mothers and just over 6% for teenage fathers/partners.

A similar finding was made when comparing local and national data for the period January – June 2003. Both sets of data showed that the vast majority of support packages were for pregnant teenagers/teenage mothers. In This region the proportion for fathers was slightly lower than nationally (5% compared to 7%).

Ethnicity

Data on the ethnicity of pregnant teenagers, teenage mothers and teenage fathers/partners in contact with Sure Start Plus show that in each of the three monitoring periods from January 2003 – June 2004 the vast majority identified themselves as White British.

Similarly, for the monitoring period January – June 2003, the vast majority of pregnant teenagers/teenage mothers and teenage fathers/partners nationally identified themselves as White. The proportion of the total was higher in this region (99%, all White British, compared to 84% nationally, nearly all White British). Figures from the 2001 Census (ONS, 2001) show that the five local authorities in which Sure Start Plus operates in this region have a higher percentage of residents from a White ethnic group than England overall (between 93.1% [Authority N] and 98.4% [Authority G] compared to 90.9% in England). Unlike in the national data, there were no cases of unknown ethnicity.

A more detailed breakdown of the percentage of the resident population in ethnic groups in these areas is given in Appendix Four.

Contact with Health Services

Of the pregnant teenagers in contact with Sure Start Plus in the period January 2003 to June 2004 a smaller proportion were in contact with health services before the 14th week of pregnancy (35.5%) than at or after the 14th week (64.5%).

During the period January – June 2003, comparison with national data shows that the proportion in contact with health services before the 14th week was lower in this region than nationally (12% compared to 37%), and the point of pregnancy unknown was higher (19% compared to 14%).

However, a comparison of the Regional figures for the three monitoring periods shows that the proportion in contact before the

14th week has increased over time (from 15% in period one to 49% in period 2 and nearly 51% in period 3). This indicates that Sure Start Plus is making increasing progress towards the target of an 'increase in numbers of pregnant teenagers in contact with health services by the 14th week of pregnancy'.

At the same time, however, there are an increasing number of instances where the point of pregnancy at which teenagers were in contact with health services is unknown.

Table 8
Number of pregnant teenagers who have been in contact with Sure Start plus in this period and in contact with health services by 14th week

	Before week 14	At or after week 14	No. unknown
Jan-June 2003	28	157	43
July-Dec 2003	46	48	48

Smoking

Data on smoking status is available for 492 pregnant teenagers and teenage mothers in contact with Sure Start Plus during the period January 2003 – June 2004. However, there is also a large number for whom smoking status is unknown (453), suggesting that advisers are having difficulty collecting this data. It is therefore difficult to draw conclusions about rates of smoking. There is also uncertainty about whether the data refers to the same young people at each time point (i.e. before and after the birth) (Rosato et al., 2004).

Table 9
Number of pregnant teenagers/teenage mothers who have been in contact with Sure Start Plus in this period who are smoking

Number smoking	During pregnancy	Number unknown	After birth	Number unknown
Jan-June '03	110	80	66	92
July-Dec '03	51	67	34	44
Jan-June '04	134	66	97	104
Total	295	213	197	240

For the period January to June 2003, there was also a high number of pregnant teenagers/teenage mothers for whom data on smoking was unavailable at national level. In this region the proportion smoking before birth was almost exactly the same as nationally, and there was a higher proportion smoking after the birth.

Breastfeeding

Data on breastfeeding is available for 44 teenage mothers in contact with Sure Start Plus over this period. However, information is not available for a much larger number of mothers – 245.

This raises the question of why this should be so. Is it because the data is difficult to collect and, if so, how could this be improved? Is it because the nature of the relationship with advisers is transient?

For each monitoring period, in the region of three-quarters of the breastfeeding teenage mothers for whom data was available were breastfeeding before six weeks and one quarter were breastfeeding at or after six weeks. However, the data should be treated with caution because of the high number of unknowns.

Likewise, national data for the period January 2003 to June 2003 shows that there was a larger number for whom data was unavailable than available. However, figures showed a higher proportion breastfeeding before six weeks in this region (77% compared to 68%) and a lower proportion after six weeks (23% compared to 32%).

Participation in education, training and employment

Of those for whom data is available, over the three monitoring periods there appears to be a decrease in the proportion of teenage mothers participating in education, training or employment in both the under 16 year olds and under 20 year olds. However, there is also a number for whom no data was available.

In England, 29.7% of teenage parents were in education, training or work in 2002-04 compared with 23.1% in 1997-99 (TPS, 2004). Figures for this region are higher than this in each of the two 6-monthly monitoring periods in 2003 (69%, 64%), with 45% in the following 6-month period January to June 2004. As Rosato et al (2004) point out, however, a large number of unknowns may provide a skewed picture of participation.

When the data is split by age, in all three periods there is a higher percentage of mothers under 16 years old participating in education, training or employment than mothers aged 16 to 19 years old.

It is not possible to give a total of the number of teenage mothers achieving NVQ Level 1 or above over this period as it is not known whether the figures in different monitoring periods could relate to the same people still in contact with the project.

Table 10

Teenage mothers in contact with Sure Start Plus over this period, and participating in education, training or employment

	Participating		Not participating		Number unknown		Achieving NVQ Level 1 or above	
Age	<16	<20	<16	<20	<16	<20	<16	<20
Jan-June '03	19	102	5	50	1	57	7	38
July-Dec '03	18	118	2	67	0	8	10	32
Jan-June '04	11	93	7	113	0	38	8	35

Comparison with national Sure Start Plus data for the period January – June 2003 shows a higher proportion of teenage mothers participating in education, training and employment in this region than nationally (69% compared to 52%). When the data is split by age group, however, this shows that this only applies to the 16-19 year old age group (67% participating, in this region, 47% nationally) and not the under 16 year old age group, where there is a slightly lower proportion participating (79% in this region, 81% nationally).

The proportion of young mothers achieving NVQ Level 1 was considerably higher in the 16-19 year old age group than in the under 16 year old age group both nationally and in this region, and the proportions were very similar (84% 16-19 in this region, 86% nationally).

Childcare

For each of the three monitoring periods from January 2003 to June 2004, the majority of the childcare places accessed by teenage mothers were for children under one year of age. The second highest proportion was for children aged one to two years of age and the smallest for children aged over two. It may be, however, that as their children are getting older mothers are having less, or no, contact with Sure Start Plus, unless they have a subsequent pregnancy/birth.

For each of the three monitoring periods, the large majority of childcare places have been accessed by mothers aged 16 to 19 years. For the period January – June 2003 this was also the case nationally, with the proportion being slightly higher than in this region (86% compared to 83% in this region). As was found locally, the majority of childcare places were accessed for children under one year of age and the smallest number for children over 2 years of age. The proportions in this region were slightly higher for children under one and over two and lower for 1-2 year olds.

Housing

For each of the three monitoring periods from January 2003 to June 2004, the majority of the teenage mothers who had been in contact with Sure Start Plus were living with their families or partners, followed by lone tenancies, then supported accommodation, then other types of housing. Over time there has been an increase in the proportion of lone tenancies and supported accommodation, and a decrease in the proportion living with families or partners and in other types of housing.

When the data is split by age, the majority of under 16 year olds in each period were living with their family or partner followed by other types of housing, with none in lone tenancies or supported accommodation. The majority of 16 to 17 year olds were living with their family or partner, followed by lone tenancies, then supported and other types of accommodation. The figures for 18 and 19 year olds were more evenly spread between lone tenancies and family/partner, with this age group showing a fairly large decrease in the proportion living with family/partner and an increase in lone tenancies and supported accommodation. None, or a very small proportion, lived in other types of housing.

Findings were similar regionally and nationally for the period January – June 2003. In both cases over half of teenage mothers in contact with Sure Start Plus in this period were living with their families or partners and the percentages were very similar (52% in this region, 54% nationally). When split by age group, this shows a higher proportion of under 16 year olds and 18-19 year olds living with their families or partners in this region and a lower proportion of 16 and 17 year olds.

However, in this region, compared to national figures, there was a larger percentage in lone tenancies (30% compared to 21%) and a lower percentage in supported housing (6% compared to 12%) and this applied to all age groups, other than that there were no under 16 year olds in lone tenancies either regionally or nationally. The overall figures for teenage mothers living in other types of housing were very similar in this region and nationally.

In summary:
The above monitoring data gives only a partial impression of the impact of Sure Start Plus; furthermore it is limited by inexactness of available statistical data and the extent of its coverage. Key points are:

- Of the total number of pregnant teenagers advised in January – June 2003 there was a smaller proportion advised under the age of 16 in this region than nationally and a higher proportion aged 16 – 17 years.
- Advisers have been coming into contact with pregnant teenagers earlier in their pregnancy.
- Of all those advised pregnancy outcomes showed that 89% gave birth and kept their child (January 2003 – June 2004).
- A total of 648 new support packages were put in place for pregnant teenagers and teenage mothers, 44 for teenage fathers/partners (January 2003 – June 2004).
- During the period January – June 2003 comparison with national data shows that the proportion of pregnant teenagers in contact with health services before the 14th week of pregnancy was lower in this region than nationally (12% compared to 37%) but increased subsequently.
- Despite an apparent decrease from January-June 2003 to January-June 2004 in the proportion of teenage mothers participating in education, training or employment in both under 16 yr olds and under 20 yr olds, figures are still higher than those for England overall.
- The number of teenage mothers accessing available childcare places has increased in this region similar to the national picture.
- The majority of teenage mothers who had been in contact with Sure Start Plus were living with their families or partners. Between January 2003 and June 2004 there has been an increase in the proportion of lone tenancies and supported accommodation and concomitant decrease in the proportion living with families or partners, chiefly 18 and 19 year olds.

Key findings

Findings from this evaluation describe the impact of Sure Start Plus i.e. five Programmes within this region, based upon interviews with key staff personnel, individual/groups of young people, observation of the programme in operation and documentary analysis of national and local Sure Start Plus material.

1. *Sure Start Plus Advisers provide one-to-one advice and group activities which are well-received by young women.*
    From the outset they have needed to carve out a role and have succeeded in providing an accessible, flexible service where they sometimes spend extensive time giving practical and emotional support to young people. They are enhancing developmental needs e.g. acquisition of skills, a feeling of self-worth and the development of appropriate relationships. Advisers tend to take a helpful, non-judgemental approach and are trusted by the young people, particularly with regard to confidentiality, an issue of central concern to pregnant teenagers/young parents. Advisers have developed a wide knowledge of relevant issues e.g. housing and financial benefits, community resources. One-to-one work with young people makes a real difference to their lives and has increased the number using all the Sure Start Plus programmes. Effects of intervention include young women being less socially isolated, gaining self-esteem and confidence and receiving benefits they are entitled to. Advisers help link with other projects and also run groups for young people. However they state that there is a difficulty in resolving tension between their organisational and professional role.

2. *Sure Start Plus Advisers have succeeded within each area in this region (N=5) in raising awareness of needs of young people among different agencies and networking with other professionals/agencies to obtain services for young people.*
    Advisers have received an increasing number of agency referrals and have developed links with a plethora of support agencies. Housing and financial benefit issues form a large part of their work. Liaison with housing agencies has been easier and more productive where there has been a named worker for young people with an interest in, and helpful attitude towards teenage pregnancy and the needs of young parents. Advisers work with

many local partners i.e. statutory service sector (health, education, social services) and voluntary sector (services concentrating on young people, families, mental health, community development, lone parents). Most common contacts were: Teenage Pregnancy Coordinators, Social Services, Sure Start, Reintegration Officers, Midwives, Health Visitors, GPs, Connexions, Housing Departments/Homeless Persons Unit, schools, Youth Services. Sure Start Plus programmes have raised awareness of needs of young parents among other professionals influencing the work of Midwives, Health Visitors, Reintegration Officers to produce a more focused and coordinated response.

3. *Sure Start Plus Programmes have helped to create additional services for young people.*

    Sure Start Plus funding has enhanced existing services in all five areas through funding or part-funding posts, thus creating new or additional opportunities such as the introduction of volunteer mentors (Authority S), additional childcare and increased availability of a lead midwife for teenage pregnancy (Authority N), additional support for training and education (Authority NS), for those in supported accommodation (Authority G) and for decision-making about the pregnancy (Authority SS). Programmes have been successful in setting up specific new services or developing existing ones e.g. setting up an effective referral system.

4. *Young fathers felt that there was a lack of information on parenting and a need for support; yet those who had obtained help from a young fathers' worker spoke positively of this.*

    The recommendation was that Sure Start Plus increases work with fathers with regard to parenting, their own needs and relationship with their partner and parents. The role of young fathers' parents has been shown to be important in their developing an early relationship with their child (Speak et al., 1997) and child-father relationships have been found to be particularly important for child adjustment in 'high-risk' families in which the mother had become pregnant as a teenager (Dunn et al., 2004). Quinton et al. (2002) found that the most important factor predicting men's postnatal involvement was the quality of their relationship with their partner rather than earlier family or social difficulties. However, the younger a father is when his baby is born, the less likely he is to remain in contact (ibid.).

5. *There was clear evidence from each Sure Start Plus Programme that there is insufficient current capacity to offer a service for all young people demanding it.*

    Findings from those interviewed suggest that the need for one-to-one support i.e. tackling problems, offering help/advice is greater than expected. Although those who received support spoke positively, anecdotal evidence suggests that there are many young people who would benefit from support of an Adviser.

Conclusion

The conclusions from this evaluation are presented in terms of implications of findings for policy/service development. The following is a glimpse of the national picture:

'The Sure Start Plus pilot projects have funding until April 2006. Evaluations are showing good results e.g. the overwhelming majority of local authorities have achieved downwards trends in their teen conception rates, sex education has improved and more young parents are returning to education (Social Science Research Unit, Institute of Education, 2004). The development and implementation of local programmes is going well and Sure Start Plus is seen to be having a substantial impact on some of its targets. It is also resulting in good joining-up of services across a range of partners including Teenage Pregnancy Coordinators and the education sector. Organisations have been seen to benefit from joined-up working by learning skills, sharing expertise, addressing joint targets, dividing labour and getting cross-referrals'. (Independent Advisory Group on Teenage Pregnancy, Annual Report 4.11: 2003/04)

1. In line with the recommendations of the Government White Paper: Choosing Health (DH, 2004:105), the National Service Framework for Children, Young People and Maternity Services (2004: Section 4), the Every Child Matters Outcomes Framework (DfES, 2004) and the Government Green Paper 'Youth Matters' (DfES, 2005a), the Teenage Pregnancy Strategy requires continued central and local government commitment and leadership. The

support needs of teenage parents need to be reflected in the Children and Young People's plans from April 2006 and action planned locally to meet the specific needs of this group of young people through mainstream service provision rather than the continuation of a pilot programme. Local teenage pregnancy strategies need to be in place which enable specialist advisers to network across agencies.

Findings of this study support broadly those of others e.g. Hanna, 2001, Rank, 2000 that teenage mothers need financial, educational and emotional support and that they are a fairly powerless group with high levels of disadvantage, social control and economic vulnerability. Young women's decisions whether to continue with their pregnancy tend to depend on the economic and social context of their lives e.g. existence of family support (Lee et al, 2004). Statham's study (2004) covering the effectiveness of services to support children in special circumstances and their families offers a number of suggestions on how support services can be made more accessible to 'hard-to-reach' groups including teenage parents. The evidence from her study correlates with our own findings e.g. the significance of young people having an advocate or champion, the beneficial effect of a link worker at the interface between agencies to facilitate communication and for family support services to have a respectful, non-stigmatising approach.

The young parents in this regional study valued positively the role of advisers particularly as some had expressed negative experiences of previous support services.

'IAG (Independent Advisory Group on Teenage Pregnancy) wants to express its concern about the future when Sure Start Plus ends. It is crucial that the many valuable elements of Sure Start Plus are retained and mainstreamed'. (op. cit 2003/4: 4.11)

Sure Start Plus mainly through its Advisers has helped to create specialist services for pregnant teenagers/young parents, by offering one-to-one advice, setting up referral systems and networking to change the role of mainstream services e.g. housing, midwifery, social services. Better information-sharing has helped service integration. The evidence from this study has demonstrated how Advisers are able to act as key figures in coordinating services and support for individual young parents.

Working interprofessionally will help to build integrated services as envisaged by the Labour Government Green Paper (Every Child Matters, DfES 2003) and the subsequent Children Act 2004. The Green Paper (op. cit, 2003) sets out the national framework for local change programmes to build services around the needs of children and young people 'to maximise opportunity and minimise risk' (DfES, 2004:2). Key proposals include:

> 'the improvement and integration of universal services (in early years settings, schools and the health services); the reconfiguration of services around the child and family in one place, for example, children's centres, extended schools and the bringing together of professionals in multi-disciplinary teams; enterprising leadership at all levels of the system and the development of a shared sense of responsibility across agencies for safeguarding children and assessing/planning service provision'. (DfES, 2004:4)

Findings from this study demonstrate that through working cross-sectorally Sure Start Plus Advisers have made significant steps in coordinating support packages for young parents.

2. All five Sure Start Plus Programmes in this region have managed to develop *young people-centred services* and 'a holistic approach to meeting the needs of children, young people and pregnant women', both highlighted as important in the National Service Framework for Children, Young People and Maternity Services (2004: 51, 16).

3. The skills learned/employed by a Sure Start Plus Adviser e.g. networking, advocacy might be used as a role model for others e.g. training/professional development, as working in an integrated way, crossing agency and professional boundaries is a future way forward (cf. Children Act 2004).

    In line with recommendations in the Common Core of Skills and Knowledge for the Children's Workforce (DfES, 2005b), skills in multi-agency working are singled out as being an important area of expertise in future training of all professionals to work in integrated services (op. cit. 18). Every Child Matters Guidance proposes that 'local leaders will want to give a strong focus to integrated workforce planning and development as part of their response to identified local needs' (2004: 3.18) and for staff 'to receive the necessary training and development to improve their professional practice .... to address the specific challenges which multi-disciplinary working poses for different professionals' (ibid. 3.23).

4. Evidence from evaluating the role of the Sure Start Plus Adviser in this region and from national sources (e.g. Independent Advisory Group on Teenage Pregnancy) suggests that Advisers would make a significant contribution to children and young people's services and therefore should be included in the Children and Young People's Plans which the Children Act requires local authorities and their partners to have developed by April 2006.

> 'All young parents should be supported by a designated personal adviser, following the success of the Sure Start Plus pilot programme: by including teenage parents in the Youth Green Paper as a group that needs targeted support, by ensuring continued funding of the existing Sure Start Plus pilots and mainstream funding of personal advisers in non-Sure Start Plus areas, including Sure Start programmes'. (Independent Advisory Group on Teenage Pregnancy, Annual Report 4.14:2003/04)

A Teenage Pregnancy Strategy needs to enhance an adviser/named person's capacity to network with relevant individuals based within different agencies who have an equivalent interest in or empathy towards supporting young parents and young people. This includes advocacy e.g. giving one-to-one support, and enhancing an adviser's role in working towards education and health targets.

Every Child Matters: Change for Children (DfES, 2004) states a commitment 'to ensure more young people stay on in education and training until they are 19', hence an adviser's ability to support this objective becomes increasingly relevant in planning future provision for young people. Evidence from the evaluation in each Regional area suggests that the Programme has helped to create additional provision e.g. crèche facilities, a young fathers worker, formation of groups/meeting places for young parents to connect with one another, gain knowledge and learn new skills. This extra provision makes a real difference to the lives of young people, yet relies partly upon social processes e.g. interagency working.

5. It is an advantage to hold a cross-agency database to assist the networking process, which would help create an identification, referral and tracking (IRT) system locally and work towards establishing outcome-focused integrated services.

   The Government is committed to providing effective services to children and young people with a focus on early intervention. A Common Assessment Framework (CAF) will help practitioners across universal and specialist services to assess children's needs earlier and more effectively. Included within the aims of the CAF are: to improve joint working and communication between practitioners by helping to embed a common language of assessment and a more consistent view as to the appropriate response; and to improve the coordination and consistency between assessments leading to fewer and shorter specialist assessments.

6. There is a need to resolve any tension arising from the Sure Start Plus Adviser performing both a strategic and operational role e.g. between contributing to planning services for young people and acting also as an advocate for individuals.

   It is difficult to envisage that a single person can perform both roles adequately and cover a relatively large geographical area. Therefore those who have responsibility for service planning need to reflect upon the scale of the task e.g. whether it is feasible to combine both roles and upon manpower requirements. As well as filling gaps in services Sure Start Plus was reported to have contributed to the identification of gaps e.g. specialist health visitors. Advisers (or equivalent) are needed to provide one-to-one support for young parents and to try and influence how mainstream services are delivered. Clearly mainstreaming of this role would enhance its effectiveness. Hence there is a need to consider capacity and how far it is possible to fulfil different aspects of the role, and how best to use Advisers' expertise and share these elements. Practice on the ground needs to inform strategic development of services for young parents and enhance joint work among agencies supporting them. Having close links with key services e.g. midwifery, social services suggests that the role of an adviser might be jointly-funded depending on local circumstances.

7. The evaluation demonstrated that Sure Start Plus has been developed differently in the five areas and that for future

development local needs and circumstances should inform planning of local teenage pregnancy services. Successful models of delivering support services have evolved, e.g. based on outreach / midwifery, including methods for co-ordinating different types of provision.

The role of the adviser has been developed in different ways across the five areas and has taken on different priorities according to local needs and circumstances. For example, in Authority G the primary focus of the adviser's work has been with pregnant teenagers who are then 'fed into' the service of the existing Young Women's Outreach Project in which she is based. Basing an adviser in an existing project for young women/young parents (Authority G, Authority S) has enabled access to a range of additional services and opportunities on site and continuity of service, as well as enhancing the support provided by these services. Sure Start Plus advisers have also provided holistic support through group work (as well as individual activity) and have undertaken extensive outreach work, e.g. running groups in Sure Start or family centres (particularly in Authority N, Authority S and Authority NS). There is evidence of Sure Start Plus taking specific steps to reshape or influence mainstream services e.g. through the reorganisation of midwifery posts in Authority NS and through the more strategic role undertaken by the Sure Start Plus Adviser in Authority SS, supported through outside funding for additional support work.

Recent guidance relating to the Teenage Pregnancy Strategy (DfES, 2006) notes the key benefits of a dedicated personal adviser for teenage parents as identified in the national evaluation of the Sure Start Plus pilot programme, notably in increased participation in education. The guidance notes its expectations that all areas should provide the successful ingredients of Sure Start Plus through Children's Centres and the targeted support in Children and Young People's Plans. It also raises the issue of ensuring that high quality support is offered to all parents under eighteen who cannot live with their own parents, through placements in a dedicated housing project or through an 'intensive floating support package, co-ordinated by a lead professional' (DfES, 2006:31), the content and length of the package being tailored to the individual needs of the young parent. The guidance also notes the need to do further work to assess what support is needed by young fathers so that they can play a positive role in their child's upbringing. This evaluation of the work of Sure Start Plus in five local authorities shows ways in which support has been successfully implemented by advisers working individually and in collaboration with other agencies, which will be of relevance to the future development of services for pregnant teenagers and young parents.

Appendix one:
Aim, objectives and targets of Sure Start Plus

Aim

Sure Start Plus aims to reduce the risk of long term social exclusion and poverty from teenage pregnancy.

Objective 1: Improving health

- In particular, by working with relevant agencies and organisations, to ensure that all teenagers, especially those who are pregnant, have access to appropriate health care, including access to contraception advice.
- By ensuring pregnant teenagers have access to comprehensive, sensitive and appropriate advice and counselling in the early stages of pregnancy so they are able to make informed decisions, including whether to continue with the pregnancy, adoption or abortion, according to their individual circumstances.
- By supporting teenage mothers and fathers in caring for their children to promote healthy development before and after birth.

Target

- Increase in numbers of pregnant teenagers in contact with health services by 14th week of pregnancy;
- Reduction in numbers of pregnant teenagers/teenage mothers smoking during and after pregnancy.

Objective 2: improving learning of teenage mothers and fathers and their children

- By ensuring teenage mothers and fathers return to or continue in education or training; by encouraging stimulating and enjoyable play for, and improving the language skills of, the children of teenage parents; and through early identification and support of children with learning difficulties.

Target

Increase in percentage of teenage mothers participating in education and obtaining qualification at NVQ Level 1 or above.

Objective 3: strengthening families and communities

By helping teenage mothers and fathers to be effective parents by involving both their families in supporting them and their grandchild.

Target

to increase the percentage of teenage mothers who report involvement of their family, father of their child, or partner in their child's upbringing.

Objective 4: improving social and emotional well-being

By supporting early bonding between teenage mothers and fathers and their children, by helping teenage parent families to function and by enabling the early identification and support of children with emotional and behavioural difficulties.

Target

increased identification and appropriate support of all teenage mothers with post-natal depression.

Appendix two: Conception data

Total under 18 conception data for England and this region, 1998-2003

	1998		1999		2000		2001		2002		2003	
	Number	Rate	Number	Rate	Number	Rate	Number	Rate	Number	Rate	Number	Rate
England	41,089	46.6	39,247	44.8	38,699	43.6	38,439	42.5	39,350	42.6	39,560	42.1
This Region	1,203	59.0	1,165	57.3	1,121	55.1	1,073	52.0	1,128	53.7	1,168	55.2
Authority G	199	57.1	182	50.7	202	56.8	152	42.3	158	44.3	174	48.3
Authority N	258	52.8	287	60.3	268	57.9	267	58.2	283	59.7	268	55.3
Authority NS	204	58.4	174	49.9	190	54.4	190	53.2	198	55.3	189	52.0
Authority SS	185	64.9	165	56.8	171	57.3	168	53.6	169	51.7	175	53.5
Authority S	357	63.1	357	63.6	290	51.0	296	51.6	320	54.9	362	62.5

Under 18 = Aged 17 and under
Rates are per 1000 female population aged 15-17

Under 16 conception data for England and this region, 1998-2002

	1998		1999		2000		2001		2002	
	Number	Rate	Number	Rate	Number	Rate	Number	Rate	Number	Rate
England	7,885	8.9	7,408	8.2	7,620	8.3	7,407	8.0	7,395	7.9
Authority G	43	12.2	32	9.0	43	12.3	32	9.1	19	5.4
Authority N	50	10.4	44	9.5	58	12.4	52	10.8	57	11.9
Authority NS	39	11.2	28	7.9	37	10.4	33	9.2	34	9.3
Authority SS	28	9.3	34	10.7	29	8.8	43	13.1	28	8.8
Authority S	79	13.8	72	12.5	71	12.1	66	11.4	56	9.9

(Sources: Office for National Statistics and Teenage Pregnancy Unit, www.teenagepregnancyunit.gov.uk)

Data from above two tables used to show numbers of conceptions divided into two age groups under 18, England and this region, 1998-2002

	1998			1999			2000			2001			2002		
	Total	<16	16-17	Total	<16	16-17	Total	<16	16-17	Total	<16	16-17	Total	<16	16-17
England	41,089	7,885	33,204	39,247	7,408	31,839	38,699	7,620	31,079	38,439	7,407	31,043	39,350	7,395	31,955
Authority G	199	43	156	182	32	150	202	43	159	152	32	120	158	19	139
Authority N	258	50	208	287	44	243	268	58	210	267	52	215	283	57	226
Authority NS	204	39	165	174	28	146	190	37	153	190	33	157	198	34	164
Authority SS	185	28	157	165	34	131	171	29	142	168	43	125	169	28	141
Authority S	357	79	278	357	72	285	290	71	219	296	66	230	320	56	264

Appendix three: Comparison of regional and national figures Jan.-June 2003

(National figures from data submitted to National Evaluation Team by 31 of the 35 Sure Start Plus Programmes, source: Rosato et al., Jan. 2004, Sure Start Plus National Evaluation, Summary of Interim Findings)

	National	This region
Total number of pregnant teenagers advised	1912	113
16-17 year olds	76%	84%
Under 16	24%	16%
Pregnancy outcomes recorded	1338	145
Birth: kept child	58%	76%
Abortions	11%	3%
Miscarriages	4%	0%
Birth: adoption	<1%	0%
Stillbirths	<1%	<1%
Unknown	22%	20%
Support packages in place for pregnant teenagers, teenage mothers and teenage fathers (new and existing)	2672	306
• Proportion already existing	37%	31%
• Proportion newly set up	63%	69%
o 18-19 year olds	28%	23%
o 16 and 17 year olds	59%	66%
o Under 16 years old	13%	11%
• Pregnant teenagers/teenage mothers	93%	95%
• Teenage fathers	7%	5%
Ethnicity		
White	84%[1]	99%[2]
Black	8%[3]	0%
Mixed	5%[4]	<1%[5]
Asian	1%	<1%
Chinese	0%	0%
Other ethnic group	2%	0%
Ethnicity unknown	297	0
Contact with health services		
Before 14th week of pregnancy	37%	12%

At or after 14th week	49%	69%
Point of pregnancy unknown	14%	19%

Smoking
No. for whom data available	1026	176
No. for whom data unavailable	800	172
Proportion smoking before birth	63%	62.5%
Proportion smoking after birth	27%	37.5%

Breastfeeding
No. for whom data available	199	13
No. for whom data unavailable	411	76
Breastfeeding before 6 weeks	68%	77%
Breastfeeding after 6 weeks	32%	23%

Participation in education, training and employment
No. for whom data available	1302	176
• Proportion participating	52%	69%
• Proportion not participating	48%	31%
o Under 16 participating	81%	79%
o Under 16 not participating	19%	21%
o 16-19 year olds participating	47%	67%
o 16-19 year olds not participating	53%	33%
• NVQ Level 1: under 20	245	45
16-19 year olds	86%	84%
Under 16	14%	16%

Childcare
Total number of places accessed by under 20s	410	78
16-19 year olds	86%	83%
Under 16	14%	17%
Proportion of total by age of child:		
Under 1	58%	61%
1-2	31%	26%
Over 2	11%	13%

Housing
With family/partner	54%	52%
Lone tenancies	21%	30%
Supported housing	12%	6%
Other types of housing	13%	12%
Under 16: With family/partner	85%	100%
Lone tenancies	0%	0%
Supported housing	8%	0%

Other	7%	0%
Under 18: With family/partner	57%	46%
Lone tenancies	21%	30%
Supported housing	13%	8%
Other	9%	16%
18-19: With family/partner	35%	54%
Lone tenancies	30%	44%
Supported housing	13%	2%
Other	22%	0%

Notes:

1. Almost all White British

2. All White British

3. Almost all Black or Black British Caribbean

4. Almost all Mixed White/Black Caribbean

5. Mixed white/other

Appendix four: Resident population data

Resident population of the local authorities in this region, and percentage of under 16 year olds and 16-19 year olds, as measured in the 2001 Census

	Total resident population	% Under 16	% 16 to 19
England and Wales	52, 041, 916	20.2	4.9
Authority G	191, 151	19.3	4.9
Authority N	259, 536	18.8	5.8
Authority NS	191, 659	19.2	4.5
Authority SS	152, 785	20.3	4.9
Authority S	280, 807	20.0	5.4

(source: ONS, 2001 Census)

Percentage of resident population in ethnic groups

	England	Authority G	N	NS	SS	S
White	90.9	98.4	93.1	98.1	97.3	98.1
of which White Irish	1.3	0.3	0.7	0.3	0.2	0.3
Mixed	1.3	0.4	0.9	0.5	0.7	0.4
Asian or Asian British	4.6	0.7	4.4	0.8	1.6	1.0
Indian	2.1	0.3	1.2	0.3	0.6	0.3
Pakistani	1.4	0.3	1.9	0.1	0.2	0.1
Bangladeshi	0.6	0.1	1.0	0.3	0.5	0.4
Other Asian	0.5	0.1	0.3	0.1	0.2	0.1
Black or Black British	2.1	0.2	0.4	0.2	0.2	0.1
Caribbean	1.1	0.0	0.0	0.0	0.0	0.0
African	1.0	0.1	0.3	0.1	0.1	0.1
Other Black	0.2	0.0	0.0	0.0	0.0	0.0
Chinese/ other ethnic group	0.9	0.4	1.2	0.5	0.3	0.3

(source: ONS, 2001 Census)

Appendix five: Interview questions for professionals regarding the impact of Sure Start Plus

Please could you describe how you (and/or your organisation) have worked with Sure Start Plus? (e.g. providing new services, funding, training, referrals, joint work; including frequency of contact)

What impact has this had on your service? (e.g. adding value, filling gaps, improving co-ordination)

Has being involved in Sure Start Plus brought about any changes in your own service?
Can you give me some examples?

Going beyond your own service, do you think Sure Start Plus has had any impact on other services for pregnant teenagers and teenage parents in your area?
Can you give me some examples?

How do you think your involvement with Sure Start Plus has affected the experience of pregnant teenagers and teenage parents?
Can you give me some examples to illustrate this?

Have you learned anything from working with Sure Start Plus that helps you in your own role?

Has your own role changed as a result of Sure Start Plus?

What are your general views about the aims of Sure Start Plus?

How do you think the Programme might be improved?

When Sure Start Plus funding finishes in April 2006 what elements of the work are likely to continue in relationship to your organisation? (e.g. further joint work, setting new plans)

7
Summary and conclusion

INTRODUCTION

From Sure Start local programmes to children's centres

In 1997 the Labour Government initiated a Cross Departmental Review of Services for Young Children which led to the creation of the national Sure Start programme in 1998. Sure Start was targeted at children under four years old and their families in areas of need and was a cornerstone of the government's strategy to end child poverty by 2020 and tackle social exclusion. Sure Start was founded on evidence that early, comprehensive and sustained support for children can help them succeed at school and help reduce crime, unemployment and teenage pregnancy and other social and economic problems (DfES, 2002). Local programmes aimed to transform the life chances of young children through better access to family support, health services and early education, and thereby break the cycle of deprivation for this generation of young children (ibid.). Sixty 'trailblazer' Sure Start local programmes (SSLPs) were set up in 1999 in areas where there were known to be high proportions of children living in poverty. 260 were underway by 2001 and by 2004 there were 524 local programmes in existence.

The following national objectives were originally set for local programmes:

- Improving Social and Emotional Development
- Improving Health
- Improving Children's Ability to Learn
- Strengthening Families and Communities.

An additional objective was later set (and became objective 1):

- Improving the availability, accessibility, affordability and quality of childcare.

Local programmes were also expected to develop local targets that were more specific to the needs of families living in the local area.

All SSLPs were expected to provide the following core services:

- Outreach and home visiting
- Support for families and parents
- Support for good quality play, learning and childcare experiences for children
- Primary and community health care and advice about child health and development and family health
- Support for people with special needs, and helping access to specialised services

Each SSLP aimed to improve existing services and create new ones as needed; however, in contrast to more narrowly delivered and highly specified early interventions, this was 'without specification of how services are to be changed or what exactly is to be delivered' (NESS, 2005b). In 2003, as part of the Every Child Matters Green Paper, the Government announced plans to create a Sure Start Children's Centre in the 30% most deprived wards in England. The centres combine early education and childcare, family support, employment advice, and health services.

In December 2004 the ten-year strategy for childcare set a target for a children's centre for every community (3, 500 centres in total) by 2010. Most of the first children's centres have been developed from existing facilities for improving services for young children including SSLPs. The first phase (2004 to March 2006) focused on establishing centres in the 20% most disadvantaged areas in the country, based on the Index of Multiple Deprivation (2000) and the second phase (2006-2008) is focusing on the 30% most disadvantaged areas, as defined by Super Output Areas. SSLPs received funds directly from the Department for Education and Skills. From 1 April 2006, the Department has provided funds to local authorities for children's centres. It sets requirements for the minimum services to be provided, but local authorities are responsible for achievement of the programme's aims. Core services that children's centres in the 20-30% most disadvantaged areas must provide (the 'core offer') are:

- Integrated childcare and early learning
- Child and family health services, including ante-natal care
- Outreach and family support services
- Links with Jobcentre Plus for training and employment advice
- Support for childminders
- Support for children and parents with special need

Children's Centres aim to improve the child outcomes set out in Every Child Matters: Be Healthy, Stay Safe, Enjoy and Achieve, Make a Positive Contribution and Achieve Economic Well-Being as well as work towards nationally set aims and indicators.

CONTRIBUTION OF THE PROGRAMMES TO THE EVERY CHILD MATTERS OUTCOMES FRAMEWORK

Introduction

This section describes how these locally evaluated programmes are working towards the five Every Child Matters Outcomes: Be Healthy, Stay Safe, Enjoy and Achieve, Make a Positive Contribution, and Achieve Economic Well-being. This is being achieved through new services that have been provided in the area and through enhancing existing service provision. Information was collected from each programme area by written questionnaire. This section also highlights some key achievements with regard to each ECM outcome over the 21-month period April 2005 to December 2006, drawn from documentary analysis of the Programme Managers' quarterly Report and Performance Review.

The five Every Child Matters outcome areas

BE HEALTHY

The Programmes provide a number of key services that contribute to the Every Child Matters (ECM) outcome: Be Healthy. These relate to:

- Pre-natal support
- Postnatal support
- Smoking Cessation
- Breastfeeding support
- Parenting and Family support
- Mental health support
- Services for disabled children
- Children's health

EXAMPLES OF SUPPORT PROVIDED BY THE KEY SERVICES:

Pre-natal support

Programmes have enhanced services in the pre-natal period through the provision of group support (Bumps to Babes, also provided in the home) and promotional sessions. Links with midwifery services have enabled more local care (midwives deliver antenatal classes; offer swimming classes at a local comprehensive school for pregnant women citywide), and increased training (for example, breastfeeding training offered by midwives across one area).

Postnatal support

The Programmes have introduced a number of new services and extended the availability and accessibility of some services. Training opportunities have enhanced services offered by health visitors. A new protocol has been developed to help identification of need

(Vulnerability Assessment Framework [HV]). Programmes have introduced Infant Massage classes and extended them into a number of outreach areas. The range of support available in the home has been increased, e.g. Infant massage, Family Nurturing, Solihull approach (citywide). The employment of extra nursery nurses has contributed to the increase in the range of services available, both through group activity and in the home (e.g. support with sleep, behaviour, diet, play and stimulation). The employment of health care assistants has also contributed to home support (e.g. promotion/sustaining of breastfeeding, promotion of smoking cessation service). The provision of local drop-in baby clinics has increased the availability and accessibility of this service. Individual programmes have introduced specific targeted groups in their area following identification of gaps in services (Stay and Play Babes, 0-1 year olds) or as a result of links with other agencies e.g. the Bright Stars group for young parents run in collaboration with Connexions.

Smoking Cessation

Health visitors offer smoking cessation support in the home and through drop-in smoking cessation clinics. Pregnant women are referred to the Specialist Smoking Cessation Service – Pregnancy, which also offers support in the home.

Breastfeeding support

New services to empower mothers to initiate and sustain breastfeeding are the La Leche group/Bosom Buddies, which provide peer support, supported by health staff.

Parenting and Family support

New courses have been introduced, e.g. Family Nurturing and Common Childhood Illnesses (a research based course developed by the Community Paediatrician, who trained local health visitors and nursery nurses as facilitators, and which has now been extended into outreach areas. One 2 One Family support is a new service provided by health care assistants and family support workers aiming to improve coping strategies. A Dental health advisor has provided training to all staff and 'brushing for life' packs are distributed to families. Increased local support is available for families with regard to general development and behaviour, and training has enhanced the skills of the health team. The paediatrician and Sure Start dietician provide research-based training to staff on nutrition and programmes provide weaning cups and bowls for families. Soft play sessions are included as part of other group activities to encourage an active lifestyle and reduce obesity in children.

Mental health support

The Parent and Child Psychology Service can be accessed through Request for Services. This offers locality based support and advice to families, including home visits. Psychologists based in local programmes have, in addition, offered support supervision to Sure Start staff. A CPN was funded by, and located in, one SSLP providing a new service working in new ways, reaching families who would not normally reach the criteria for mainstream services.

Services for disabled children

Portage training and supervision has been provided and availability of the Portage service has been extended enabling a more rapid response. The service provides locality based intensive home visits. New sensory play sessions have been introduced for children with complex needs. Hydrotherapy pool sessions are run twice a week, and soft play sessions are provided in school holidays for children with complex needs.

Children's health

The Community Paediatrician receives referrals from any team member and sees children in children's centres or in their own home in an attempt to help those families who would not usually access mainstream health services. In one Sure Start area in 2005 there was only a 4% Failure to Attend rate, which compares with a rate of over 20% at Hospital Outpatients. The Paediatrician also provides evidence based training to all staff to ensure consistency of correct advice to parents, for example Community Nursing staff were trained in the current guidelines on weaning.

Key findings from evaluation of infant massage at one SSLP

Classes have helped support the bonding process; massage provides 'quality time' for mother and child, which can encourage the development of a good relationship.

Classes have helped develop communication between mother and baby, e.g. recognising and responding to the baby's expressed needs and signals.

Massage was reported to have had a positive impact on babies' well-being and to increase relaxation for mother and child.

Learning massage techniques provides parents with a new skill and an additional way of responding to babies' needs, thus promoting a sense of parental competence.

The classes take place in a relaxed, informal setting, which also provides opportunities for socialisation for carers and babies, and valued peer support with regard to parenting; also opportunities for valued informal support from a health professional regarding babies' health and development.

Infant massage classes are providing a positive (often initial) introduction to Sure Start, and are providing information on other Sure Start services, of which there has been a high take-up rate. In some cases families would not otherwise have used these services, and have been encouraged to do so through starting with other mothers they had got to know whilst participating in the course.

The Programme has since followed up recommendations in the report to increase take up following initial expression of interest by parents, by group leaders telephoning prior to commencement of a course and by exploring whether community parents could accompany new parents and babies. As not all participants were completing the course they are now offered one to one sessions in the home.

Key findings from evaluation of Stay and Play Babes group within one SSLP

Stay and Play Babes is a 'group activity for 0-1 year olds encouraging play and stimulation for mother and child' and 'to offer advice, support, and empower parents in developing a close bond with their child through play and peer support'.

The purpose of this evaluation was to ascertain what impact Stay and Play Babes was having on children's development and how it was supporting parents. Parents reported positively on the impact of the group on their child's development (e.g. social and physical skills) and also on their relationship with their baby. The staff are supporting parents through providing information and advice themselves and through visiting speakers, and responding to queries in an informal, non-threatening environment; through increasing confidence; through providing opportunities for peer support and the formation of friendships; through encouraging personal development; through responding to and encouraging parents' ideas (walking group) and through easing transition to toddler groups. The group is supporting learning in the home through providing age appropriate activities that are followed up at home and providing information on other services and activities that are taken up by some families, e.g. the Toy Library and other library services.

Key findings from an integrated model of health visiting within one SSLP

This evaluation examined the 'Sure Start for All' model for health visiting, which aimed to adopt a collaborative, integrated and inclusive approach in order to ensure equal access to services, equal workload for all health visitors, and the opportunity for all staff to deliver the Sure Start and Public Health agendas.

Strengths of the Integrated Health Visiting model included:

Reduced caseloads for all health visitors in the Coaldown area, through the provision of a larger workforce, have contributed to their capacity to deliver the Sure Start and Public Health agendas.

Working as a team across the area has avoided a 'postcode lottery' for Sure Start services and ensured a more inclusive approach. Links formed with outreach venues, the provision of crèche facilities and transport have increased the availability and accessibility of local support. Targeted services have been provided for specific groups such as young parents. The health visiting team provide multiple forms of service delivery (outreach, individual support in the home, and groups). The activities place emphasis on health promotion, prevention and intervention for medical or social reasons. Staff reported that they have become able to adopt a more family and community oriented model and a more 'holistic' approach to working with families.

The diversity of the services available within and beyond the health visiting team has enabled the team to offer greater choice to families and a more varied approach according to needs and circumstances.

Additional training has increased knowledge, skills and expertise and led to a more diverse workforce. Groups of staff have developed expertise in particular areas (e.g. Infant Massage) and are able to share ideas and good practice. The increased availability of 'cover' through the larger workforce and the training of several staff in the same area of expertise have contributed to the smooth running of services (e.g. delivering courses).

The employment of nursery nurses has made a positive contribution to the working of the team.

Joint working between mainstream and Sure Start health visiting teams ensures good knowledge of Sure Start services and work with families is facilitated by ease of referral both through ongoing contact with a range of professionals and through Request for Services.

The networks formed with other agencies have led to joint initiation, planning and delivery of groups targeted at specific groups (e.g. fathers, young parents), have enhanced input into groups (e.g. Stay and Play) and have made the team better informed. Links with other agencies (e.g. a domestic violence support project, Barnardos and community access points) are also enabling sharing of expertise and access to venues that are better used by the community.

Representatives from other agencies reported ease of access to Sure Start, improvement in communication and co-ordination and impacts on their service delivery and work with families.

Staff reported satisfaction with their work, through the ability to offer a wider range of resources to families, greater integration with the community and other agencies and improved communication, greater opportunities for professional development, and opportunities and support to try new ideas. Improvements in job satisfaction and professional development are important as they have implications for the retention and recruitment of staff.

Parents have generally been well informed about Sure Start health and family support services. The majority found the services of the health visiting team easy to access, relevant and useful. They had benefited from practical support, general and specific advice and from social opportunities for themselves and their children, making friends and sharing ideas, increased relaxation, confidence and ways of coping, and bonding with their child.

STAY SAFE

Key services that are contributing to the ECM outcome 'Stay Safe' are:

- Request for Services (multi-agency approach to provide support packages for families)
- Domestic Violence Support
- Safety Schemes
- Family Support

EXAMPLES OF SUPPORT PROVIDED BY THE KEY SERVICES:

Request for Services

Regular multi-agency meetings are held to plan and review work with families in a way that improves interagency working and communication. The system allows for a rapid response that supports families using a holistic approach.

Domestic Violence Support

Two domestic violence outreach workers have been employed in two Sure Start areas and provide emotional and practical support for families experiencing domestic abuse. Support is provided with regard to housing, the legal system, safety planning, and mental health services. This is a service that targets hard to reach families. A weekly drop-in has recently been set up at a community venue to create an informal setting in which people can access support and be signposted to appropriate agencies. In addition, they deliver the Choices programme, which provides women with the opportunity to meet up weekly and offers support in a group setting. It explores a variety of issues relating to domestic violence and isolation and has guest speakers from legal services, the police service and mental health. It also aims to help women understand the effect of domestic violence on children. In addition to this, a Children's Support Worker, part-funded by Sure Start, does outreach work with children in the area on issues of abuse, providing a safe environment for children to explore their feelings and plan for their safety. An Advice Circle, has been established in partnership with the local domestic violence support project and the legal services commission, and operates weekly from a community venue, providing free legal advice and support for families experiencing domestic abuse.

Safety Scheme

Safety equipment schemes operate in all programme areas, providing equipment and advice and aiming to reduce childhood accidents. The schemes also provide sun protection cream. Safety Matters courses have been run in Early Years settings to raise awareness of accidents with young children in nursery classes, as well as being run for parents. 'Whoops' training is a new service delivered through the Common Childhood Illnesses course that aims to raise awareness of childhood accidents.

Family Support

Flexible funded childcare places are available to parents requesting short-term childcare, subject to meeting clearly defined criteria, and there is a clear pathway to request these places through Request for Services. One 2 One Family Support aims to alleviate parental stress and postnatal depression and reduce risks to children and is available via multi-agency teams.

Key Findings from evaluation:
The role and contribution of the domestic violence outreach workers

Between December 2003 and December 2006 the domestic violence outreach workers worked with 255 women and 405 children. There has been some flexibility to support women with no children or with children over four years of age. They have also worked with 107 women and 162 children from other Sure Start programmes. The Children's Services Manager has worked with children from 30 families.

Through both individual and group work, women have been supported to develop ways of coping and to gain greater understanding of their situation, including the effects of domestic violence on children, and make choices about their future. The majority of women interviewed (total *n*=9) reported that working with a DVOW had increased their knowledge of what other services provide, and a small number commented that it was easier to access other services due to a change in their attitude as a result of the support received (e.g. feeling less ashamed or embarrassed). The majority also reported that working with a DVOW had made a difference to how they viewed relationships, and that they felt more enabled to keep themselves safe. All would recommend the service to others in a similar situation and women commented particularly on the confidentiality, accessibility and non-judgmental nature of the service. Women who had attended the Choices group (*n*=3) found it helpful and supportive to be with people who had been in a similar situation to themselves, welcomed the emotional and practical support provided through the group and noted similar outcomes.

There have been several benefits to locating the service within Sure Start. These include the ability to offer a non-stigmatising approach, the ability to offer services locally with a good choice of timing and location of support and opportunities to access crèche facilities, and knowledge and experience of the service being passed by word of mouth in the local area. There has been quicker and easier access to the DVOWs, who have also been able to access other Sure Start services for their clients. There has been increased information sharing between different disciplines, both informally and through Request for Services. The shared base has enabled easier communication and networking between DVOWs and Sure Start staff, making liaison and monitoring of work easier. DVOWs and other Sure Start staff have benefited from learning about each other's roles and there has been opportunity and greater willingness to discuss domestic violence. It was felt that understanding and promotion of, and referral to, the service had taken longer to develop in one programme than the other, but that the situation was improving over time. It was noted that there were now strong policies and procedures with regard to domestic violence. There were some disadvantages, such as opening times, lack of privacy (e.g. for confidential and sensitive phone calls) in one programme, and limitations regarding geographical boundaries and target population, although Sure Start's flexibility in this matter was appreciated.

Interprofessional working between the DVOWs and other members of the Sure Start team has involved shared learning, the ability to offer a more integrated service and a more holistic approach, opportunities for mutual referral and for information sharing and joint work. Working within two agencies has provided additional support for the outreach workers, whose work could be isolating, although there were some challenges, such as dealing with dual policies, procedures and bureaucracies, and differences in training objectives, which were being addressed.

The DVOWs were considered to have made a positive contribution to the work of other agencies through their extensive specialist knowledge, through contributions to meetings (e.g. core groups, Child Protection review meetings) and keeping agencies informed about changes in family situations; through their willingness to discuss cases informally and give their opinion on whether they or other Sure Start services or other agencies were the most appropriate to become involved with the family.

All representatives from other agencies (n=5) reported finding the service accessible, both in terms of making contact and in terms of being proactive in providing information for themselves and their clients, e.g. regarding appropriate services.

The work of the DVOWs has impacted on other services through e.g. providing an easily identifiable and easily accessible extra support, impacting on Child Protection work, improving multi-agency working and continuity of services, providing clearer routes to information and better signposting, and increasing their knowledge of domestic violence issues.

The most commonly noted way in which domestic violence support in the area could be improved was through the employment of a male worker to work with male perpetrators and thus provide a more comprehensive service.

ENJOY AND ACHIEVE

Key services that are contributing to the ECM outcome 'Enjoy and Achieve' are:

- Speech and language support
- Family learning activities
- Childminding support
- Toddler group support
- Toy Library

- Support to Early Years settings
- Services for disabled children

EXAMPLES OF SUPPORT PROVIDED BY THE KEY SERVICES:

Speech and language support

A training package has been developed and delivered to Sure Start staff and community to raise awareness of and identify language delay and thus enable earlier detection and earlier and quicker intervention, and reduce the need for speech therapy. One cluster area employs a speech and language nursery nurse and training has also enhanced the skills of health visitors and other nursery nurses providing support. In some cases, Chatterbox bags are introduced into the home by health visitors to promote the development of communication skills with the support of an adult taking an active role in using the resource bags with the child. Group support is also provided for children who have speech and language delay in an informal setting. Chatterbox sessions (group work with children and parents working with Chatterbox bags) have been run at a local public library (now with input from a Health nursery nurse) as well as from the Children's Centre.

Family learning activities

Programmes have introduced a large number of family learning activities into their areas to promote children's development with involvement from their parents/carers.

Talk Talk

Talk Talk and Chatterbox bags are provided for home loan in local nurseries and schools (Chatterbox also in toddler groups), and more settings have been included over time.

Busy Bodies and soft play

Busy Bodies and soft play aims to help children become social and effective communicators, promote skills in listening and responding appropriately to language and instructions, and respond creatively to the world around them by connecting ideas.

Time for Rhyme

Time for Rhyme sessions aim to develop a bond between parents/carers and children through action rhymes and nursery rhymes, to promote listening and responding skills and help the child become a confident and competent language user. In one area the service has been extended to support a local school with a high number of children from a minority ethnic community, working alongside an interpreter to provide support for children whose first language is not English. The group is also run in a local library as well as the Children's Centre to support the extended community. The programme has also purchased books and resources to provide a loan service to parents and carers.

Messy Play sessions

Messy Play sessions are a new activity designed to encourage creative, mathematical, intellectual, social and emotional development and develop language skills. Staff training on Birth to Three Matters has influenced the planning and evaluation of these sessions to enhance service delivery.

Story Time

In one SSLP, story time sessions are delivered at toddler groups with the aim of signposting parents to the story time sessions at the public library. In another SSLP, story time sessions are delivered in the local library to nursery classes/schools. In Folde the service is offered by the Sure Start Early Years Librarian in the local Children's Centre, three local libraries and 14 local schools/nurseries, and the service has been increased to include the extended area. The Early Years Librarian also works with an interpreter in a nursery with a high number of children from a minority ethnic community.

Bookstart (and Bookstart Plus)

Bookstart (and Bookstart Plus) is a national project that aims to encourage parents to share books with children from an early age to help develop language and listening skills and to foster a love of books. The packs have been given to parents at the child's hearing test, but as this test is now to be carried out neo-natally, health visitors will give them out at the 9-month check in future. This will potentially increase uptake of the service. Bookstart Plus packs, given out at the 2-year check, now contain a £1 voucher for certain bookshops to encourage parents/carers to purchase books to read to their children from a young age. In Folde a new service, Bookstart Treasure Boxes, is being delivered directly to education nurseries, supported by the Early Years Librarian when requested.

Childminding support:

Programmes use childminders to look after children from Request for Services as a means of offering choice and flexibility of childcare for the families requesting provision. One SSLP is working with the Childminding Development Officer to develop a drop-in group/ session.

Toddler group support

In two areas there have been monthly development visits to toddler groups, including activity sessions, to help ensure sustainability through the provision of advice/network meetings and resources; to make the groups aware of the importance of keeping children safe, setting up stimulating environments for children; and to support adults in the provision of play activities that stimulate and challenge children, using Birth to Three Matters as guidance. Staff training in all programmes in Birth to Three Matters and from SALT has enhanced service delivery. Training in Birth to Three Matters was provided to toddler group leaders via the Toddler Group Network.

Toy Library

Toy Libraries have been established and extended in all areas, and attempts have been made to improve access. In one SSLP the Toy Library has been relocated to a more prominent position close to the entrance to the building and the opening hours have been extended, leading to an increase in membership figures. In addition, craft materials are now available to purchase in small quantities and at reasonable prices. In the Coaldown area Toy Library users can now access provision across the three sites and outreach sessions are provided.

Key findings from Talk Talk evaluation (summary of two evaluations)

In the academic year 2004-2005, take up rates of Talk Talk home loan Bags in the six schools in one area were all over 75%, ranging from 75.86% to 95.55%. In the five schools in the other Sure Start area they were 86% and over, and in three schools there was 100% take-up.

Whilst some staff in one school in one area reported that they would have welcomed the money spent on the Talk Talk project to have gone directly into the school to enable them to decide how to spend it, the parents, children's first educators, have clearly supported the scheme and found it beneficial.

Whilst acknowledging that children's language is likely to have matured over the year and to have benefited from family, school and community influences, Talk Talk does appear to have contributed to children's language development. This is demonstrated through child assessments showing increased word recognition and through parental reports. For example, a large majority of families felt that Talk Talk had helped their child to learn new words and use longer sentences; to listen, concentrate and follow instructions; to talk and ask questions about pictures in books; ask questions about the story or facts in the books; retell the events in a story, and to talk about activities when playing. The activities provided in the bags (e.g. jigsaws, activity sheets) are also contributing to the development/practice of other skills such as shape and colour recognition, counting and number recognition and coordination/fine motor skills.

The Talk Talk scheme has contributed to home learning through increasing the amount of time families spend with their child on reading and doing activities together; facilitating conversations on the wide range of topics covered by the bags; increasing families' knowledge of suitable books and activities for their child's age, and providing ideas for activities that are then carried out in the home.

Talk Talk is enabling Sure Start to reach families who are not using other Sure Start services, and therefore providing a means of helping the Programme to work towards its objective of improving learning by promoting high quality care and education which supports children's development and early education.

Both programmes have been working towards recommendations of the reports to ensure age appropriate activities, explore the introduction of dual language books, in particular Bengali, to explore how communication can be improved between family learning assistants, parents and/or children and nursery staff; to review monitoring systems to assist the ongoing development of the service; to address the lower uptake of Bags in some schools in one area e.g. through introductory coffee mornings, and to develop greater communication with schools and parents regarding individual children's needs and interests and to increase familiarity with the contents of the Bags.

Key findings from evaluation report:
The impact of Sure Start on toddler group provision in one SSLP

Through working together with toddler groups, Sure Start is increasing the availability and accessibility of a wider range of activities for children planned to develop skills in line with Birth to Three Matters and to promote shared activity with parents/carers, and of services to support children's learning (e.g. library books, Toy Library, Chatterbox), and, in some cases, children's health and safety (Health Visitor drop-in, access to safety equipment). Regular visits to the groups are enabling easier access to advice and information for parents.

As well as providing a pack to support the running of the group, Sure Start, through the Early Years Practice Development Officer (EYPDO), is providing easier access to advice and support for toddler group leaders in running and resourcing their group, e.g. through support for accessing grants for new equipment. This is potentially contributing to the sustainability of toddler groups, as is the promotion of toddler groups undertaken by the Programme. Groups have had varying needs and the EYPDO has clearly responded to the individual needs of each group.

Sure Start's work with toddler groups is part of the Programme's outreach activity, which is an activity emphasised in the Sure Start: Children's Centre Practice Guidance (2005) along with home visiting. Workers have increased the accessibility of services by taking them to toddler groups and visited groups to promote Sure Start services, in addition to the ongoing information and promotion carried out by the EYPDO in regular visits. The EYPDO has also signposted some parents to training, including childcare training. Through providing access to activities to be carried out at home (Chatterbox, library books) and through the EYPDO working with parents/carers and children together in toddler groups, the Programme is contributing to 'helping parents to support early learning' (Sure Start, 2005:19).

The role of the EYPDO with regard to childminding was not in the remit of this evaluation. However, with the expectation that children's centres will provide a childminder's network and 'support networks of childminders giving them access to advice and materials through the centre which will improve the experiences and outcomes for children in their care' (Sure Start, 2005:17), this will clearly be an important area of work for the Programme.

MAKE A POSITIVE CONTRIBUTION

Key services that are contributing to the ECM outcome 'Make a Positive Contribution' are:

- Parental Involvement
- Community Development
- Volunteering
- Training
- Fathers work

EXAMPLES OF WORK CARRIED OUT UNDER THE KEY SERVICES

Parental Involvement

In one SSLP there has been an active committee, Family Focus, which became a constituted group, allowing it to fundraise, and has appointed recognised officers, i.e. Chairperson, Treasurer, Secretary. Three parents are represented on the Citywide Parents Group, where parents participate in training events and planning sessions. Twenty-four parents have attended roadshows, raising awareness of this group. Parents are represented on the Partnership Board in two SSLPs, where there is a parent Chair, and in both areas staff are involved in the appointment of staff.

Community Development

New groups have been established by and for the community. In one SSLP, parents and carers have established 'Walking with Little Wheels', which has been introduced into the services programme. Two parents/carers gained a recognised qualification to lead walks. A 'Little Ducklings' swimming group has also been developed.

Volunteering

Community Parents have been trained in three SSLPs.

Training

'Listening to Children' training is to be delivered in all cluster areas. The Community Involvement Officer has attended training.

Fathers work

In one SSLP a Dads and Kids group is run on a weekly basis, offering one-to-one work and group support, e.g. in their relationship with their partner and their role as a parent. There are also weekly five-a-side football sessions. There is also a Dads and Kids group in another area, run on Saturdays during school summer holidays in collaboration with Leisure Services at a local Sport Complex .

Key Findings:
The Involvement of Fathers in one SSLP

There was early commitment from team members to working with fathers, involving consultation and events and leading to the establishment of a dads' group. Subsequently a fathers' worker was appointed and took over leadership of the group, supported by the Toddler Power worker and crèche workers, and worked to further develop the group and support individuals within it, and to promote the further involvement of fathers.

Figures for a snapshot four-week period in 2005 showed that the programme was reaching a large number of fathers (52), either individually (the majority, 27), with their partner, with their child or with both, although only five staff reported any contact with fathers that month. As a result of the contact, fathers were receiving information and support (e.g. on employment services and rights, tax credits, budgeting, childcare), treatment for their health/well-being, knowledge regarding their baby's development (weight), training (including football training) and self development, and one was involved in a consultation meeting regarding volunteers. Some internal referrals were made as a result of the contact, e.g. to the Health team, and some fathers were referred or signposted to other agencies such as Job Linkage and childcare settings.

Ways in which fathers using Sure Start services noted that Sure Start was making a difference to them and hence their families related to: Support for families and parents; Support for good quality play, learning and childcare experiences for children; Primary and community health care.

The dads' group was reported to be having an impact on the father and child relationship. Two fathers reported that coming to the group had brought about a change in how they felt about their relationship with their child. Some fathers reported that they did different activities with their child, such as painting. Five fathers reported greater involvement with their child as a result of the dads' group. It was also having an impact on fathers' own life. Some fathers reported that their involvement in the group had helped develop skills that could be important in the future. Regular attendance had also led to an increase in confidence. For some it was having an impact on family life, for example through becoming able to handle their children's behaviour or through a more equal sharing with their partner.

The Programme has worked towards the recommendations of the report e.g. to support staff in ensuring that working with fathers is the responsibility of the whole team, to promote fathers' services, to further develop activities and support for fathers from identified wants and needs, to maintain ongoing review of information and publicity and how this is provided to fathers, to increase accessibility of services, promote a welcoming ethos, to monitor use of services, and to explore participation at management level.

ACHIEVE ECONOMIC WELL-BEING

Key services that are contributing to the ECM outcome 'Achieve Economic Well-being' are:

- Information
- Training and Education
- Volunteering support

EXAMPLES OF SUPPORT PROVIDED OR SIGNPOSTED BY THE KEY SERVICES:

Information

Programmes have worked to increase provision of information and signposting to other services, e.g. Jobcentre Plus, training, debt advice services, other community services, housing, benefits advice, and childcare information.

Training and Education

A Basic Skills tutor has been employed to work with the Children's Centres ('Early Start'). Additional training undertaken by parents in

Folde has been Basic English Level 2 (10 week course), Working with Children with Special Needs (10 weeks), Teaching Assistant Diploma Level 2 (36 weeks), Arts and Crafts (10 weeks), and a Family History Scrapbook course (10 weeks).

Volunteering support

Programmes introduced La Leche training for volunteers (breastfeeding peer support). In one SSLP volunteers have been supported to carry out risk assessments and lead walks ('Walking with Wheels') and two have achieved a recognised Volunteer Walk Leaders certificate. Three volunteers run the Triple F After Schools Project which provides activities for children once a week after school hours and during school holidays.

Key Findings on the role of the Employment Counsellor and the outcomes of the service

The Employment Counsellor service had unique features not within the remit of other employment related services, i.e. it enabled concentration and sustained intervention at a time in people's lives when their financial position, rights and needs are likely to be changing, it enabled home visits and a flexible, accessible approach, and it enabled the development of trusting relationships which can make families more open to accessing other services (e.g. through visiting childcare settings together).

The service proved to be an effective way of reaching families who are in great need and providing a quick response and solution-focused approach, through which they see positive results. The service was also successful in reaching a large number of fathers/male carers. In some cases this led to further engagement with Sure Start services, including the Dad's and Kid's Group.

There was strategic commitment through Partnership to providing employment related support to families with young children at the Programme's inception. Operationally, there was good collaboration between the Employment Counsellor and local agencies to provide appropriate targeted support to families.

The service was adult-focused but the work had implications for the wellbeing of children and families. As noted in the Children's Centre Practice Guidance 'Living in a household where nobody is working is a significant indicator of poor outcomes for children' (Sure Start, 2005:37) and the ECM Outcomes highlight the need for support whereby 'parents, carers and families are supported to be economically active'. This in turn may have an impact on children's achievements and aspirations for education, employment or training as well as their more immediate health, well-being and learning, for example through an increased ability to support children's learning through addressing basic skills. The work of the Employment Counsellor not only supported parents through, for example, ensuring that they received the correct financial and work entitlements, helping them consider options and work towards aspirations and supporting them through the process, but also developing confidence and self esteem and developing a trusting relationship that in several cases encouraged further engagement with Sure Start services for health, family support and children's learning.

The evaluation highlighted the importance, in addition to centre-based services, of a flexible, accessible outreach and home based approach that addresses a far wider range of barriers to work than those highlighted in the Children's Centre Practice Guidance. It showed the complex issues surrounding employment and low income for families with young children and how much could be achieved through a dedicated worker within Sure Start, whose role encompassed a wide range of issues including, for example, preventative work (i.e. helping parents stay in employment, e.g. through knowledge of and access to employment rights and benefits) and helping parents consider their options (e.g. those on maternity leave). The evaluation also highlighted the number and variety of outcomes that had been achieved by families through this approach, which were enhanced through strong links with the Sure Start team and other agencies.

Conclusion

NESS includes as one of its 18 indicators of effective implementation of programmes that 'service delivery reflects the guidance requirements for the provision of core services in support, health, and play & childcare' (NESS, 2005b:58). This section has demonstrated not only how this has been achieved but also how the introduction of new services and enhancement of existing services will contribute to the five ECM outcomes and areas identified in the Sure Start Children's Centre Practice Guidance. In considering the future development of services these outcomes and the second edition of the Guidance (Sure Start, 2006) must remain at the forefront of planning.

However, there have been barriers to development relating to staffing, some unavoidable due to long-term sickness, others due to staff shortage and staff turnover. Another indicator of effective implementation is that 'staff turnover is low' (ibid: 57). Ratings range from 1-7:

1   Chaotic and erratic staffing and/or turnover in staff.
2   Interviewees report that staff turnover is high because of difficulties within the SSLP.
3   Reported problematic vacancies in staffing.
4   Has acceptable levels of turnover for the area (e.g. some geographical and discipline areas may have issues related to local skill shortages, maternity leaves).
5   Staff stability.
6   Evidence of strategies for recruiting and retaining staff (e.g. targeted training for individual staff development).
7   Evidence of high levels of job satisfaction amongst wide range of SSLP staff and volunteers.

Children's Centre management will need to work hard to overcome staffing shortage and to overcome employment uncertainty to achieve high levels of job satisfaction.

The following further recommendations were made for consideration with regard to working toward the five ECM outcomes and Children's Centre Practice Guidance.

Be Healthy

- Continue to improve links with midwifery service, in particular in relation to breastfeeding support
- Increase antenatal and postnatal support to teenage parents, and provide training to staff
- Increase focus on nutrition and diet
- Explore ways in which to increase communication between agencies with regard to early support for disabled children

Stay Safe

- Maintain and extend outreach domestic violence support and address the need for a male perpetrator worker
- Make increased efforts to engage with minority ethnic families

Enjoy and Achieve

- Continue to develop speech and language support, in particular by maximising opportunities for early assessment and accessing hard to reach families
- Increase services and activities for adults and children whose first language is not English and provide further training for staff and volunteers as necessary
- Further develop support for childminders through training, drop-ins and networks

Make a Positive Contribution

- Increase involvement of parents with disabled children
- Increase involvement of parents from minority ethnic backgrounds
- Increase parental representation at Partnership and other decision-making groups and increase efforts to involve fathers at this level
- Extend work with fathers, including young fathers, and provide training and support to staff as necessary
- Encourage male representation in Children's Centres, including male volunteers
- Examine promotional materials to encourage male participation
- Undertake consultation work with teenage parents

Achieve Economic Well-Being

- Explore offering more male-orientated courses through Children's Centres

- Increase awareness of courses available to parents
- Further develop links with Jobcentre Plus
- Provide more individualised support for parents seeking employment and benefit advice, including in the home
- Explore how the ways of working and benefits of the Employment Counsellor service can be transferred to Children's Centres

CROSS CUTTING ISSUES

Engaging service users

As noted by Garbers et al (2006),

> 'The facilitation of access to services represents a universal challenge for all those policy-makers and practitioners responsible for designing and delivering services for children and their families in the community' (Garbers et al, 2006:287).

It was a fundamental requirement for all SSLPs to reach all families and children living in the areas of high deprivation in which they were set up. A key Sure Start principle has been that 'every family should get access to a range of services that will deliver better outcomes for both children and parents, meeting their needs and stretching their aspirations'. There was a particular emphasis on reaching those families who were most in need and/or 'hard to reach'.

The Sure Start Children's Practice Guidance acknowledges that there are barriers to service use and that families most vulnerable to poor outcomes, and other families, may not want to use the services that are on offer for a variety of reasons. They 'may not see themselves as needing services or not know there are services that could help them' (Sure Start 2005: 29). They 'may find the attitudes of the professional staff in the services off-putting or not feel that the services are relevant to their needs' (ibid.). They 'may be fearful of using services in case they are judged as not being able to cope' (ibid.). They 'may be worried about possible interference in their lives, about their control being undermined, about being patronised, or that their privacy will be invaded' (ibid.).

The guidance on participation in multi-agency working also points out that families' needs will vary between families and over time, which will mean offering a variety of ways for parents and carers to be involved in the service and influence what is on offer. Further, 'Outreach, home visiting and drop-ins can provide a non-threatening gateway to other more specialist services'. The Sure Start Children's Centre Practice Guidance (2005) has recommended that there should be 'a greater emphasis on outreach and home visiting as a basis for enabling greater access to services for families who are unlikely to visit a centre' (Sure Start, 2005:3).

Every Child Matters: Change for Children guidance on participation in multi-agency working comments that 'Engaging with parents and carers is resource intensive – but not engaging them can be wasteful, because families are unlikely to take up any service provision that they feel has been imposed on them'. Further, Garbers et al comment that 'labelling them [parents] as 'hard to reach' can be simplistic, and sometimes a way of avoiding confronting and undertaking the necessary tasks' (Garbers et al, 2006: 295).

As a first step in assessing the impact of SSLPs on child and family functioning, the Impact Study of the National Evaluation of Sure Start (NESS) conducted a study of 9- and 36-month old children in 150 SSLP areas and 50 comparison areas which were to become SSLPs later (NESS 2005a). The NESS Programme Variability Study (NESS 2005b) set out to consider links between aspects of SSLP implementation and the level of effectiveness on child and parenting outcomes for the 150 SSLPs in the Impact Study. It rated programmes on 18 dimensions of implementation relating to what was implemented, the processes underpinning proficient implementation of services and holistic aspects of implementation. It found that SSLPs tended to score consistently low, average or high across all the 18 dimensions and the three broad domains and noted that 'The proficiency with which the *whole* model is implemented has a direct bearing on effectiveness, with implications for services delivered by Children's Centres' (NESS, 2005b:iii).

In each of the three domains, there were dimensions relating to engaging service users, such as *identification of users, reach, reach strategies, service flexibility, access to services, empowerment* and *ethos*. Ratings in some of these dimensions showed specific effects. For families with a 9 month old, more *empowerment* by SSLPs was related to higher maternal acceptance. For families with a 3-year-old, better *identification of users* by SSLPs was related to higher non-verbal ability for children, and stronger *ethos* and better overall scores on the 18 ratings were related to higher maternal acceptance. However, the report also points out that the 18 ratings are related to each other. For example, those SSLPs with high *empowerment* are likely to be high on all the other ratings. Those scoring high on the *identification of users* rating will also tend to score more highly on all other ratings, in particular *reach strategies, leadership* and *ethos*.

These dimensions were explored as follows:

- What strategies are in place to identify new users?
- What strategies does the Programme have to improve/sustain use of services over time?
- How are specific groups targeted?
- To what extent is there a welcoming and inclusive ethos within the Programme?
- Do communication systems reflect and respect the characteristics and languages of the community?
- In what ways do services accommodate the needs and preferences of a wide range of users, i.e., accessibility and availability, venues, access points, opening times)?

Identification of users and 'reach'

Strategies for the identification of users

NESS (2005b) refer to the dimension of *identification of users* as relating to strategies for identifying potential users; information exchange and shared record keeping systems by professionals; location and support of children with disabilities or additional needs; and links between agencies to locate families in the programme area.

All new births are identified through the Health Visiting Service who visit all new births at 10-14 days. Children aged 0-4 moving into the area are identified by health visitors and GPs. The database enables all Sure Start workers 'reaching' a family to enter details of services accessed. In some areas, links with other agencies have facilitated identification of users. For example, one area reported that health care assistants secure links with the Midwifery service, the Special Needs Support Worker ensures links with, e.g., the Children with Disabilities Team and SALT, and the Social Worker ensures links with Social Care Teams. Another SSLP has established some links with other organisations i.e. Housing, Children with Disabilities team and the Young Parents' Project, but has noted that these could be strengthened as it sometimes depends on relationships individual staff have developed, rather than common practice. One area has identified that exploration is required to establish what other services may know of families new to the area. There is some self-identification of users and Request for Services helps identify appropriate services for families with a higher level of need than that for universal services.

Reach

It is difficult to assess improvement in reach over time as quarterly figures fluctuate for various reasons, including a decrease due to some services not running during school summer holidays or staff sickness, and an increase due to extra activities over the Christmas period or one-off special events e.g. open days.

There has been a substantial improvement in providing publicity information to families in the local programme areas. There is now a centralised publicity team and all families in each programme area receive a Newsletter three times a year containing overall and programme specific information. The Newsletter informs families of what services and activities are available and how to access services. There is an established database and all families who access services are asked for consent to enter their details on this database. Links have been established with the Children's Information Service.

Programmes have promoted services through information days and events, through links with voluntary, private and statutory sectors. Over time, increasing parental involvement (e.g. parents' groups), the increasing involvement of volunteers and 'word of mouth' have helped promote services in the area. Programmes have sought to reach families through delivering services in a variety of ways, e.g. home visiting, group work, drop-in sessions, events and fun days, and in a variety of locations

Strategies to improve/sustain use of services over time

Improving reach relates to strategies to identify and target hard-to-reach groups and strategies to extend services to particular target groups, e.g. those with special needs. Identification of particular target groups takes place via information provided on consent forms and through health visitor contact with families. Request for Services provides a forum for multi-agency discussion of suitable services to offer families over and above universal services. Link workers for children with Disabilities and young parents act as a bridge between mainstream/specialist services and Sure Start. Some programmes employ a Special Needs Support Worker and in one area, this Worker has established links with the Specialist Health visitor, the Child Development Unit, the Children with disabilities Team, SALT and Paediatric Physiotherapy Services. A pathway of services has been developed via the Disability Link Forum.

One SSLP has supported a parent in establishing and running the 'Ups and Downs' group on its premises, to provide support for families with children with Downs Syndrome. It introduced Hydrotherapy Pool sessions for children with a disability/special need and their parents, initially one day a week, since increased to two sessions a week in response to demand. Sensory Play sessions are offered for children with complex needs. The availability of the Portage service has been extended in all programme areas and provides locality based intensive visits and supervision and training for staff. One area has developed links with schools where there is a high population of minority ethnic families and/or asylum seekers. In some cases, groups been established in partnership with other agencies. In one area, for example, Leisure Services and Sure Start jointly created and developed a Dads & Kids Club, and a health visitor was invited by Connexions to jointly develop the Bright Stars group for young mums and pregnant school students that they had originally set up.

Ethos

As stated earlier, a stronger *ethos* and better overall scores on the 18 ratings have been found to relate to higher maternal acceptance (NESS, 2005b). *Ethos* relates to whether, overall, the SSLP has a 'welcoming and inclusive ethos'.

Programme staff attend a range of training to enable them to have an inclusive approach throughout the programme including customer care and equality and diversity. A buildings audit has been carried out to identify standards parents can expect when accessing children's centres in the area, such as telephone answering, hospitality and common courtesy. These are minimum standards that centres are expected to deliver (Sure Start Children's Centre Practice Guidance).

The local evaluation reports have consistently shown that users of Sure Start services have found staff approachable, easy to contact by telephone and willing to seek information or signpost to other workers or services when they are unable to answer queries themselves.

Outreach and home visiting

The first edition of the Sure Start Children's Centre Practice Guidance recommended that there is 'a greater emphasis on outreach and home visiting as a basis for enabling greater access to services for families who are unlikely to visit a centre' (Sure Start, 2005:3).

The programmes provide an expanded home visiting service, i.e. a service beyond the mainstream health visiting service. For example, health care assistants provide breastfeeding and other support for new mothers; health nursery nurses conduct home visits for Portage intervention; Infant Massage and Family Nurturing are offered in the home for those who are not able or do not wish to attend a group. Family support workers, Special Needs Support Workers, the Community Paediatrician, psychologists and domestic violence workers offer home visits and one-to-one appointments in accessible venues. There is also a volunteer community parent programme to provide support in the home. The funding of additional health visitors, and the integration between Sure Start and mainstream health visitors enable more intensive home support for those who need it and enable health visitors to deliver a range of groups in a variety of venues. These groups include Family Nurturing, Common Childhood Illnesses, Infant Massage, La Leche breastfeeding support groups, and smoking cessation.

Programmes provide outreach services from between approximately 12 and 30 sites in the community. These include schools, nurseries and other early years settings; toddler groups; medical centres; community associations, centres and organisations; sports and leisure centres, and libraries. All Programmes intend to work towards the recommendation for a greater emphasis on outreach and home visiting (Sure Start Unit, 2005, 2006) by, for example:

- Using monitoring data to identify postal areas where little contact has been made with families and compare this information to the location of the sites where services are being delivered and to the population figure for under fives in that area. This will be followed by an assessment of why families are not engaging, leading to the targeting of services.
- Working with mainstream organisations to access children and families who do not access centre-based services
- Further liaison with existing networks e.g. toddler groups and childminder support groups.

Taking the views of parents/carers into account

Programmes hold consultation events and have established parent groups. Parents are represented on some planning groups (e.g. publicity, events planning). There is parental representation on Partnership Boards and in there is a parent Chair. Parents are also involved in the recruitment of staff.

There is also parent representation on some city wide groups, e.g. the City Wide Parents Group, the Disability Link Forum, the City Wide Community Parents Group, the City Wide Breastfeeding Strategy, and the Early Years and Childcare Strategic Partnership.

The Sure Start Children's Centres Planning and Performance Management Guidance stresses that community and user involvement must be built firmly into new arrangements for Children's Centres. Local authorities 'must ensure that there are effective mechanisms for the involvement of fathers and mothers and carers in the planning and delivery and governance of services. Structures should include significant parental representation' (DfES, 2006:15). Evaluations of parental involvement carried out in two local programmes have highlighted the following areas for consideration that could apply to all local children's centres:

Parental involvement in one SSLP

- Staff reported that they would welcome more volunteers and expansion of their role. Volunteers noted that it can be daunting meeting a group and that it is important to start with something small. The evaluation found that a gradual approach appears to work best, supported by staff with whom parents have developed a relationship.
- Considering how best to develop and share the skills of the local community for the benefit of the local programme, the community and individuals (e.g. through developing employment skills) is an important area for the future development of services for children and families.
- The Programme had shown commitment to consulting parents through a survey of a sample of service users to ascertain whether, and in what ways, they would like to be further involved in service use, service planning and service delivery. At the same time, it is important that consultation extends to those who may not access the Centre and targets particular groups. Parents suggested that input via website/e-mail could be considered. The Sure Start Children's Centre Practice Guidance (2005) specifically mentions consulting expectant parents, parents of disabled children, minority ethnic parents and lone parents.
- It will be important for Programmes to maintain and extend working groups of parents and professionals and a parents' forum. Every Child Matters documentation differentiates between 'general consultation' ('Important though this is') and 'involvement in real service planning and delivery', noting that 'consultation may reach many people, though sometimes not in any great depth'.
- Local Programmes and other services need to consider how best to facilitate effective parental participation in meetings. Issues such as the timing of meetings, childcare, preparation/training, understanding roles, use of jargon, ensuring members feel that their views are important need to be taken into consideration.

Parental participation in one SSLP

- Every Child Matters documentation recognises that securing the participation of the local community can be challenging and notes that it takes time and expertise to carry out consultation and planning work. In some cases parents in this study had become involved directly as a way to have a voice in Sure Start, and in other cases active involvement had been a gradual process leading on from the use of services for a specific need (e.g. domestic violence, managing behaviour, extending knowledge and developing own practice), from the desire to socialise, or from the desire to help others in a way that had not been available to them (e.g. breastfeeding peer support). For individuals, parental involvement is often a gradual process and is best fostered as such.

- Parental involvement is influenced by the 'ethos' of the Programme i.e. its atmosphere and the attitude of staff. The 'ethos' of a programme has also been related to outcomes with regard to parenting (NESS, 2005b).

- 'Effective participation' has been encouraged and there have been many achievements, which could still be further developed in the future. The style of meeting rooms needs to be conducive to participation; the crèche and meeting should be located within the same building to enable full participation in the meeting and enable immediate access in case of emergency or a child needing their parent's attention. For parents, consistency of staff and venue are important. An appropriate level of informality needs to be encouraged; jargon, acronyms and abbreviations need to be avoided or explained (e.g. flipchart, information for files), and steps need to be taken to help parents know who group members are (e.g. name and organisation on table) and to enable some social interaction at more formal meetings. Communication is key to effective participation. Parents need to be clear about the aims and purpose of management groups, their own and others' roles, and the decision-making powers and processes of the group. They also need to be well informed about the Programme's targets and objectives to understand the context in which decisions are made and to enable them to contribute to ways of achieving these. Communication with the wider community is also crucial for disseminating information and accessing the views of those who are unable, or do not wish, to attend meetings. It is important that parents are well prepared for meetings through receiving agendas, minutes and papers to be tabled in advance of the meeting to enable understanding and discussion. Training is clearly important, and will be key to involvement in Children's Centres. Parents felt that participation needed to be beneficial to 'both sides' and that training needed to be flexible and to recognise people's existing skills and experience. If attendance at subgroups was organized by having three volunteers for each subgroup these volunteers could be offered regular informal training specific to that group, e.g. how finances operate, jargon used, issues that are likely to come up, and how decisions are made. Parents suggested that, if feasible, it would be helpful for minutes to be placed on a website to refer back to. They also suggested a system for people to send in comments through the website, which would enable working mothers to contribute and possibly encourage more male participation. Co-operation, trust and a feeling of equality are important for effective participation, as is the opportunity to learn from others with similar and dissimilar views, and need to be evident in all groups in which parents participate. It is important for parents to feel that they are important to the success of the group and their role is valued. It was considered important for professionals to openly and directly express their appreciation rather than pass this on through another worker. Praise, and a feeling of doing something right, is important to parents.

- Parents have been influential in the decision making process. It was stressed by parents that decision-making processes need to be transparent and that involvement needs to take place from the first discussions.

- Parents have gained new knowledge and skills through service use and through their active involvement in Sure Start. They considered that, as well as courses facilitating participation (e.g. committee skills, interview training) other courses and training they had undertaken through Sure Start all *'indirectly help you have a voice because they give you more specialised knowledge and enable you to make a more informed decision'. In addition, 'courses empower parents to help other parents'.*

- Parents feel that their involvement has helped to break down barriers between parents and professionals and led to new ways of working. This has been supported through the development of a Parental Involvement Subgroup that has worked on a definition of parental involvement and what it means for the Programme and on a Strategy for achieving this. Workers in multi-agency teams have very different professional backgrounds. There may be a need for training for professionals working in partnership with parents to increase understanding of community development and participation and ensure effective communication. Parents felt that the amount of support they received varied, and depended on personalities and professional role. The support of workers 'on the ground' has made parents feel valued. Some felt that their local knowledge, experience, contacts and expertise could be more fully utilised, for example in encouraging the involvement of more parents and working alongside staff in some areas.

- Participation is linked to the empowerment of parents and of professionals. Parents have been empowered through specific procedures and support for parents to be involved in the planning of services and represented on the partnership and other groups, through training offered to both paid and voluntary staff which contributes not only on their own knowledge and skills but also *'empowers us to help other parents'* and enables better informed active participation in the Programme. Sure Start Children's Centre Guidance also sees consultation with parents as a means to enhance the professional skills of local workers.

Interprofessional and multi-agency working

Multi-agency teamwork

One of the dimensions used for exploring variability in the proficiency of implementation of SSLPs (NESS, 2005b) was that 'Multi-agency teamwork is established in the SSLP'. The National Evaluation of Sure Start identified positive aspects of multi-disciplinary working as 'greater flexibility, opportunities to work beyond rigid professional boundaries, sharing good practice and being better able to inform parents about the range of support available to them' (NESS, 2004:3). Staff interviews were analysed to seek answers to the question: 'What is it about interprofessional working that contributes to working towards the objectives and targets?' This led to the identification of several main ways in which interprofessional working appeared to be contributing towards achievement of the objectives.

Widening the repertoire of possible interventions and responses e.g.

- through providing interventions, support and guidance in the home from a range of professionals, e.g. health visitor, nursery nurse, community paediatrician, family support workers.
- through providing a range of courses and activities in venues across the local area (facilitated in part by smaller health visitor caseload)
- through having the time and flexibility to offer support in the home to those who do not wish to attend a class, e.g. baby massage (facilitated in part by change in nursery nurse role)
- through training and supporting mainstream health visitors, nursery nurses and health centres to extend Sure Start activity and enhance services offered
- through the Request for Services system (e.g. offering to accompany parents to groups/sessions)
- through liaison with outside agencies to increase participation of families in Sure Start activity

One SSLP has offered an accessible whole team approach to family support at a church hall drop-in, with staff from all teams providing parent support and information covering the range of Sure Start services, e.g. health visitor: baby weighing, monthly health information theme (e.g. healthy eating); nursery nurse: play and stimulation; admin team: issuing baby milk; Domestic Violence worker; Early Years librarian; Toy Librarian; Child Safety worker.

Accessing a range of professional perspectives

- through the Request for Services system
- quick and informal pathways to other professionals within the team to discuss problems/ideas and provide mutual support
- support from other experts in the field (e.g. SALT)
- the contribution of outside agencies to training and parent support groups

Co-location and office sharing facilitated quick and informal sharing of problems and ideas and provided support across teams. In one Programme, a Buddies system (pairing with colleague from another team) enabled informal discussion of work on a flexible basis.

Providing access to networks of different professionals involved

- through the Request for Services system
- links with hospital consultants and children's ward staff to improve communication and information sharing and ensure consistency of advice
- through representation on Sure Start sub-groups e.g. for access to trainers and knowledge of opportunities in the area
- raising awareness of Sure Start services in different agencies and organisations
- whole staff training extends knowledge and informs practice in individual or group settings, including through informal discussions and subsequent referral, and enables consistent messages to be given

Easing referral and support pathways

- informal contact with parents, e.g. in toddler groups, at Centre, enables discussion of concerns and offers of referral / support
- co-location of staff facilitated information sharing and referral and reduced waiting time for parents
- close links with PNC as employing agency facilitate referral between agencies.
- community paediatrician support facilitated access e.g. for advice, information and referral, providing quicker response and more efficient pathway

This was facilitated by co-location of staff in a centred base, office sharing and informality, which made referrals, raising queries, requesting information easier and reduced waiting time for parents. The range of professionals with different backgrounds and expertise 'on tap' provided help for staff on queries outside their area of expertise and enhances what they can offer/ suggest to families.

Using community networks to extend activity into the community

- staff access community groups to increase knowledge of services and offer a range of input

One Programme, for example, worked closely with local organisations and agencies (e.g. re. funding, venues, trainers) to: introduce new services and extend activity across the area and thus increase opportunities and enhance accessibility for families (e.g. baby clinics; courses such as First Aid; outreach access points for Domestic Violence worker, paediatrician, Health Visitors); gain input into existing groups, thus benefiting from a range of expertise outside the Programme to increase knowledge and skills; and increase accessibility through the provision of community transport.

Supporting community groups / networks to promote sustainability

- through providing or enabling access to training opportunities and advice
- through developing play provision within toddler groups
- through working with the Under Fives Forum to devise draft standards for toddler groups

The Programmes have added value to existing toddler groups and childcare e.g. through contributing expertise and developing play practice.

Pooling expertise to enhance family support and promote parental learning

- joint planning and running of groups for parents; joint diary planning; use of Service Delivery Request form
- involving experts from outside agencies, e.g. Healthy Cities, to enhance service delivery
- producing leaflets/packs

In one SSLP, staff proposed new activities via a Service Delivery Request form, which was taken by the Programme Manager to a whole team meeting to provide an opportunity for others to co-present or provide information. The system facilitated pooling of the team's expertise and personal and professional development; it also promoted consultation with partners/outside agencies for further support.

Joint planning and delivery of courses and joint organisation of diaries have encouraged the pooling of expertise and provision of input from a range of professional backgrounds. In some Programmes this has been facilitated by co-location and office sharing by e.g. Health and Play and Learn, which has promoted informal sharing of ideas for sessions and for work with individual families.

Mutual promotion of activity

- knowledge of range of Sure Start services and activities, detailed timetable and communication between staff enable promotion of activity in a variety of settings

The Administration team are often the first point of contact for parents at Reception and develop relationships through their involvement with e.g. Affordable Children's Essentials shop, safety scheme, milk distribution, sometimes leading to their informally suggesting other activities e.g. soft play. Staff from different teams access a range of community groups (e.g. toddler groups, community centres) and professional bases (e.g. Health Centre, clinics, nurseries), which facilitates the distribution of Sure Start information and leaflets and provides opportunities for staff to become familiar faces and for parents to ask about Sure Start.

Sharing practice across Sure Start boundaries

- learning from pilot schemes in other local programmes
- linking with other local programmes in particular areas of activity e.g. La Leche, Community Parents
- linking with networks of professionals, e.g. Citywide team of safety workers, Toy Library network.

The evaluation suggested that the Programmes may wish to consider: 'How can the Programme maintain, enhance and extend these features of interprofessional working for the benefit of families and the community and to further help progress towards the Sure Start objectives?' This remains pertinent to progress towards Children's Centre aims and objectives and Every Child Matters outcomes.

Multi-agency teamwork and clear pathways for users

As stated above, one of the dimensions used for exploring variability in the proficiency of implementation of SSLPs (NESS, 2005b) was that 'Multi-agency teamwork is established in the SSLP'. Another dimension was that 'There are clear pathways for users to follow in accessing specialist services' (ibid.). The evaluation of the Request for Services system shows how clear pathways have been developed and important features of this dimension have been achieved, i.e. guaranteed response time; proven systems for routinely sharing specialist knowledge among all workers; all SSLP workers have an understanding of appropriateness of referring users beyond generic to specialist help.

The Request for Services system developed from a pilot system (the Referral and Allocation Project) initiated by a group of professionals from different disciplines working in a Sure Start trailblazer local programme. As workers were appointed to the programme and took up work with families, it gradually became evident that referrals were being made to Sure Start from a variety of sources and that different systems were in operation for handling referrals. Staff had come to Sure Start with different experiences of allocation, assessment, planning and review systems, or no experience at all. The group identified that there was no clear referral process, a lack of co-ordination and restricted information sharing and opportunity for creative use of knowledge and skills or rethinking of professional boundaries. It sought to develop, through regular meetings, a whole-team interagency focus on discussing the needs of families who had been referred, or had referred themselves, to Sure Start and on suggesting ways in which support or advice could be offered and accessed in order to meet their needs. New documentation was introduced and refined over the first year. Issues regarding, for example, professional anxiety, hierarchy and the danger of dominant representation, personal impact of complex cases, changing relationships with clients, the tension between traditional practice and different models of working (e.g. dealing with wider family and community concerns), tensions over the way meetings were used (i.e. multi agency case management/group supervision) and overt and covert resistance by team members were identified and ways were sought to address these. It was also recognised that despite the process, some families were still 'hard to reach'. Evaluation highlighted the importance of shared aims and collective responsibility, of periods of experimentation and adjustment, and the recognition that teamwork is an evolving and negotiated process.

The process was subsequently introduced in later wave local programmes (Rounds 2, 4, 5 and 6). Over time it was identified that the process was operating in different ways in different programmes, and with different forms of participation, i.e. whole team/co-ordinators only/professional leads, and only two parents attending. Professional anxiety was still evident; there was still some reluctance to share information and there were issues regarding attendance and agency approval. A cross programme team was established to review the process, including a review of purpose, attendance, roles, paperwork, review dates and the accessibility of the meetings for parental attendance. In July 2005 the process was re-launched under a common name 'Request for Services' and staff were re-trained. The following principles were established for the Request for Services process:

Sure Start seeks to operate a process of requests for services that:

- Takes a multidisciplinary approach
- Involves parents and families in the process
- Takes a broad view of the families' needs and circumstances rather than focusing on the specific request made
- Provides a preventative service
- Has a clear pathway, with a working agreement and targets which are reviewed regularly
- Avoids duplication of effort and reduces confusion for families
- Provides feedback to agencies and individuals requesting services and seeks to keep them involved in work with families where appropriate
- Recognises that 'Request for Services' meetings attended by parents need to meet their individual and family needs.
- Are made with the full involvement and consent of the parent or family.
- Appoints a key worker to take work forward with the family.
- Is deemed to be sensitive and attuned to the needs of the family.

Key findings of request for services evaluation phases one and two

Professionals identified benefits of the Request for Services approach to be easy and direct access to a range of professionals, providing a holistic approach, improvements in communication, monitoring processes through a key worker, consistency of messages given to parents, additionality for external referrers accessing extra services outside their own remit, and continuity of services. Some expressed concerns regarding the process, including personal and professional discomfort, a view of the process as time consuming, concerns over membership of the group and tensions regarding information sharing, which indicated a need for ongoing discussion and training.

The majority of families reported that they would not have gone looking for support themselves. Not all families were aware of whether they had been invited to a meeting. Perceived benefits of the process related to communication between families and professionals, including informed decision-making, pacing and control; co-ordination of services (liaison and communication); providing a single point of contact and convenience.

In all cases, families and professionals were able to identify outcomes of the process for children and families. Outcomes related to engagement with services on a regular basis/better relationship with services; child development; improvements in family relationships and communication; skills and learning; financial well-being; and social and emotional well-being.

The evaluation highlighted the need for the referrer to attend the meeting to gain a full understanding of the Request for Services system and the nature of the information-sharing and decision-making processes, and the initial stated needs of the family in order to have a full debate on the issues and needs of the family. Some professionals noted the value of preliminary discussions with the family about possible services prior to the meeting as this gave the opportunity to gauge the reaction of the family and whether/which services might be acceptable.

There is not yet parental attendance at meetings in all the cluster areas. Some professionals felt it inappropriate in the current format. Further thought needs to be given to how best to explain the purpose and function of meetings to parents and how to make the format and ethos of the meetings welcoming and family friendly. It was also pointed out that the nature of the support requested might make it difficult for families to attend (e.g. depression). In some cases it might be appropriate to have a separate meeting with the family involving only those professionals who are directly involved with the support being offered.

Acting as Chairperson is a complex role that requires objectivity and needs to maintain a clear focus on child and family needs throughout the initial discussion and subsequent reviews. This requires training and support and develops with experience. Training has now been delivered and peer group support and supervision are in place. A training course has also been delivered to minute takers to ensure effective practice across cluster areas.

The number of external referrals has been increasing, but still varies across Programmes. There is an ongoing need to ensure that all partner agencies are aware of the Request for Services policy and procedures and how to access services for the benefit of their clients.

Request for Services has an important part to play in supporting integrated services which, according to ECM, 'act as a service hub for the community by bringing together a range of services, usually under one roof, whose practitioners then work in a multi-agency way'. Integrated working comprises a way of improving outcomes for children and families and involves delivery of integrated frontline services supported by more integrated processes which include: the Common Assessment Framework (CAF), the Lead Professional and better information-sharing. The CAF consists of three elements grouped into the themes of development of the child, parents and carers, and family and environment and is intended to provide a process to assess the additional needs of a child or young person and to give a holistic view that considers strengths as well as needs. Request for Services encompasses a process for child/family referral and assessment and combines improved information-sharing among different disciplines, holistic assessment and nomination of a lead professional to act as a single point of contact who is able to support the child/family in making choices and in navigating their way through the system. It contributes to a key part of the reform of children's services: the integration of systems and processes so that the needs of children and families are met in a more appropriate way, for example,

'Children and families are supported most effectively when CAF, the lead professional and information sharing procedures are planned and delivered in a co-ordinated way, to offer integrated support across the continuum of needs and services' (DfES 2006:7).

Effective integrated working is cited as being underpinned by workforce reform and by multi-agency working, so that

'a network of services is in place, configured according to local needs, to enable professionals from different agencies to come together to meet the needs of children and families and jointly agree the delivery of the action plan arising from a common or specialist assessment. This will include appropriate procedures for ensuring links and smooth transitions between different agencies and services' (ibid:8)

The DfES vision for the lead professional is that:

'All children and young people with additional needs (including complex needs) who require integrated support from more than one practitioner should experience a seamless and effective service in which one practitioner takes the lead to ensure that services are co-ordinated, coherent and achieving intended outcomes' (ibid:11)

The Lead Professional Managers' Guide notes that evidence from practice suggests that appointing a lead professional is central to the effective frontline delivery of integrated services for children with a range of additional needs. 'Delivered in the context of multi-agency assessment and planning, underpinned by CAF or relevant specialist assessments, it ensures that professional involvement is rationalised, co-ordinated and communicated effectively' (ibid:12). More importantly it helps overcome some of the frustrations traditionally experienced by service users with a range of needs, requiring input from a range of practitioners, e.g. numerous lengthy meetings; lack of co-ordination; conflicting and confusing advice; not knowing who to speak to; the right support not being available at the right time. It can also help alleviate the frustrations often felt by practitioners e.g. difficulties in accessing specialist help; inadequate, misleading or inappropriate referral information; barriers to information sharing and communication problems; over-large and bureaucratic case conferences and management meetings, to the detriment of delivering early intervention support.

The lead professional is not seen as a job title or a new role, but as a set of functions to be carried out as part of the delivery of effective integrated support. These functions are: to act as a single point of contact for the child or family, to co-ordinate the delivery of the actions agreed by the practitioners involved, and to reduce overlap and inconsistency in the services received. An important principle underpinning these functions is that the lead professional should 'ensure that the child and family remain central to any decisions made, and should provide them with sufficient information to empower them to make their own decisions, acting as a sounding board if necessary' (ibid:13). The City's Children and Young People's Plan 2006-2009 states its intention 'to improve services to children and families by introducing the CAF and the role of the Lead Professional across the city' from April 2008.

The Request for Services evaluation has shown that many of the proposed functions of, and principles underlying, the lead professional role are already in evidence in the Request for Services process. In addition, Request for Services is already incorporating the CAF pre-assessment checklist, which links to the Every Child Matters outcomes. Further work is currently being developed to ensure that the CAF and Lead Professional role are an integral part of the process. CAF training has been held for the Chairs and co-ordinators who attend Request for Services, and will subsequently be cascaded to all staff working with children and families.

RECOMMENDATIONS

Our recommendations focus upon *how* to engage families and *how* to strengthen inter-professional working. On the former, there is a need to identify hard to reach groups using local data sources and to ensure that there are reliable methods for monitoring take-up, to track which families are using services and to monitor trends in service usage by different groups. This involves using monitoring data to identify postal areas where little contact has been made with families and compare this information to the location of the sites where services are being delivered and to the population figure for under fives in that area. There is a need to ensure that strong outreach and home visiting are offered and to further extend work with mainstream organisations to access children and families who do not access centre-based services. On the latter, the suggestion is that Operational Management Groups will need to support the continued development of multi-disciplinary working by providing regular opportunities for further multi-agency training incorporated into future plans. Above all there is a need to continue the development of Request for Services incorporating the Common Assessment Framework and Lead Professional.

Progress towards targets

As the transition is made towards establishing Children's Centres the process of setting clear and concise objectives and ensuring that they are specific, measurable, achievable and realistic becomes urgent. Local programme managers and senior representatives from partner agencies should be involved in setting the objectives and be aware of evidence needed to monitor progress against these objectives. In this city this has been achieved through the development of a 'Local Outcomes Framework for Early Childhood Services' which identifies the local service objectives and targets and how the key services offered relate to these local objectives and targets, to national Children's Centre aims, and to national ECM aims and outcomes. Progress is required in information gathering on baseline statistics and in data monitoring as programmes continue to develop better systems for gathering accurate statistical information and identifying information gaps.

Partnership working

Consideration ought to be given as to how those agencies that have not as yet fully embraced the principles of Sure Start can be encouraged and supported to contribute to the strategic direction and development of future work. In re-structuring Children's

Services a core staffing structure requires clarity as do Governance and Partnership arrangements in the context of Children's Trust arrangements for Children's Centres and Extended Services.

Our evaluations have recognised that at a local programme level Sure Start has supported the involvement of voluntary and community sector organisations in the planning and delivery of services and plans for future work should seek to sustain current levels of involvement and explore opportunities to develop further the scope for partnership working with the voluntary sector. Programme managers need to review the purpose and the aims/objectives of Local Partnership Boards as part of the transition process to Children's Centres, taking into consideration which agencies need to be represented, the purpose of their involvement and the level of representation from within the organisation that is required to ensure that meetings are productive.

Evaluations have shown that multi-agency training has proven to be an effective tool for encouraging workers from different backgrounds and disciplines to work collaboratively, and regular opportunities for further multi-agency training should be incorporated into future plans. Local training arrangements will be influenced by core training required for staff working in Children's Centres, hence a need to undertake city-wide commissioning of multi-agency training to maximise use of resources and provide wider opportunities. The development of Children's Centres will provide further opportunities for staff sharing and cross programme working, and although there are clear benefits to staff sharing, the capacity of workers to deliver across programmes needs to be monitored carefully. It is envisaged that the commissioning of services city-wide will ensure consistent delivery of services and that detailed Service Level Agreements will ensure generic practice across all cluster areas, with workers delivering specific service provision. Staff re-structuring will ensure clarity of roles and service reviews will identify resource issues. Centralisation of some core functions e.g. processes for monitoring and evaluation, needs consideration to ensure greater consistency across all Children's Centres.

Inter-professional working

Our evaluations demonstrate that there has been significant progress in the development of integrated working practices and a belief that development is cumulative hence the need to sustain effort to support and encourage inter-professional working as Children's Centres develop and as new workers are recruited to core and virtual staff teams. Ongoing development is required to promote and enhance good practice through integrated working. The move to Children's Centres is involving changes to staffing structures and changes to the ways that some Sure Start services are delivered. The importance of support to existing staff through the change process, and of induction of new staff, particularly those who will continue to work within mainstream agencies i.e. Health Visitors, Midwives, Social Workers but who may not be permanently based within Children's Centre buildings is critical to the success of the programme. Evaluations have identified factors that have had a positive influence on inter-disciplinary working i.e. providing regular opportunities for team-building both within and across cluster areas, maximising opportunities for the co-location of staff, encouraging and supporting role flexibility to maximise skill levels within teams, providing opportunities for joint training, and ensuring programme managers have the capacity to offer appropriate support to individuals within their teams.

Parental involvement and accessibility

Programme managers should consider how consistent practice can be developed across all local programmes with regard to parental involvement, i.e. the provision of childcare places, transport, volunteer and training opportunities; also to review the role of Community Development Workers/Parental Involvement Workers to help ensure that practice is consistent across all programmes. There needs to be a particular effort to review and re-define community development roles and to establish practice models for community development workers that dovetail with core business. Further investment is required to provide appropriate training opportunities for parents/carers involved in decision-making groups and to create a volunteering strategy to formalise and standardise volunteering opportunities available via local programmes which explores possibilities for accreditation and a volunteer pathway of training. The process of volunteering needs to be strengthened through robust supervision and through expanding the range of volunteering opportunities. There is a need for strategies to engage traditionally difficult to reach groups i.e. those who 'choose not to access services' as such families may be vulnerable and most in need of support as regards child-rearing.

Programme management

The move from SSLPs to Children's Centres entails a period of change with implications for management with regard to e.g. the future role of management groups, training, the management of change, support for staff including those from voluntary organisations, and job satisfaction. In this city cluster based Operational Management Groups replacing Local Partnership Boards have been established and are in operation by April 2007. Their purpose is to *co-ordinate* services within different settings, and to support local delivery and the city wide commissioning of services. Consideration should be given to the training of key individuals from voluntary organisations who are involved in the delivery of Sure Start services to ensure they fully understand the changes and the impact those changes will have on their current systems/methods of delivery. Detailed Service Level Agreements need to inform voluntary organisations and partner agencies of the requirements in their delivery of services e.g. data collection procedures. There has been a high turnover of staff in the SSLPs hence the suggestion is that all staff employed by or seconded to Sure Start Children's Centre local programmes need to have standardised job descriptions and terms and conditions of work, and that staff turnover across local programmes needs careful monitoring.

Finally, our findings from evaluating SSLPs tend to focus more upon processes rather than outcomes and demonstrate clearly that an *infrastructure* is in place for advancement of the Sure Start Children's

Centre ethos as expressed in Government guidelines. The term *infrastructure* in this instance refers to inter-professional working and methods for engaging parents and supporting families. The evaluations provide strong evidence of *how* inter-professional working and parental involvement in particular provide a foundation for integrated services. Sure Start Children's Centres will be an important part of all Local Authorities' strategies to improve services for families and children, particularly to those families needing extra help through for example providing access to structured parenting programmes. The NESS illustrates that well-led local programmes have tended to be more effective i.e. leadership starts with governance and different models of multi-management are evident from both NESS and our local evaluations. A recent report from the Commission for Social Care Inspection (April 2007) recommends practice leaders, service leaders, system leaders, and future leaders across the whole sector of social care. There is a strongly voiced view from relevant sectors to promote research utilisation to model and advance evidence-informed practice and our evaluations have illustrated how practitioners have used research to develop their practice. The direction is towards integrated working and our evaluations illustrate significant change to culture and practice across the workforce serving children and families.

References

Acheson, D. (1998) *Independent Enquiry into Inequalities in Health.* London, The Stationery Office.

Adams, R. (1996) *Social Work and Empowerment.* London, Macmillan.

Anderson T and Sim, D (2000) (eds) *Housing and Social Exclusion. Context and Challenges.* Coventry: Chartered Institute of Housing and Housing Studies

Arnstein, S.R. (1969) A ladder of citizen participation. *Journal of the American Institute of Planners,* 35 (4) pp. 216-224.

Allen, S.M. and Hawkins, A.J. (1999) 'Maternal Gatekeeping: Mothers' Beliefs and Behaviour That Inhibit Greater Father Involvement in Father Work'. *Journal of Marriage and the Family,* 61, 199-212.

Anderson T and Sim, D (2000) (eds) *Housing and Social Exclusion. Context and Challenges.* Coventry: Chartered Institute of Housing and Housing Studies

Anning, A & Edwards, A (1999) *Promoting children's learning from birth to five: developing the new early years professional.* Buckingham: Open University Press

Association of Directors of Social Services/NCH - Action for Children(1996) Children Still in Need

Atkins, J (1998) Tribalism, loss & grief; issues for multiprofessional education, *Journal of Interprofessional Care,* 12(3): 303-7

Atkinson, M, Wilkin, A, Scott, A, Kinder, K (2001) *Multi-agency activity: an audit of activity.* Local Government Association Research, Report 17. Slough: National Foundation for Education & Research

Audit Commission (2000) *A fruitful partnership. Effective partnership working.* London: Audit Commission.

Ball, C (1994) *Start Right. The Importance of Early Learning.* London: RSA

Balloch, S and Taylor, M (2001) *Partnership Working; Policy and practice.* Bristol: The Policy Press.

Barnes, M and Bowl, R (2001) *Taking Over the Asylum: Empowerment and Mental Health.* London: Palgrave

Barr, H & Ross, F (2006) Mainstreaming interprofessional education in the UK: a position paper, *Journal of Interprofessional Care,* March 20(2)

96-104

Belsky, J. (1985) 'Experimenting with fathers in the newborn period'. *Child Development*, 56, 407-414.

Belsky, J, Melhuish, E, Barnes, J, Leyland, A, Romaniuk, H (2006) Effects of Sure Start Local Programmes on children & families: early findings from a quasi-experimental, cross-sectional study, *British Medical Journal* 10: 1136, bmj.38853.16 June

Beresford, P. (2003) 'A missed chance to listen to the child', *Guardian Society*. 5.2.03

Biggs, S. (2000) User Voice, Interprofessionalism and Postmodernity in C. Davies, L. Finlay and A. Bullman (Eds.) *Changing practice in Health and Social Care* (London, Sage).

Blair, T (1998) *The Third Way*. London: Fabian Society

Boehm, A. and Staples, L.H. (2004) 'Empowerment: The Point of View of Consumers'. *Families in Society: The Journal of Contemporary Social Services*, 85 (2): 270-280.

Boreham, N. and Samurcay, R. (1999) *Models for the Analysis of Work Competence: A Critical Review*, Paper presented at the European Conference on Educational Research, Lahti, Finland, 22-25 September, 1999.

Botting, B., Rosato, M. and Wood, R. (1998) 'Teenage mothers and the health of their children'. *Population Trends*, 93, Autumn, pp.19-28.

Brown, G (1999) "Equality- Then and Now" in Dick Leonard (ed) *Crosland and New Labour*. Basingstoke: Macmillan

Brown, M, Conaty, P and Mayo, E (2003) Life Saving: Community Development Credit Unions. London: New Economics Foundation

Buchanan, A & Hudson, B (eds) (1998) *Parenting, schooling & children's behaviour*. Ashgate: Aldershot

Bucholz, E.S. and Korn-Bursztyn, C. (1993) 'Children of adolescent mothers: Are they at risk for abuse?' *Adolescence*, 28, pp. 361-382.

Burchardt, T LeGrand, J and Piachaud, D (2002) "Introduction" in *Understanding Social Exclusion* Hills, J, LeGrand, J, Piachaud, D. (eds) Oxford: Oxford University Press.

Burgess, A. (2002) *Fathers and families* (In practice paper). London, Parenting Education and Support Forum.

Burke, P and Cigno, K (1996) Support for Families. Aldershot: Ashgate

Byrne, D (1999) Social Exclusion. Buckingham: Open University Press

Cameron, R and White, M (eds) (1982) *Working Together: Portage in the UK*, Windsor: NFER

Campbell, B (1988) *Unofficial Secrets : Child Sexual Abuse - The Cleveland Case*, Virago

Chawla-Duggin, R. (2006) 'Exploring the role of father development workers in supporting early years learning'. *Early Years*, 26 (1), 93-109.

Clarence, E and Painter, C (1998) Public services under New Labour: collaborative discourses and local networking, *Public Policy and Administration*, Vol 13, no 1, 8-22

Clarke, K. (2006) 'Childhood, parenting and early intervention: A critical examination of the Sure Start national programme'. *Critical Social Policy.* 26 (4): 699-721.

Clarke, J & Newman, J (1997) *The managerial state.* London: Sage

Collett (2001) 'Working with Men in Family Centres'. In L. McMahon and A. Ward (eds.), *Therapeutic Work in Family Centres.* London, Jessica Kingsley.

Commission on Social Justice (1994) Social Justice: Strategies for National Renewal. London: Vintage

Cook, J.L. (2005) 'Revisiting men's role in father involvement: the importance of personal expectations'. *Fathering: A Journal of Theory, Research and Practice about Men as Fathers,* Spring 2005.

Cooley, C.H. (1918) *Human Nature and the Social Order* (New York, Scribner).

Coren, E., Barlow, J. and Stewart-Brown, S. (2003) 'The effectiveness of individual and group-based parenting programmes in improving outcomes for teenage mothers and their children: a systematic review'. *Journal of Adolescence,* 26, pp. 79-103.

Crittenden, P (2001) *Care-Index (Coding Manual)* Family Relations Institute, Miami FL 33176 USA

D'Amour & Oandasan (2005) Interprofessionality as the field of interprofessional practice & interprofessional education: an emerging concept, *Journal of Interprofessional Care,* May Supplement, 8-20

Daniel, B. and Taylor, J. (2001) *Engaging Fathers: Practical Issues for Health and*

Social Care. London, Jessica Kingsley.

David, T (1996) Curriculum in the Early Years. In Pugh, G (ed) *Contemporary Issues in the Early Years. Working Collaboratively for Children.* London: National Childrens Bureau

Dawson, N. (1997) 'The Provision of Education and Opportunities for Future Employment for Pregnant Schoolgirls and Schoolgirl Mothers in the UK'. *Children and Society,* 11(4), pp. 252-263.

DfEE (1999) *Sure Start. Making a difference for children & families.* Suffolk: DfEE Publications

DfES (2002) *Early Experiences of Implementing Sure Start,* Sure Start National Evaluation Report 01, June 2002. Nottingham, DfES

Publications (Ref:NESS/FR/01).

DfES (2003, September) *Every Child Matters* (Cm5860). London, The Stationery Office.

DfES (2004) *The Children Act 2004.* London, The Stationery Office.

DfES (2004) *Every Child Matters: Change for Children.* Nottingham, DfES Publications.

DfES (2005a) *Youth Matters* (Consultation: Cm 6299). London, The Stationery Office.

DfES (2005b) *Common Core of Skills and Knowledge for the Children's Workforce.* Nottingham, DfES Publications.

DfES (2006a) *The lead professional: managers' guide.* London, DfES, www.everychildmatters.gov.uk/leadprofessional

DfES (2006b) *Sure Start Children's Centres. Planning and Performance Management Guidance.* www.surestart.gov.uk

DfES (2006c) *Teenage Pregnancy: Accelerating the Srategy.* Nottingham, DfES Publications.

DfES/DH (2004) *National Service Framework for Children, Young People and Maternity Services. Supporting Local Delivery.* London, DH Publications.

DoH (1991) Working Together under the Children Act 1989, London, HMSO

DoH (1995) Child Protection: Messages from Research, London, HMSO

DoH (1998) *Modernising health & social services: National Priorities Guidance.* London: The Stationery Office

DoH (1998) *Modernising Social Services: Promoting Independence, Improving Protection, Raising Standards.* London: The Stationery Office

DoH (1998) *Supporting Families: A Consultation Document.* London, The Stationery Office.

DoH (1999a) *Saving Lives: Our Healthier Nation.* London, The Stationery Office.

DoH(1999b) *Making a difference: strengthening the nursing, midwifery and health visiting contribution to health and healthcare.* London, The Stationery Office.

DoH (2002) *National Service Frameworks: best practice.* London, The Stationery Office.

DoH (2003) *Liberating the Talents of Community Practitioners and Health Visitors.* London, The Stationery Office.

DoH (2004) *National Service Framework for Children, Young People and Maternity Services. Supporting Local Delivery.* London, The Stationery Office.

DoH (2004) *National service framework for children & families.* London:

DOH

DoH (2004) *White Paper: Choosing Health. Making healthy choices easier* (Cm 6374). London, DH Publications.

DoH/DfES (2004) *National Service Framework for children, young people and maternity services.* London, DH Publications.

De Jonge, A. (2001) 'Support for teenage mothers: a qualitative study into the views of women about the support they received as teenage mothers'. *Journal of Advanced Nursing,* 36 (1), pp. 49-57.

DSS (1998) *Households Below Average Income 1979-1996/7.* London: Corporate Document Services

DSS (1999) *Opportunity for All: Tackling Poverty and Social Exclusion, Cm. 4445* (London, TSO).

Dombeck, M (1997) Professional personhood: training, territoriality & tolerance. *Journal of Interprofessional Care,* 11(1): 9-21

Drysdale, J and Purcell, R (1999) Breaking the Culture of Silence: Groupwork and Community Development. *Groupwork* 11(3) 70-87

Duffy, K (1997) *Review of the International Dimension of the Thematic Priority on Social Integration and Exclusion,* Report to the Economic and Social Research Council. Swindon: ESRC

Duggan, AK, McFarlane, EC, Windham, AM, and Rohde, CA (1999) Evaluation of Hawaii's Healthy Start Program. In *The Future of Children* 9(1): 66-90. David and Lucile Packard Foundation: Los Altos

Dunn, J., Cheng, H., O'Connor, T.G. and Bridges, L. (2004) 'Children's perspectives on their relationships with their nonresident fathers: influences, outcomes and implications'. *Journal of Child Psychology and Psychiatry and Allied Disciplines,* 45 (3), pp. 553-566.

Earle, S. (2000) 'Why some women do not breastfeed: formula feeding and fathers' role'. *Midwifery,* 16, 323-330.

Easen, P, Atkins, M & Dyson, A (2000) Interprofessional collaboration & conceptualisations of practice. *Children & Society,* 14, 335-367

Edgley, A & Avis, M (2006) Interprofessional collaboration: Sure Start, uncertain futures, *Journal of Interprofessional Care,* 20(4) 433-435

Eisenstadt, N. (2002) Sure Start: key principles and ethos. Editorial, *Child: Care, Health and Development,* 28 (1) pp.3-4.

Ermisch, John, E. (2003) 'Does a 'Teen-birth' have Longer-Term Impacts on the Mother? Suggestive Evidence from the British Household Panel Study', *Working Papers of the Institute for Social and Economic Research,* paper 2003-32. Colchester, University of Essex.

Erskine, A. (1998) The Approaches and Methods of Social Policy. In P. Alcock, A. Erskine and M. May *The Student's Companion to Social Policy.* Oxford, Blackwell.

Evans, R (1998) *Housing Plus and Urban Regeneration: What Works, How, Why and Where?* Liverpool: European Institute for Urban Affairs, Liverpool John Moores University

Farrell, C. and Gilbert, H. (1996) *Health Care Partnerships* (London, King's Fund).

Faugier, J (1996) The supervisory relationship, in Butterworth, T & Faugier, J (eds) *Clinical supervision & mentorship in nursing*, London: Chapman & Hall

Featherstone, B. (2001) 'Putting Fathers on the Child Welfare Agenda: a research review'. *Journal of Child and Family Social Work*, 6 (2), 179-186.

Fergusson, R (2004) Discourses of Exclusion: reconceptualising participation amongst young people, Journal of Social Policy, 33, 2, 289-320

Field, J. (2003) *Social Capital*. London, Routledge.

Flouri, E. and Buchanan, A. (2003) 'What predicts good relationships with parents in adolescence and partners in adult life: Findings from the 1958 British birth cohort'. *Journal of Family Psychology*, 16, 186-198.

Fox Harding, L (1997) *Perspectives in child care policy* (2ⁿᵈ Ed) Harlow, Addison Wesley Longman

Freeman, M, Miller, C & Ross, N (2002) The impact of individual philosophies of teamwork on multiprofessional practice & the implications for education, *Journal of Interprofessional Care*, 14, 237-247

Frost, N, Johnson, L, Stein, M & Wallis, L (2000) Home Start & the delivery of family support. *Children & Society*, 14, 328-342

Gambetta, D (1988) Can We Trust Trust? In Gambetta, D (ed) *Trust: Making and Breaking Cooperative Relations*, 213-238. Oxford: Blackwell

Gambrill, E (2001) Social work: an authority-based provision, *Research on Social Work Practice*, 11(2), March: 166-75

Garbers, C., Tunstill, J., Allnock, D. and Akhurst, S. (2006) 'Facilitating access to services for children and families: lessons from Sure Start Local programmes'. *Child and Family Social Work*, 11: 287-296.

Garmezy, N (1985) Stress-resistant Children: the search for protective factors. In Stevenson, J (ed) *Recent Research in Developmental Psychopathology*, Oxford: Pergamon Press, 213-233

Ghate, D. and Hazel, N. (2002) *Parenting in Poor Environments: Stress, Support and Coping.* London, Jessica Kingsley.

Ghate, D., Shaw, C. and Hazel, N. (2000) *Fathers and family centres: Engaging fathers in preventive services.* York, Joseph Rowntree Foundation/YPS.

Giddens, A. (1991) *Modernity and Self-Identity.* Cambridge, Polity Press.

Giddens, A (1998) *The Third Way: The Renewal of Social Democracy.* Cambridge: Polity

Gilchrist, A. (2003) 'Community development in the UK - possibilities and paradoxes' *Community Development Journal.* 38 (1): 16-25.

Glass, N (1999) Sure Start: The Development of an Early Intervention Programme for Young Children in the UK. *Children and Society,* 13 (4) 257-264

Gough, D (1993) *Child Abuse Interventions: A Review of the Research Literature.* HMSO: London

Halsey, A (1978) Government against Poverty in School and Community, in Bulmer, M. (ed.) *Social Policy Research.* London: Macmillan

Halvorsen, K. (2003) 'Assessing the Effects of Public Participation'. *Public Administration Review,* 63 (5): 535-541.

Hanna, B. (2001) 'Negotiating motherhood: the struggles of teenage mothers'. *Journal of Advanced Nursing,* 34 (4), pp. 456-464

Harker, R, Dobel-Ober, D, Berridge, D & Sinclair, R (2004) More than the sum of its parts? Interprofessional working in the education of looked after children. *Children & Society,* 18, 179-193

Health Development Agency (2001) *Teenage pregnancy; an update on key characteristics of effective interventions.* London, Health Development Agency.

HM Government (2004) *Children Act 2004.* London, The Stationery Office.

HMSO (1998) *"Report of the Inquiry into Child Abuse in Cleveland"* Cm 412

Hewstone, M. and Brown, R. (Eds.) (1986) *Contact and Conflict in Intergroup Encounters* (Oxford, Blackwell).

Hobcraft, J. (1998) *Intergenerational and Life-Course Transmission of Social Exclusion: Influences of Childhood Poverty, Family Disruption, and Contact with the Police.* CASE paper 15, Centre for Analysis of Social Exclusion. London, London School of Economics.

Hobcraft, J. and Kiernan, K. (1999) *Childhood Poverty, Early Motherhood and Adult Social Exclusion.* CASE paper 28. London, London School of Economics.

Home Office (1998) *Supporting Families: A Consultation Document.* London, The Stationery Office.

Hudson, B (1999) Primary health care & social care: working across professional boundaries, Pt 2: models of interprofessional collaboration, *Managing Community Care,* 7(2): 15-20

Hudson, B (2005) Information sharing & children's services reform in England: can legislation change practice? *Journal of Interprofessional Care,* December. 19(6): 537-546

Hunter, D (2000) Pitfalls of arranged marriages. *Health Service Journal,* 23

Nov, 22-3

Huxham, C (2000) The Challenge of Collaborative Governance, *Public Management*, Vol 2, no 3, 337-57

Independent Advisory Group on Teenage Pregnancy (2004) *Annual Report 2003/04*. London, DfES Publications.

Johnson, Z, Howell, F and Molloy, B (1993) "Community Mothers" Programme: randomised control trial of non-professional intervention in parenting. *British Medical Journal*, 29 May, vol 306, 1449-1452

Johnson, P, Wistow, G, Schulz, R & Hardy, B (2003) Interagency & interprofessional collaboration in community care: the interdependence of structures & values. *Journal of Interprofessional Care*, 17, 69-83

Jones, G (1995) Education and Assessment Services, in (ed) Malin, N, *Services for People with Learning Disabilities*, 125-154. London; Routledge

Kettle, M (Guardian June 19, 2003) "New Labour's big idea is that there is now no big idea"

Kidger, J. (2004) 'Including young mothers: limitations to New Labour's strategy for supporting teenage parents'. *Critical Social Policy*, 24 (3), pp. 291-311.

Kiernan, K.E. (1980) 'Teenage motherhood: Associated factors and consequences'. *Journal of Biosocial Science*, 12 (4).

Kiernan, K.E. (1995) *Transition to parenthood: young mothers, young fathers – associated factors and later life experiences*. STICERD Discussion paper WSP/113. London, London School of Economics.

Kiernan, K.E. (1997) 'Becoming a Young Parent: A longitudinal study of associated factors'. *British Journal of Sociology*, 48 (3), pp. 406-428.

King, C.S., Feltey, K.M. and O'Neill Susel, B. (1998) 'The Question of Participation: Toward Authentic Public Participation in Public Administration'. *Public Administration Review*, 58 (4): 317-326.

Lacey, P (2001) *Support partnerships: collaboration in action*. London: David Fulton

Lacey, P and Lomas, J (1993) *Support Services and the Curriculum: A practical guide to collaboration*. London: David Fulton Publishers

Lamb, M. E. and Tamis-Lemonda, C. S. (2004) 'The role of the father: an introduction'. In M.E. Lamb (Ed.) *The role of the father in child development* (4th edn.). Hoboken, New Jersey, John Wiley & Sons.

Lazar, I and Darlington, R (1982) Lasting Effects of Early Education : a Report from the Consortium for Longitudinal Studies. *Monographs of the Society for Research in Child Development*, 47, 2-3 serial no.195

Lea, R and Mayo, E (2003) *The Mutual Health Service: How to Decentralise the NHS*. London: Institute of Directors and New Economics Foundation

Leathard, A (ed 1994) *Going Interprofessional: Working Together for Health and Welfare*. London; Routledge

Lee, E., Clements, S., Ingham, R. and Stone, N. (2004) *A matter of choice? Explaining national variations in teenage abortion and motherhood*. York, Joseph Rowntree Foundation.

Le Grand, J (1998) "The Third Way Begins with Cora" New Statesman, 6 March: 26-7

Lenoir, R (1974) *Les Exclus*. Paris: Seuil

Lewis, C. (2000) *A man's place in the home: Fathers and families in the UK* (Foundations ref: 440). London, Joseph Rowntree Foundation.

Lewis, C. and Warin, J. (2001) 'What Good are Dads?' *Fatherfacts*. 1 (1), London, Fathers Direct/NFPI/NEWPIN/Working with Men www.fathersdirect.com

Liao, Tim Futing (2003) 'Mental Health, Teenage Motherhood, and Age at First Birth among British Women in the 1990s'. *Working papers of the Institute for Social and Economic Research,* paper 2003-33. Colchester, University of Essex.

Lister, R (2000) From Equality to Social Inclusion: New Labour and the Welfare State, Critical Social Policy, 18: 215-25

Lister, R (2004) The Third Way's Social Investment State in Lewis, J and Surender, R (eds) *Towards a Third Way*? Oxford: Oxford University Press

Lloyd, E (ed, 1999) *Parenting matters; what works in parenting education?* London: Barnados

Lloyd, N., O'Brien, M. and Lewis, C. (2003) *Fathers in Sure Start*. National Evaluation of Sure Start, Birkbeck, University of London.

Lockett, T (1997) Traces of Evidence. *Healthcare Today*, July/August 16

Lorenz, E (1988) Neither Friends nor Strangers: Informal Networks of Subcontracting in French Industry, in Gambetta, D (ed) *Trust: Making and Breaking Cooperative Relations*. Oxford: Blackwell

Lowery, M. (2004) *Sure Start for All. An Integrated Healthcare Model*. Sure Start Hetton and Houghton.

Lowndes, V and Skelcher, C (1998) The Dynamics of Multiorganisational Partnerships, *Public Administration*, vol 76, 313-33

Loxley, A. (1997) *Collaboration in health and welfare: working with difference* (London, Jessica Kingsley).

Lund, B (2002) *Understanding State Welfare: social justice or social exclusion*? London: Sage Publications

Lupton, R and Power, A (2002) Social Exclusion and Neighbourhoods, in Hills, J, LeGrand, J and Piachaud, D, (eds) *Understanding Social Exclusion*, Oxford: Oxford University Press

McCool, S.F. and Guthrie, K. (2001) 'Mapping the Dimensions of Successful

Public Participation in Messy Natural Resources Management Situations'. *Society and Natural Resources.* 14: 309-323.

Macdonald, I (2005) Theorising Partnerships: Governance, Communicative Action and Sport Policy, *Journal of Social Policy,* 34, 4, 579-600

Mack, J and Lansley, S (1985) *Poor Britain.* London; Allen and Unwin

Masten, A, Best, K, Garmezy, N (1990) Resilience and Development: contributions from the study of children who overcome adversity. *Development and Psychopathology* 2: 425-444

Menzies Lyth, I (1988) *Containing anxiety in institutions: selected essays.* London: Free Association Books

Miller, T. (2002) 'Adapting to motherhood: care in the postnatal period' *Community practitioner.* 75 (1): 16-18.

Mitchell, S and Shortell, S (2000) The Governance and Management of Effective Community Health Partnerships. *The Milbank Quarterly,* vol 78, 241-89

Molyneux, J (2001) Interprofessional teamworking: what makes teams work well?

Journal of Interprofessional Care, 15(1) 29-35

Mooney, G (ed) (2004) *Work: Personal Lives and Social Policy,* Bristol: Policy Press

Moorman, A. and Ball, M. (2001) in C. Henricson (ed.)*Understanding parents' needs, a review of parents' surveys.* London, National Family and Parenting Institute.

Morrow, G. and Malin, N. (2004) 'Parents and professionals working together: turning the rhetoric into reality'. *Early Years,* 24 (2): 163-177.

National Commission of Inquiry into the Prevention of Child Abuse (1996) *Childhood Matters.* Stationery Office: London

NESS Research Team (2002) *Early Experiences of Implementing Sure Start.* Nottingham, DfES Publications.

NESS Research Team (2004) *Towards understanding Sure Start local programmes.* Ref.NESS/FR/2004/006. Nottingham, DfES Publications.

NESS Research Team (2005) *Early Impacts of Sure Start Local Programmes on Children and Families.* Report submitted to DfES Sure Start Unit.

NESS Research Team (2005a). *Variations in Sure Start Local Programmes' Effectiveness: Early Preliminary Findings.* Report submitted to DfES Sure Start Unit. Nottingham, DfES Publications.

NESS Research Team (2005b) *Early findings on the impact of Sure Start Local Programmes on child development and family functioning: Final report of the cross-sectional study of 9- and 36-month old children and their families.* Report submitted to DfES Sure Start Unit.

NFPI (1999) *The Millenial Family.* London, National Family and Parenting Institute.

NPCL/NHSA (2000) *Father-Friendliness Organizational Self-Assessment and Planning Tool.* www.nhsa.org/program/fathers/parents_father_assess.htm

New Economics Foundation (2001) *Time Banks: A Radical Manifesto for the UK.* London: New Economics Foundation

Nicholas, E, Qureshi, H & Bamford, E (2003) *Outcomes into practice: focusing practice & information on the outcomes people value: a resource pack for managers & trainers.* York: SPRU, University of York

O'Brien, M. (2004) *Fathers and Family Support. Promoting involvement and evaluating impact.* London, National Family and Parenting Institute.

O'Brien, M. (2005) *Shared caring: bringing fathers into the frame.* Working Paper Series No. 18, Manchester, Equal Opportunities Commission.

ONS (2004) *Health Statistics Quarterly 24,* Winter 2004, London, The Stationery Office.

Orelove, F & Sobsey, D (1991) *Educating children with multiple disabilities: a transdisciplinary approach.* Baltimore: Paul Brookes

Parkin, M (1979) *Marxism and Class Theory: A Bourgeois Critique.* London: Tavistock

Parton, N (ed) (1997) *Child Protection and Family Support: Tensions, Contradictions and Possibilities,* London: Routledge

Paugam, S (1993) Poverty and Social Disqualification: a Comparative Analysis of Cumulative Social Disadvantage in Europe, *Journal of European Social Policy,* 6/4: 287-303

Pease, B. (2002) 'Rethinking Empowerment: A Postmodern Reappraisal for Emancipatory Practice' *British Journal of Social Work.* 32 (2): 135-147.

Penn, H. and Gough, D. (2002) 'The Price of a Loaf of Bread: Some Conceptions of Family Support' *Children and Society.* 16 (1): 17-32.

Penn, H and Randall, V (2005) Childcare Policy and Local Partnerships under Labour, *Journal of Social Policy,* 34, 1, 79-97

Pleck, J.H. (1997) 'Paternal Involvement: Levels, Sources and Consequences', in Lamb, M.E. (ed.) *The role of the father in child development,* 3rd edn. New York, Wiley.

Powell, M and Exworthy, M (2002) Partnerships, quasi-networks and social policy, in Glendinning, C, Powell, M and Rummery, K (eds) *Partnerships, New Labour and the Governance of Welfare.* Bristol: The Policy Press

Pugh, G (1981) *Parents as Partners.* London: National Children's Review

Pugh, G (1996) A Policy for Early Childhood Services? In Pugh, G (ed) *Contemporary Issues in the Early Years. Working Collaboratively for Children.* London: National Childrens Bureau.

Pugh, G (1999) Parenting Education and the Social Policy Agenda. In Wolfendale, S, Einzig, H (eds) *Parenting Education and Support: New Opportunities.* London: David Fulton Publishers

Pugh, G, De'Ath, E, Smith, C (1994) *Confident Parents, Confident Children.* National Children's Bureau: London

Quinton, D. (2004) *Supporting Parents. Messages from Research.* London, Jessica Kingsley.

Quinton, D., Pollock, S. and Golding, J. (2002) *The Transition to Fatherhood in Young Men.* End of Award ESRC report. www.regard.ac.uk

Rainforth, B et al (1992) *Collaborative Teams for Students with Severe Disabilities.* Baltimore: Paul Brookes

Rank, M. (2000) Poverty and economic hardship in families. In D. Demo, K. Allen and M. Fine (eds.) *Handbook of Family Diversity.* New York, Oxford University Press.

Roaf, C (2002) *Coordinating services for included children.* Buckingham: OUP

Robinson, M & Cottrell, D (2005) Health professionals in multidisciplinary & multiagency teams: changing professional practice, *Journal of Interprofessional Care*, December 19(6): 547-560

Robinson, P and Oppenheim, C (1998) *Social Exclusion Indicators: A Submission to the Social Exclusion Unit.* London: Institute for Public Policy Research

Rosato, M., Wiggins, M., Austerberry, H. and Oliver, S. (2004) *Summary of Interim Findings.* Sure Start Plus National Evaluation, London, Social Science Research Unit Report, Institute of Education.

Rowlingson, K. and McKay, S. (2005) 'Lone motherhood and socio-economic disadvantage: insights from quantitative and qualitative evidence'. *The Sociological Review,* 53 (1), pp. 30-49.

Rutter, M (1987) Psychological Resilience and Protective Mechanisms. *American Journal of Orthopsychiatry* 57: 316-331

Ryan, M. (2000) *Working with Fathers.* Abingdon, Radcliffe Medical Press.

Salmon, G & Rapport, F (2005) Multi-agency voices; a thematic analysis of multi-agency working practices within the setting of a child & adolescent mental health service, *Journal of Interprofessional Care*, 19(5) 429-443

Sawtell, M., Wiggins, M., Austerberry, H., Rosato, M. and Oliver, S. (2005) *Reaching out to pregnant teenagers and teenage parents: Innovative practice from Sure Start Plus pilot programmes.* London, Social Science Research Unit Report, Institute of Education.

Schweinbart, L , Barnes, H and Weikart, D (1997) *Significant Benefits: The High/Scope Perry Preschool Study Through Age 27.* Ypsilanti, Michigan:

The High/Scope Press

Schweinhart, L, Weikart, D and Larner, M (1986) Consequences of Three Pre-School Curriculum Models through age 15. *Early Education Research Quarterly*, April

Sennett, R (1999) *The corrosion of character*. London: Norton

Sennett, R. (2003) *Respect. The Formation of Character in an Age of Inequality* (London, Penguin Press).

Shemmings, D. and Shemmings, Y. (1995) Defining participative practice in health and welfare in R. Jack (Ed.) *Empowerment in Community Care* (London, Chapman and Hall).

Shepherd, P and Farrington, D (1995) *The National Child Development Study. An Introduction, Its Origins and the Methods of Data Collection.* Working Paper Nr 1: SSRU, City University, London

Singh, D. and Newburn, M. (2000) *Becoming a father: men's access to information and support about pregnancy, birth and life with a new baby.* London, National Childbirth Trust in association with Fathers Direct.

Sloan, G (1999) Understanding clinical supervision from a nursing perspective, *British Journal of Nursing*, 8, 524-529

Smith, R (2005) *Values & practice in children's services*. Basingstoke: Palgrave Macmillan.

Smith, T (1999) Neighbourhood and Preventive Strategies with Children and Families: What Works? *Children and Society*, vol 13, 265-277

Smith, T, Smith, G, Coxon, K , Sigala, M, Sylva, K and Mathers, S (2007) *National Evaluation of the Neighbourhood Nurseries Initiative (NNI)* Sure Start, March

Social Exclusion Unit (1998) *Bringing Britain Together: A National Strategy for Neighbourhood Renewal.* Cm 4045. London: The Stationery Office

Social Exclusion Unit (1999) *Teenage Pregnancy.* (Cm 4342) London, The Stationery Office.

Social Exclusion Unit (2001) *Preventing Social Exclusion.* London: The Stationery Office

Solutions 4 Community Consultants (2006) *Sure Start Sunderland: Summative Evaluation.* Report presented to Sure Start Sunderland.

Sparkes, J and Glennerster, H (2002) Preventing Social Exclusion: Education's Contribution, 178-201, in (eds) Hills, J, LeGrand, J and Piachaud, D. Understanding Social Exclusion, Oxford: Oxford University Press

Speak, S., Cameron, S. and Gilroy, S. (1997) *Young single fathers: Participation in fatherhood – bridges and barriers.* London, Family Policy Studies Centre.

Statham, J. (2004) 'Effective services to support children in special circumstances'. *Child: Care, Health and Development*, 30 (6), pp. 589-598.

Stevenson, O and Parsloe, P (1993) *Community Care and Empowerment.* Joseph Rowntree Foundation.: York

Sunderland Children's Trust (2006): *Sunderland Children and Young People's Plan2006-2009*, www.sunderlandchildrenstrust.org.uk

Sure Start Development Project (1999) Report to the Sure Start Unit

Sure Start Plus Tyne and Wear (2001) *Mid Year Progress Report.*

Sure Start Unit (2001) *Sure Start. A guide for fifth wave programmes.* Nottingham, DfES Publications.

Sure Start Unit (2002) *Sure Start: a guide to planning and delivering your programme: Sixth wave guidance.*

Sure Start Unit (2003) *Sure Start Local Evaluation*, Nottingham: DfEE Publications

Sure Start Unit (2003) *Start-Up Guidance, Children's Centres: Developing Integrated Services for Young Children and Their Families*, August

Sure Start Unit (2005) *Sure Start Children's Centres: Practice Guidance.* www.surestart.gov.uk/publications/?Document=1500

Sure Start Unit (2006) *Sure Start Children's Centres Practice Guidance.* Revised version. www.surestart.gov.uk/publications/index.cfm?document=1854

Sylva, K and Wiltshire, J (1993) The Impact of Early Learning on Children's Later Development: A review prepared for the inquiry "Start Right". *European Early Childhood Education Research Journal*, 1, 17-40

Sylva, K (1994) The Impact of Early Learning on Children's Later Development. In Ball, C (ed) *Start Right: The Importance of Early Learning.* London: Royal Society of Arts

Sylva, K, Melhuish, E, Sammons, P, Siraj-Blatchford, I, Taggart, B and Elliott, K (2003) *The Effective Provision of Pre-School Education (EPPE) Project: Findings from the Pre-School Period* (www.ioe.ac.uk/coll/eppe/pdfs/eppe brief 2503 pdf, accessed August 2003)

Taylor, A. (2003) 'Sure Start chief fears government control could damage initiative' *Community Care.* Issue 1455: 14.

Teenage Pregnancy Strategy (2004) *Progress Report December 2004.* www.teenagepregnancyunit.gov.uk

Thoburn, J, Wilding, J, Watcons, J (2000) *Family support in cases of emotional maltreatment & neglect.* London: The Stationery Office

Townsend, P (1979) *Poverty in the United Kingdom.* Harmondsworth: Penguin

Tunstill, J (1996) Family Support: past, present and future challenges, *Child and Family Social Work*, 1, 151-8

Tunstill, J & Aldgate, J (2000) *Services for children in need: from policy to practice.* London: TSO

Tunstill, J , Allnock, D, Akhurst, S and Garbers, C (2005) Sure Start Local Programmes: Implications of Case Study Data from the National Evaluation of Sure Start, *Children and Society* Vol 19, 158-171

Tunstill, J (2006) Outline Proposal: Evaluation of a CSV pilot scheme in two local authorities which engages volunteers in work with families where children are on the Child Protection Register

Utting, D (1995) *Family and Parenthood: Supporting Families, Preventing Breakdown.* Joseph Rowntree Foundation: York

Wakschlag, L.S. and Hans, S.L. (2000) Early parenthood in context: Implications for development and intervention. In C.H. Zeanah (ed.) *Handbook of Infant Mental Health.* 2nd edn. New York, Guilford Press.

Waldfogel, J (1999) *Early Childhood Interventions and Outcomes.* CASE paper 21. London: LSE/STICERD

Ward, L (1982) *People First: Developing Services in the Community for People with Mental Handicap: A review of recent literature.* London: Kings Fund Centre

Warren, M. (1992) 'Democratic Theory and Self-Transformation'. *American Political Science Review,* 86 (1): 8-23.

Washington, J and Paylor, I (1998) Social Exclusion, Empowerment and Civil Society, Socrates European Module: Social Work

Wenger, E. (1998) *Communities of Practice. Learning, Meaning, and Identity* (Cambridge, Cambridge University Press).

Werner, E and Smith, R (1982) *Vulnerable but Invincible: A Longitudinal Study of Resilient Children and Youth.* McGraw-Hill: New York

West-Burnham, J. and Otero, G. (n.d.) *'What are we learning about . . .? Community leadership in networks: Leading together to build social capital'.* Cranfield, National College for School Leadership. www.ncsl.org.uk

Whalley, M. (1997) *Working with Parents.* London, Hodder and Stoughton

White, S (2001) "The Ambiguities of the 3rd Way" in S. White (ed) *New Labour: The Progressive Future?* London: Palgrave

White, S (2004) Welfare Philosophy and the Third Way, in J. Lewis and R. Surender (eds) *Welfare State Change: Towards a Third Way?* Oxford: Oxford University Press

Wiggins, M., Austerberry, H., Rosato, M., Sawtell, M. and Oliver, S. (2003) *Service Delivery Study: Interim Findings.* Sure Start Plus National Evaluation, London, Social Science Research Unit Report, Institute of Education.

Wiggins, M., Rosato, M., Austerberry, H., Sawtell, M. and Oliver, S. (2005) *Sure Start Plus National Evaluation: Final Report.* London, Social Science Research Unit Report, Institute of Education.

Williams, B (1988) Formal Structures and Social Reality, 3-14 in Gambetta, D (ed) *Trust: Making and Breaking Cooperative Relations,* Oxford: Blackwell

Wilmot, S. (1995) Professional values and interprofessional dialogue *Journal of Interprofessional Care* 9 (3) pp. 257-266.

Wilson, E (1996) *Consentience: The Unity of Knowledge.* New York: AA Knopf

www.everychildmatters.gov.uk/delivering services/multiagencyworking

www.everychildmatters.gov.uk/parents/participationinmultiagencywork ing

www.surestart.gov.uk/improvingquality/guidance/guidanceresources/

Index

www.ingramcontent.com/pod-product-compliance
Lightning Source LLC
Chambersburg PA
CBHW060140280326
41932CB00012B/1583